Banks of the Future

AF895511

Sohella Thuiner

Banks of the Future

Putting a Puzzle Together Creatively

Springer

Sohella Thuiner
Swiss Banking Advisory – Ella Thuiner
Zurich
Switzerland

ISBN 978-3-319-07553-2 ISBN 978-3-319-07554-9 (eBook)
DOI 10.1007/978-3-319-07554-9
Springer Cham Heidelberg New York Dordrecht London

Library of Congress Control Number: 2014949204

© Springer International Publishing Switzerland 2015
This work is subject to copyright. All rights are reserved by the Publisher, whether the whole or part of the material is concerned, specifically the rights of translation, reprinting, reuse of illustrations, recitation, broadcasting, reproduction on microfilms or in any other physical way, and transmission or information storage and retrieval, electronic adaptation, computer software, or by similar or dissimilar methodology now known or hereafter developed. Exempted from this legal reservation are brief excerpts in connection with reviews or scholarly analysis or material supplied specifically for the purpose of being entered and executed on a computer system, for exclusive use by the purchaser of the work. Duplication of this publication or parts thereof is permitted only under the provisions of the Copyright Law of the Publisher's location, in its current version, and permission for use must always be obtained from Springer. Permissions for use may be obtained through RightsLink at the Copyright Clearance Center. Violations are liable to prosecution under the respective Copyright Law.
The use of general descriptive names, registered names, trademarks, service marks, etc. in this publication does not imply, even in the absence of a specific statement, that such names are exempt from the relevant protective laws and regulations and therefore free for general use.
While the advice and information in this book are believed to be true and accurate at the date of publication, neither the authors nor the editors nor the publisher can accept any legal responsibility for any errors or omissions that may be made. The publisher makes no warranty, express or implied, with respect to the material contained herein.

Cover image: Painting "Beautiful Lake" by Sohella Thuiner

Printed on acid-free paper

Springer is part of Springer Science+Business Media (www.springer.com)

Foreword by Matthias Kröner

A thought-provoking book on the future of the banking industry could start with a number of shrewd men and their even shrewder quotations. Benjamin Franklin is often quoted in such cases, who knew as early as the eighteenth century that "*Well done is better than well said*". The words of Charles Darwin, too, impress us even today, such as "*It is not the strongest of the species that survives, nor the most intelligent, but the one most responsive to change*", even if his quotations were not directly conceived in reference to the modern banking industry. Or one could turn to a living business legend such as Jeff Bezos or Bill Gates, for whom "*unhappy customers are [the] greatest source of learning*". For me, however, the most fitting quotation to begin this book is not taken from a politician, scientist or entrepreneur—instead, I find that the American folk rock duo Simon & Garfunkel encapsulated the ideal strategy for tomorrow's financial industry when they sang,

> Keep the customer satisfied.

But do banks know what their customers need? Obviously, with things as they are, financial service providers and customers are no longer compatible, seeming to have drifted apart. Untold headlines on banking and financial crises have led a greater and greater percentage of customers to distance themselves. Trust in financial service providers has plummeted. Yet, although major banks are currently suffering a severe lack of credibility, the financial industry continues to be intensely self-absorbed. In many places, the realisation has yet to sink in that it will take more than a few TV advertisements and sophisticated corporate image campaigns to respond to customer alienation. The route leading away from this crisis of confidence must be different. It is imperative that a solution be found for a fundamental lack of customer focus, along with an insufficient understanding of specific customer issues. Service quality and procedures which affect customers must be improved. Innovative ideas must be promoted in order for customers to have real benefits in their day-to-day banking activities. A new corporate culture must be established, characterised by openness, honesty, transparency, dialogue and participation. In a nutshell, the spotlight must be pointed at the customers.

People are the most important human capital of a bank operating as a service provider.

Customers, their requests and their requirements should always take top priority. Instead of leaving them out in the cold, customers should be included. In the past several years, banks have trained their customers to stop talking, but this is entirely the wrong route. Financial service providers, instead of asking "What can we sell?", should be posing the question "What do our customers want to buy?" A wide variety of options are available for communicating with customers, among them Web 2.0.

Yet use of social media in the financial services sector is nothing less than underdeveloped, while customer focus is rarely more than a platitude. Although many banks have recognised that having an Internet presence is indispensable, social networking continues to be misunderstood by most companies. Instead of using social media as a source of feedback to better understand what customers want, Twitter and its ilk are frequently used only for PR and marketing, or companies' Facebook pages may be half-baked, with a few weeks of activity being followed by silence. The problem is that no serious examination has taken place of what options and opportunities are available to banks from the Internet.

Having a presence in social media portals and mobile apps is set to exert an increasing influence on customer satisfaction.

Most customers will increase their expectations that banks should make full use of these technological possibilities. Being with the spirit of the times and offering modern banking to modern customers could be crucial to survival. If banks continue to shy away from setting a new course, ignoring the requirements and preferences of their customers, the financial industry will continue to have an uphill battle. But if financial service providers take another path and focus once again on their customers, bolstered by their Web 2.0 options, they may have a chance at winning back lost confidence.

The future could see the rise of "social banking", where customers and banks could meet on equal footing once again. Exchanging ideas instead of being talked down to, transparency instead of devious transactions—it will be exciting to observe how the financial industry positions itself over the coming years. Simon & Garfunkel may have hit the nail on the head here once again—their debut album contains a skilled rendition of a Bob Dylan song whose title has lost none of its pertinence:

The Times They Are a-Changin'.

München, Germany

Matthias Kröner

Foreword by Thomas Schmidt

"The future of Banking"—what a big statement! Not the future of one Bank, the author wants to show us the future of a whole universal industry. Is this mission impossible? I hope not, even it is fair to say, that the future will never be what we expect from it.

Why is it important to think about the future, if we cannot predict it anyway and as we all know from any prospectus accompanying investment vehicles: "the past is not a predictor for the future and the value of your investment might go up as well as down." However, thinking about the future forces us, the writer as well as the reader, to face the issues and challenges of the present. And in banking there are overwhelming issues and challenges, which have to be tackled.

The list of challenges can be divided into three groups. First is the "theoretical group". Questions about the role of the bank in the capitalistic system, the "correct" definition of a Bank, the distinctive factors vs financial institutions, the economical and expected purpose of Banks, e.g. risk transfer, are keywords surrounding this group.

Another area of concerns which needs to be explored is the "stakeholder group". What does Bank's customer want? How did it change over time and what are the requirements of the future? Why is the reputation and perception of Banks so bad and what can be changed? What do the investors/shareholders want? Do both expectations match? And what about the managers and employees of banks, what is on their agenda. And last but not least, the role of the regulators and the influence of opportunistic politicians on them! What is their current raison-d'etre and what will be their remit in the future? How can an industry prosper, with so many diverse goals of its many stakeholders?

However, the biggest challenge in my opinion is the lack of invention in Banking. The only original invention in the last 25 years which was customer focused and added operational efficiency to the Bank was the introduction of the ATM! Nevertheless, customers do normally not complain of less invention if they rail against Banks. So for me, one of the unanswered questions is, do customers really want invention from Banks or do they want something less tangible?

I am looking forward reading the book, I am sure it will not solve all problems of the banking industry, but I am also convinced that each of us readers will be confronted with some mind-buckling thoughts which hopefully helps us to shape the future of our institutions in a positive way.

Union Bank
Vaduz, Liechtenstein

Thomas Schmidt

Foreword by Sandro Schmid

The World Is Enough

Do you remember when you were a child and everything was managed for you by your loving parents, and you were a strong believer that our world and its systems are equally managed by great leaders? It was the time when you spent your day mainly for learning or playing, and the future was bright anyway, somehow. If things turned sour, there was always someone to fix it for you, and you had this comfortable feeling of trust.

Today, as reader of this book, you take care yourself of the system and its future; eventually you might even be worried, considering the health of today's financial world. Why did so many massive failures happen in the past? I am thinking here of the sub-prime crisis, of all the bank scandals, including libor manipulation and unexpected losses from trading activities, but also of all the Ponzi schemes, beginning with Madoff and others. Is the financial system healthier today than in the past? How will the next crisis impact your life?

Looking today at the world after the last financial crisis, it is still not running well at all! The political tensions have increased, no one has been able to fix what went wrong in 2008, and most countries handled the crisis badly and time-delayed. We have very large unemployment rates. Especially many young people fresh out of school and with lots of dreams about their future, must learn day by day that no matter how brave and smart they are, the future will barely look bright for them. Further, most large countries still face increasing debt to an unreached high level, with the only hope that growing the economy might at any rate pay the debt, i.e. about at least 2 % GDP in Europe—a challenging target for most countries in the near future. In order to help the economy, central banks offer money almost for free, a peculiar situation since only things that are rare are normally valuable.

When reading the newspaper or watching the news, we get the impression that those who approach us with their solutions have a plan on how to get back on track. But do they truly understand the impact of prosperity, liquidity glut, or a long-lasting low-interest environment? Do we hear them explaining what risks their course includes and which scenarios can be handled with which instruments?

I believe the financial and economic world is getting more and more complex and demanding. Its developments are no longer directly manageable or are known systems. We enter a new world in which overview, control and directions are inherent in a complex system and in which interactions and intentions cannot just be designed and implemented.

We will continue to stabilize the shaky system through interventions from central banks and through a number of new regulations for financial institutions such as Mifid2, Fidleg, Dodd-Frank act, EMIR, Basel III and more to come. Some changes will have a massive impact on the business model of most financial institutions. Clearly, the changes expected from the new regulations are designed in good faith to stabilize the financial market. However, it is no longer possible to fully understand their impact on a single institution, not to mention—in a larger context—how these new regulations will interact with the other regulations.

Hence, banks must operate in a daily mode of change. They need to run a flexible business model, supported by a modern IT system in an environment where the corporate culture is dynamic, creative but still thorough and precise, so that employees may cope with the must-changes deriving from regulations and the need-changes necessary to adapt to the client's wishes and new expectations.

I am convinced that once the financial industry returns to less rough waters, where it can sail along with ease, banks will be managed more professionally and will better contribute to the overall economy; they will hopefully even reduce the magnitude of the next crisis. Therefore, more than ever we need research, discussions and publications from those who care and can contribute to the hopefully brave new world we all need to work on.

Board of Aaaccell Ltd
Zürich, Switzerland

Private Bank
Zürich, Switzerland

Sandro Schmid

Preface

In this book I have put my focus on key factors in banking, such as technology, human interaction, and processes, which can help to eliminate future crises in the banking industry. They are also the reason behind operational risks and numerous reputational actions over the past few years. This book is combining input from numerous sources which I have put in a new context. My aim was to provide a new way of integrating a wide range of banking-related topics, which should inspire the reader to develop the ideas further, based on his or her background. The readers of this book are clients, employees and partners of banks. They will have their own creative journey after starting to read their favorite topics in the book.

The reason for me to focus on project management was that it enabled me to cover the topics of innovation and creativity. As the role of a project manager requires the continuous improvement of soft skills, the understanding of different corporate cultures, pro-activity, authenticity, and the ability to develop a supportive culture in the context of teamwork, it enables the project manager to deal with high levels of complexity and is the most suitable approach to deal with the challenges of today's complex banking systems.

I think that our economies still need traditional banking, but changing customer habits requires banks with cutting-edge technology. I personally prefer to have accounts with both types of banks, which allows me to choose a combination of services from both types of financial institutions.

My intention was to make this book accessible for readers who have no or only little knowledge about information technology and banking, but are nevertheless able to understand the content. I have used a combination of pictures and text to enable key information to be easily understood and helpful for readers who do not find the time to go through the whole text.

According to numerous experts who have been quoted in the book, a mixture of pictures, colors, and text supports our brain to gather information with little effort. This is also going to be the way we will go in the future in order to be better able to cope with large amounts of information.

Zurich, Switzerland — Sohella Thuiner
May 2014

Thank You

Thank you to all my family members, especially to my husband and our son, for all their support I have received during my research, preparation and completion of this book.

Contents

About the Author

Sohella Thuiner has a lifelong interest in art and enjoyed working as a painter before she started working in IT in 1992. In 1996, her first role at a bank was as a systems administrator for Sybase and Unix and later became responsible for a derivative trading system on the trading floor. In 1998 she was the project manager in charge of implementing a trading system worldwide after two of the largest banks in Austria merged. She worked as a trader for derivatives, as an auditor, as a business analyst, a test manager and as a project manager in different countries. Since 2007, she works as an entrepreneur and was also responsible for working as a business analyst for different areas such as trading, management accounting, tax, IT as well as managing a number of interesting projects for financial institutes. During this time several articles in newspapers and magazines reported about her ideas, especially about the combination of banking and art.

Abbreviations and Acronyms

AI	Artificial Intelligence
APP	Applikation Software
ASE	Accelerated Solutions Environment
BOFB	Brain Of Future Bank
BPL	Business Project Lead
Brain	BOFB or Brain Of Future Bank
Brain	Human Brain
CMMI	Capability Maturity Model Integrated
ETF	Exchange-Traded Funds
FT	Financial Times
FX	Foreign Exchange
GPS	Global Positioning System
GUI	Graphical user interface
HBR	Harvard Business Review
ITPL	IT Project Lead
MtM	Marked-to-Market
OTC	Over-The-Counter
PMO	Project Management Office
PnL	Profit and Loss
RRA	Risk Reduction Analyst
SOX	Sarbanes-Oxley
VaR	Value at Risk
XML	Extensible Markup Language

1 Introduction

This book aims to present to banks how to apply new ways of dealing with existing issues and to formulate new solutions. It intends to keep readers engaged, simply through the presentation of new ideas. The intention of this book is also to develop a vision for banks about the future in the context of transformational changes in societies, and to make the book readable and understandable by people who work in the banking business, no matter what their expertise or rank in the organization is. Therefore, my aim is not to impress the reader by the use of IT jargon or banking language, but to introduce readers to a new way of thinking about financial institutions, regardless of whether the reader is a manager in a bank, an employee, a client, consultant or the provider of another financial service.

There are numerous pictures included throughout the book in order to illustrate a concept or idea and to facilitate the understanding. The idea was to combine a picture with text for each major topic, with the pictures providing the reader with an overview about the text and the following benefits: the picture can be considered as a management summary of the topic and it can also save time for those readers who lack the time to go through every detail. The pictures should be read in the following order:

© Springer International Publishing Switzerland 2015
S. Thuiner, *Banks of the Future*, DOI 10.1007/978-3-319-07554-9_1

Throughout the book, creativity is always kept in mind in the context of the various topics, with the intention being to provide an alternative point of view to the dimensions of a particular issue we are already familiar with. Most of my research was based on the study of literature and on audio books as well as interviews.

The content of the book is focused on innovations, projects, and creativity in finance by presenting an outside-the-box view of the current situation and potential future developments. The examples in the book are supposed to support a better understanding of a particular topic. They are mainly taken from projects which I managed during my time as an employee or independent consultant. The content of the project is supposed to provide an overview of upcoming changes and what the missing skills and solutions are so that we can harmonize the changes in a practical way around all areas of an organization. Furthermore, an audio version of the book might be provided at a later stage for those who would like to listen rather than read.

Below are some of the questions that will be handled in this book:

What were the important developments during the past 20 years? How can financial institutions operate more practically and avoid hidden risks naturally? What is the role of the internet in the daily banking business today, and what are the missing innovations? What is the desirable IT landscape of the future, and what is the maintenance of such a landscape? What kind of outsourcing and insourcing solutions will be used in the future, and what does this mean for today's IT issues and business-related controls? What is the culture of future banking in terms of attracting and supporting clients and employees, both old and new? How will banks of the future collaborate with third parties, such as consultants? What is their relationship to other financial institutions? What are prospective developments that will make collaborations with future banks more attractive? What are the new ways of education and innovation? Is there a link between complex brain functionalities and complex banking operations? How can we access creativity so that new ideas are generated on a continuous basis? What is the future market value of a creative banking solution?

1.1 After the Crisis

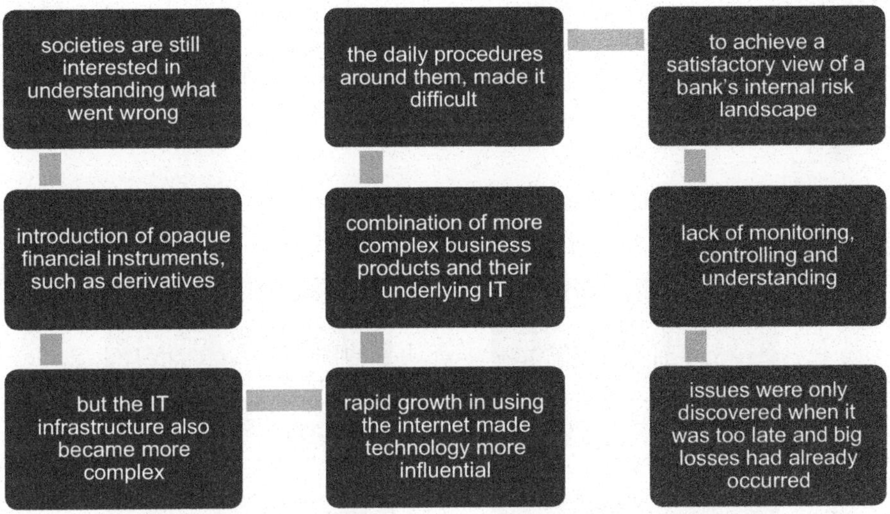

Creative minds in the movie business have been busy turning the subject of banking into entertainment. Accordingly, two movies concerning the banking crisis were nominated for Oscars in 2014. Societies are still interested in understanding what went wrong in the banking industry and what is missing. If there was a brief explanation of what the issues behind the banking crisis were, the explanation would be as follows:

During the past 20 years, not only did financial services become more complex, due to the introduction of opaque financial instruments, such as derivatives, structured products etc., but the IT infrastructure that was introduced into all areas of banking also became more complex. The rapid growth in using the internet and the creation of social networks and smart phones made technology more influential in the world of finance. The combination of more complex business products and their underlying IT infrastructure solutions, as well as the daily procedures around them, made it difficult to achieve a satisfactory view of a bank's internal risk landscape. Due to a lack of monitoring, controlling, and understanding, the issues that came about were only discovered when it was too late and big losses had already occurred.

In order to make the trading of derivatives safer, Stafford (2014) argued in a FT article titled "Swaps and derivatives: Tougher capital rules boost traders' feelings of security" the following: "The transparency of the global over-the-counter (OTC) market is improving."..."However, there are a lot more obstacles till we meet the [G20's] vision."

After 2008, the main focus in the banking business was on discovering issues around monitoring and controlling and solving them as quickly as possible. The culture in respect of change in the organizations was re-defined and innovation was no longer seen as a luxury, but as a necessity. Although revolutionary improvements have still not taken place, the daily business is continuously interested in finding better controlling mechanisms. Many of yesterday's blueprints of daily business operations were reviewed again and adjusted where needed. Financial institutions became more sensitive towards risks and costs than ever and needed to accept a stronger involvement of external regulators in their businesses.

1.1.1 Current Situation

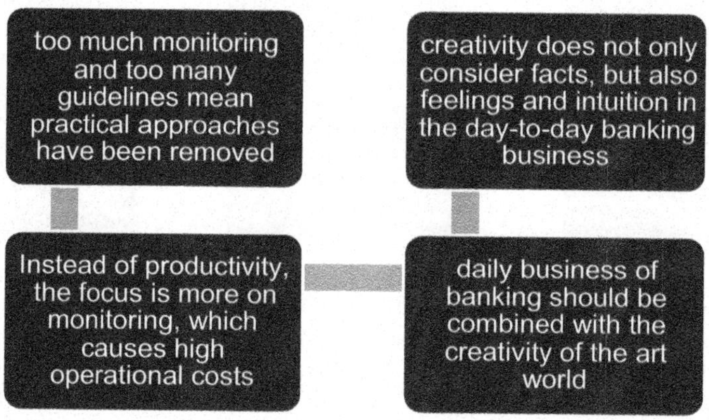

Today, too much monitoring and too many guidelines mean practical approaches have been largely removed from many organizations. Instead of efficiency and productivity, the focus is more on monitoring, which causes high operational costs and also slows down daily business. The main question in our world today is how banks can remain focused on avoiding risks and becoming more practical.

This book argues that the daily business of banking should be combined with the creativity of the art world. Such a combination could result in extraordinary solutions to any bank's forthcoming issues. Creativity does not only consider facts and rules, but also feelings and intuition in the day-to-day banking business in order to better control business as well as paying attention to emotions and relationships, such as the relationships with clients.

1.1.2 Discovering Weaknesses in Daily Processes

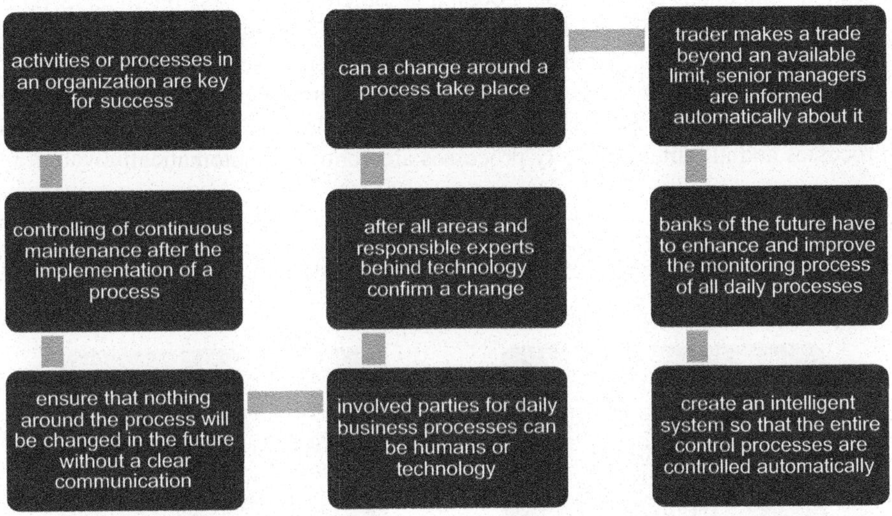

Daily activities or processes in an organization are key for success and any deviation from the originally agreed upon processes during daily activities can cause risks. The main part of a successfully implemented process is the controlling of continuous maintenance after the implementation of a process to ensure that nothing around the process will be changed in the future without a clear communication to the owners of the process and their confirmation. Monitoring and controlling daily processes also means the continuous communication between all involved areas around one particular process, as a process is normally only a part solution of an overall solution and therefore any changes must be communicated to all involved parties.

The involved parties for daily business processes can be humans or technology. Only after all areas and responsible experts behind technology confirm a change to an existing process can a change around a process take place. A good example of the importance of processes in banking is the controlling of limits. All activities in a financial institution, such as securities trading, are based on many pre-defined processes, such as checking of the limits of the currency being traded for a particular financial instrument and only executing the trade if it would remain within the limit framework. In case a trader makes a trade beyond an available limit, senior managers are informed automatically about it.

For example: Before a trade is executed, the following checks must be performed by the trader to ensure that the guidelines are followed and there are no issues after the trade is concluded. Traders must check if limits are available in their areas, for instance, when buying Euros, check the availability of a limit with the counterparty in the organization and check the limit of your open position in the trading book.

If the answers to all checks outlined above allow the trade to be executed and there are no other restrictions, the trade can be done. Even with modern technology solutions implemented on trading floors, it is sometimes not possible to let technology control all steps around the process of checking limits, as counterparty limit checking may be managed in a different system than the checking of currency limits. The banks of the future have to enhance and improve the monitoring process of all daily processes and create an intelligent system so that the entire control processes and all other key daily processes are controlled automatically.

1.1.3 What's Missing in Control Mechanisms

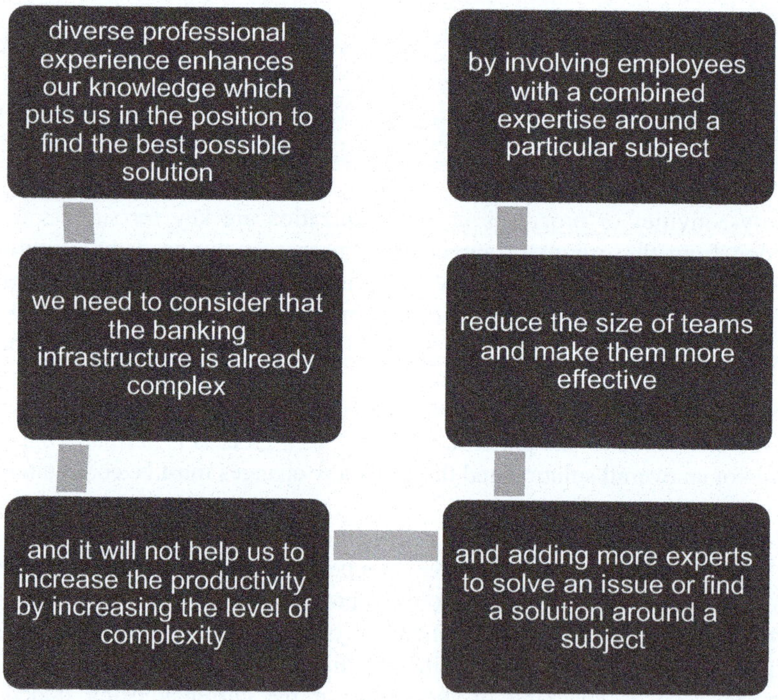

A control mechanism should be performed within well-tested daily processes and involve qualified experts with a diverse expertise in order to remain practical. A diverse professional experience around one subject enhances our knowledge which puts us in the position to find the best possible solution. In case we are looking for the best possible solution to control the limits of a trading system, a diverse expertise around this subject would be one where you may have worked as a trader, as an expert in the back-office or as an IT expert on the trading floor. With each additional experience, you not only acquire new knowledge about daily processes in those areas, but also learn about job-related emotions and work cultures.

Following the financial crisis, there was a tendency of involving too many internal as well as external experts in the process of finding the best possible solution to a problem which contributed to declining productivity and the complication of processes. We need to consider that the banking infrastructure is already complex and it will not help us to increase the productivity by increasing the level of complexity and adding more experts to solve an issue or find a solution around a subject. We can reduce the size of teams and make them more effective by involving employees with a combined expertise around a particular subject.

Example

Here is an example: Today's ways of running a project are already regulated by internal guidelines, but a project manager can still allow himself to become practical by understanding the scope and not only the needs of senior managers and his project team. Understanding the scope means to also understand the needs of all stakeholders and what is expected to be delivered. In many cases project managers are so busy following the guidelines and keeping everyone happy that they forget to focus on the actual requirements, why the project has been initiated, and who the stakeholders of his project are in order to be able to end their project with success.

The project should clarify which documentation needs to be provided, based on the guidelines and mainly focus on the scope of the project, the project team, and the project deliveries. Based on the project type, only a number of documentation will be needed, and it is important to keep it as practical as possible. The practical approach is to re-use the current documentation, for instance, for an Agile project and to copy and paste your information into it or to add pictures instead of a long text.

1.1.3.1 Administrative Tasks

Documentation or presentations in a project should remain as practical as possible, as extensive documentation does not generate much value for the organization after a project has been finished successfully. If the project manager is able to remain practical regarding administrative tasks, the chance of ending a project successfully will increase. The practical approach is not only applied to administrative tasks, such as documentation and reporting, but also to the way the core team of the project is managed and communication within the project team as well as with all external areas is handled. A project manager with work experience in some of the involved areas of his project will be able to raise the chance of a successful project finish.

1.1.3.2 Remain Practical

The project manager should be able to control the daily processes around his project in a pragmatical way and to provide all needed documentation, including reporting, about the ongoing status of the project so that he can freely decide whom to involve formally, informally, or not at all. If the project manager, for instance, does not bring along a diverse work experience, he will encounter difficulties to focus on a practical approach, which can make a simple and straightforward project become more complex than necessary. By understanding the different cultures in different areas of an organization, a project manager is able to ease the collaboration within his project and will finish the project smoothly by avoiding conflicts.

1.1.3.3 Bottom Line

The bottom line here is that a project manager must focus on a practical approach at every stage of his project in order to avoid unnecessary complexity. Furthermore, a project manager must be sufficiently confident to exclude or include internal experts in discussions and to avoid involving groups of too many people with similar knowledge and background. Also, involving too many line managers in discussions about details can be a risk, as the project team is continuously trying to explain every single topic to everyone to make sure that they understand it and have no objections regarding the status.

This is what happens in numerous projects with senior management attention. Although the content of certain discussions is not more challenging than the rest of the project, since the project has the attention of senior managers, more and more line managers (all the layers between the project's core team and senior management) want to understand the project. The best way to approach this kind of projects is to hire project managers who are senior enough to communicate with senior managers. They also need to have the courage and confidence to exclude line managers from the project and to keep them informed informally. It is well known that large groups require higher time efforts and more management attention.

In case we are not able to remain practical, a project will increase in complexity, costs will rise, and the involvement of possibly too many managers and experts will result in the project team continuously trying to explain every single topic to everyone and trying to ensure that they understand the content and have no objections to the status. I think that this is also a sign of inexperienced project managers, as they lack the confidence to say occasionally "no."

1.1.4 Adjustments of Regulations

In order to avoid risks, Tuveson and Ruffle (2014) argue the following in an FT article titled "Diversity is the way to avoid cyber collapse": "Regulators have poured vast amounts of intellectual capital into formulating the best measures for preventing taxpayer bailouts of collapsing institutions." According to the article, banks should worry about systemic risks, because of the breach of customer credit card data or a software error with high-frequency trading solution that created losses of USD 440 million in less than an hour. The reasons for issues like these are different, such as cyber-attacks, hardware break-downs, or software issues. Diversification of IT solutions and system providers of a financial institution could reduce the risks for banks from cyber-attacks.

1.1.4.1 Regulating Risks

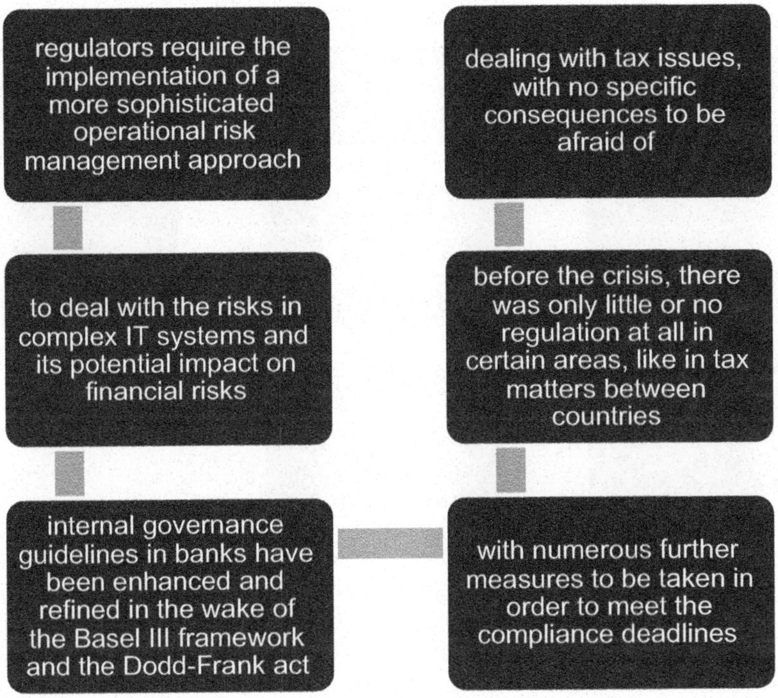

Enhanced regulatory requirements for banks (Basel III) as well as changing business models and customer behavior require a better control of the risks emanating from IT systems. Regulators require the implementation of a more sophisticated operational risk management approach to deal with the risks in complex IT systems and its potential impact on financial risks. Since 2008 internal governance guidelines in banks have been enhanced and refined in the wake of the Basel III framework and the Dodd-Frank act, with numerous further measures to be taken in order to meet the compliance deadlines. All the rules and regulations which have been designed in the aftermath of the financial crisis of 2008 intend to make the banking sector more stable by establishing more sophisticated and sound risk management practice and principles and to regain the public trust towards the banking sector.

What is often forgotten is that before the crisis, there was only little or no regulation at all in certain areas, like in tax matters between countries. This contributed to a certain carelessness by banks when dealing with tax issues, with no specific consequences to be afraid of.

1.1.4.2 Bottom Line

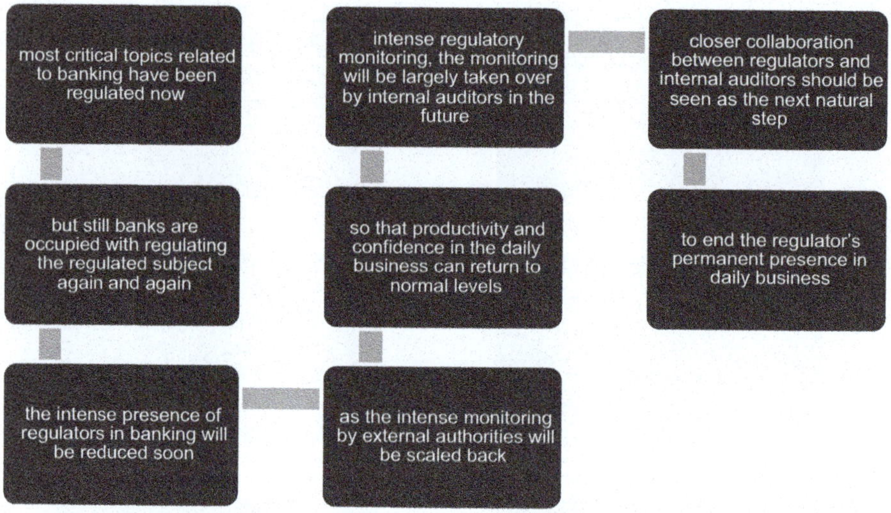

Most critical topics related to banking have been regulated now, but still banks are occupied with regulating the regulated subject again and again. I think that the intense presence of regulators in banking will be reduced soon, as the intense monitoring by external authorities will be scaled back so that productivity and confidence in the daily business can return to normal levels. Instead of intense regulatory monitoring, the monitoring will be largely taken over by internal auditors in the future, and a closer collaboration between regulators and internal auditors should be seen as the next natural step to end the regulator's permanent presence in daily business.

1.1.5 Re-evaluating Ethics

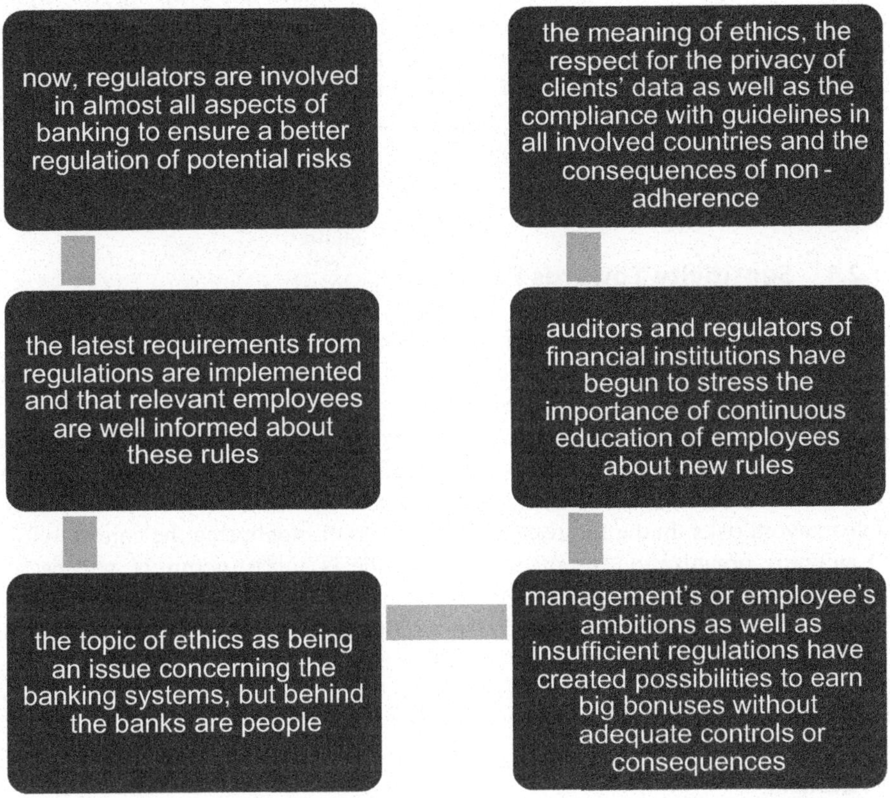

Before 2008, fewer aspects of the interactions between countries, banks, and their clients were regulated. After the crisis, the need for more stringent banking regulations gained momentum. Now, regulators are involved in almost all aspects of banking to ensure a better regulation of potential risks. All financial institutions must ensure now that the latest requirements from regulations are implemented and that relevant employees are well informed about these rules to ensure that they are followed.

We tend to see the topic of ethics as being an issue concerning the banking systems, but behind the banks are people. In the past, management's or employee's ambitions as well as insufficient regulations have created possibilities to earn big bonuses without adequate controls or consequences for bad behavior. Since the crisis senior managers, auditors, and regulators of financial institutions have begun to stress the importance of continuous education of employees about new rules, the meaning of ethics, the respect for the privacy of clients' data as well as the compliance with guidelines in all involved countries and the consequences of non-adherence.

1.2 Sensitivity Towards Hidden Risks

After the crisis, a lot of attention has been paid to hidden and evolving risks in the day-to-day business of financial institutions. Banks are interested in finding new solutions to avoid hidden risks naturally. Risks can be based on a diverse range of subjects and can always cause an unexpected increase of costs in an organization. As mentioned before, the main drivers of risks are the processes behind the daily activities and the underlying systems.

1.2.1 Sensitivity Towards Processes

A process is usually defined based on the following factors: The understanding of a task, the steps of how it is performed, its underlying IT systems, internal guidelines, internal experts, and the owner of the task.

The reason why a continuous review of implemented processes is so important is that they represent a small part of a comprehensive solution in an organization. There are many small parts which must be in harmony with each other in order to be able to avoid risks. In the future, the daily process of monitoring the core activities of an entire organization, no matter how old the IT infrastructure is, will be run automatically and will combine different systems and areas if necessary.

The main reason for getting lost in the complexity of banking is that we have still inadequate controls in the bank's core activities. We need to develop a sensitivity towards the core activities or processes of a banking business and automate the control process around them first.

Example

Controlling a limit in a trading area is a core activity of bank, as a hidden risk around this process can harm the organization as we saw it several times during the last couple of years. Therefore the future monitoring of the entire limit system should be run automatically. Processes will be designed to allow or prohibit a certain trade automatically, based on a number of checks, and there will be no need for traders to check anything by themselves. Many steps of this monitoring process are already automated today, but in the near future, manual controls will disappear and activities such as controlling the limit of an open position for complex trades will be done automatically. The future system will be able to allow an automatic hedge for critical positions overnight if needed.

1.2.1.1 Controlling Core Processes

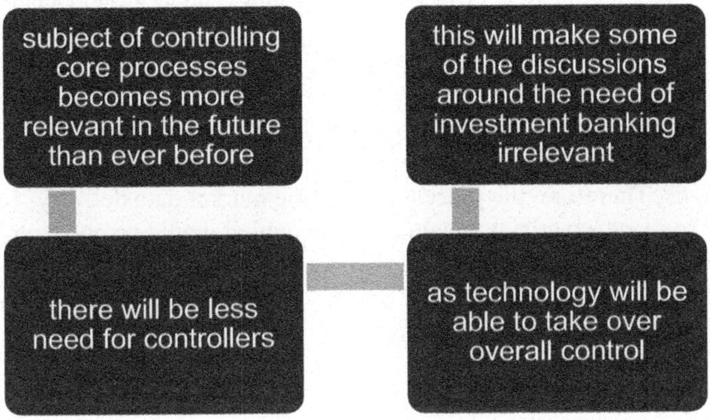

The subject of controlling core processes becomes more relevant in the future than ever before. There will be less need for controllers, as technology will be able to take over overall control of the for instance entire trading activities of a financial institution. This will make some of the discussions around the need of investment banking irrelevant, as there will be a way to run a controlled open position and remain in the market by simplifying IT and focusing on core processes.

In case of a change of the process itself, the system must be able to show by when it will be changed, who has agreed to change it and who has been informed about the change. The processes around trading must be reviewed and adjusted automatically from time to time, as the limits might have been changed and new currencies, countries, or products may have been added or managers might have been assigned new responsibilities in the organization or might have left it.

Example 1

Even though it might confuse the reader, I need to add that behind each process there is another process which can be all controlled by available IT solutions automatically. Here is an example to make it understandable: In the case of a trading limit, there is a process behind the setup of a limit, which might be defined by the following logical steps: Find out what the limits are, set up the limits in the systems over the weekend to ensure that there will be no mixture in using old and new limits during a working day, communicate the change to all relevant business areas and maintain a list of relevant areas to ensure awareness of who is using the limit and for which purpose.

As can be seen from the example above, there can be sub-processes behind each process. The main question here is how complicated it is for an organization to have an overview of their process landscape today. In order to avoid hidden risks in a new solution, the involved experts need to have a clear understanding of the dependencies to a particular core process. The best way to get a clear understanding of the dependencies to a particular core process is to involve at least one expert with a diverse work experience in IT as well as in business areas around a particular core activity.

Example 2

A portfolio manager needs to ensure that the process of running the portfolio for his client is aligned with the rest of the activities and processes of the day-to-day operations. Therefore, the process behind the market data delivery, for instance, must take place exactly at the agreed time, which would be confirmed when the solution for the data delivery is implemented. It is assumed that since the system implementation has taken place, IT teams have kept the process unchanged and new implementations or any changes followed the old agreement.

1.2.1.2 The Future

I think that in the future companies will be equipped with superior process knowledge via the right group of experts and customized tools in order that processes can be designed and monitored smoothly and risks avoided naturally. Therefore controlling processes of daily activities will be managed almost effortlessly.

1.2.2 Sensitivity Towards Costs

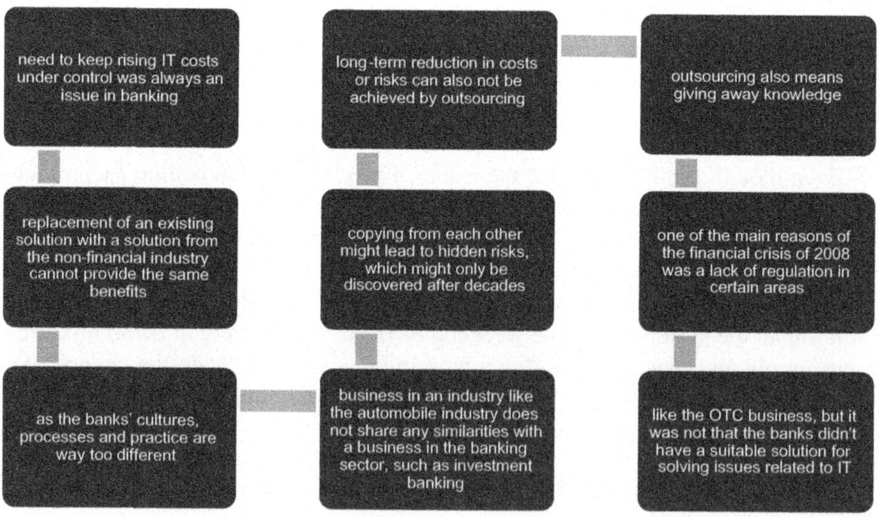

The sensitivity towards costs started to rise after the crisis and the need for more cost efficient solutions became more relevant. The need to keep rising IT costs under control was always an issue in banking. Great work was done in optimizing existing solutions over the last couple of years. Some industry solutions, such as lean management, were already implemented in some areas in order to minimize defects and control risks. I think that the replacement of an existing solution with a solution from the non-financial industry cannot provide the same benefits, as the banks' cultures, processes, and practice are way too different. A business in an industry like the automobile industry does not share any similarities with a business in the banking sector, such as investment banking. Copying from each other might lead to hidden risks, which might only be discovered after decades.

Transferring methodologies and systems from non-financial industries to banks will not reduce the costs for a bank. It is a wrong approach to implement cost reductions, which seems to be based on a lack of understanding of the banking business. A long-term reduction in costs or risks can also not be achieved by outsourcing. Simply outsourcing the IT activities will not help to reduce costs and there are also risks attached to such measures. Outsourcing also means giving away knowledge; after a number of years, who in the organization will be able to ensure that the effort put in the entire development of a project is correct or realistic?

In the optimal case, outsourcing is only done partly, which means that development or testing is only partly performed by the company to which the application has been outsourced to and partly by internal employees. Large projects can be implemented as planned and resources made available for work in your project, but you also need internal experts to work closely with the outsourcing company so that the performance standards remain high and the level of expertise from the outsourcing company meets expectations.

In case there is a complete dependency on the external company, you will always run the risk that your project will not deliver the promises on time and on budget. Banks have served their clients successfully for a long time by having full control over their systems, processes, and the quality of their services, which might not be sustainable if outsourcing is falsely considered as a solution for a different problem than the level of costs. One of the main reasons of the financial crisis of 2008 was a lack of regulation in certain areas, like the OTC business, but it was not that the banks didn't have a suitable solution for solving issues related to IT.

Example

During my time as project and test manager, I once provided support to my line manager by taking over some of his tasks, with one of it being issue tracking in the context of a major trading system implementation. At the time I also made my first experience in collaborating with an outsourcing company in India. I needed to ensure that five to eight internally employed developers were engaged with supporting our project. I assume that I got this task from my manager after he found out that one of my closest friends in London was of Indian/British origin who also happened to be my client adviser at my bank.

These developers (from the outsourcing company) were very bright specialists, and although we sometimes had difficulties in understanding each other's working cultures, we managed to make the project work. Even the collaboration with experts in Singapore who were testing the system worked well. Although we sometimes had to deal with frustrations arising from misunderstandings between IT and business or between internal and external experts, the project was completed successfully by keeping the formal interaction among the involved experts as low as possible. We were more than happy to communicate informally. It helped us to create an efficient communication between the developers and the rest of the group by summarizing what was discussed casually and copied-in the relevant experts in the project in emails. It took time to get used to the fact that the shaking of one's head means "yes" and not "maybe." Fact is that outsourcing will not always cut costs. Make sure to retain the critical knowledge in the organization in order to keep the dependency on outside expertise low.

1.3 Bank and Insurance Regulation

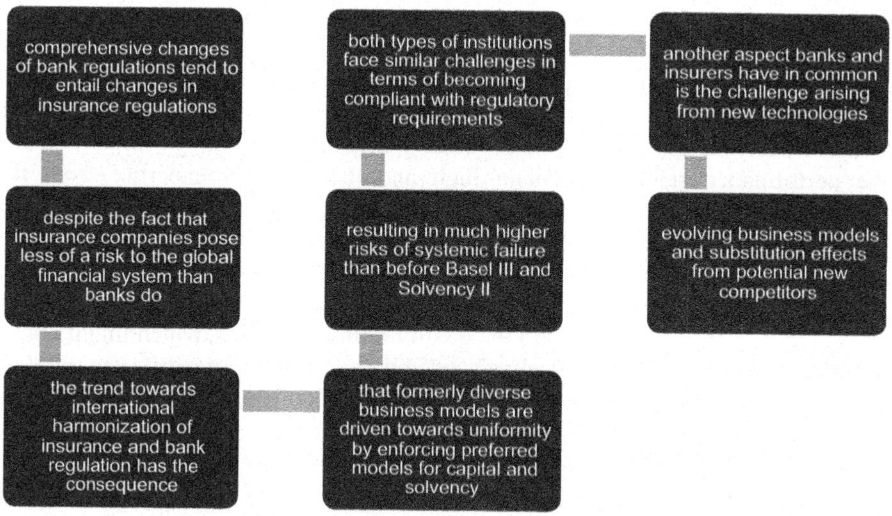

Comprehensive changes of bank regulations tend to entail changes in insurance regulations, despite the fact that insurance companies pose less of a risk to the global financial system than banks do. For example, in insurance risks are exogenous (outside of the system) and independent in occurrence, while in banking risks are very often endogenous (within the system) and correlated in unpredictable ways. Therefore, a single bank failure can have systemic consequences for the banking system, while a single insurance company failure does not trigger systemic consequences.

The trend towards international harmonization of insurance and bank regulation has the consequence that formerly diverse business models are driven towards uniformity by enforcing preferred models for capital and solvency, resulting in much higher risks of systemic failure than before Basel III and Solvency II.

Both types of institutions face similar challenges in terms of becoming compliant with regulatory requirements and regarding the control of the rising costs thereof. Another aspect banks and insurers have in common is the challenge arising from new technologies, evolving business models, and substitution effects from potential new competitors.

1.4 The Role of Innovations

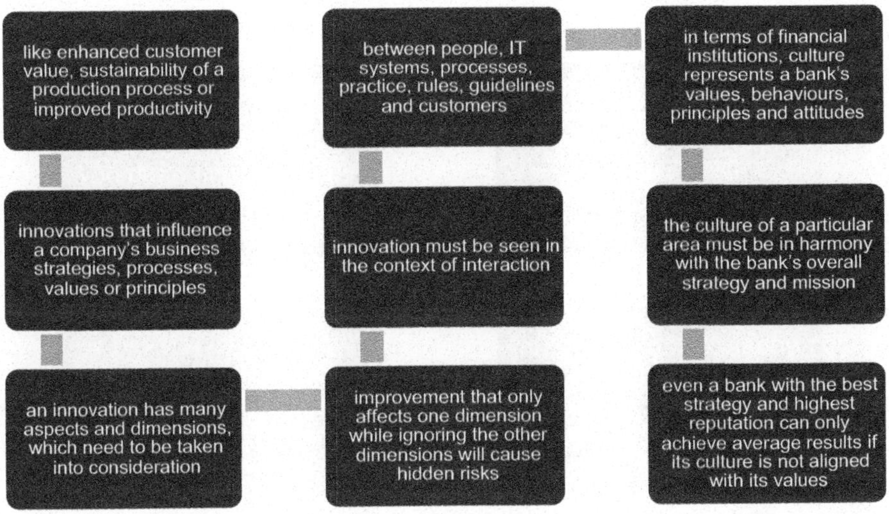

Innovations should be considered as an improvement and can thus be introduced for particular reasons, like enhanced customer value, sustainability of a production process, or improved productivity. There are innovations that influence a company's business strategies, processes, values, or principles. There are also innovations that introduce new business or IT solutions. In other words, an innovation has many aspects and dimensions, which need to be taken into consideration. An improvement that only affects one dimension while ignoring the other dimensions will cause hidden risks. An innovation must be seen in the context of interaction between people, IT systems, processes, practice, rules, guidelines, and customers.

In today's banking world, there is a need for innovations, but not every bank provides the culture that enables or encourages change. The word "culture" is associated with the traditions and history of people related to a particular country. In terms of financial institutions, culture represents a bank's values, behaviors, principles, and attitudes in interactions among its employees and between the bank and its clients. Therefore, the culture of a particular area must be in harmony with the bank's overall strategy and mission.

A mix of existing cultures in the various areas of a bank evolves into an overall culture that features different aspects, depending on the observer. Due to different activities and objectives, each area in a bank has its own culture which aims to attract employees that support its goals. Here it is believed that even a bank with the best strategy and highest reputation can only achieve average results if its culture is not aligned with its values.

1.4.1 The Meaning of Innovations

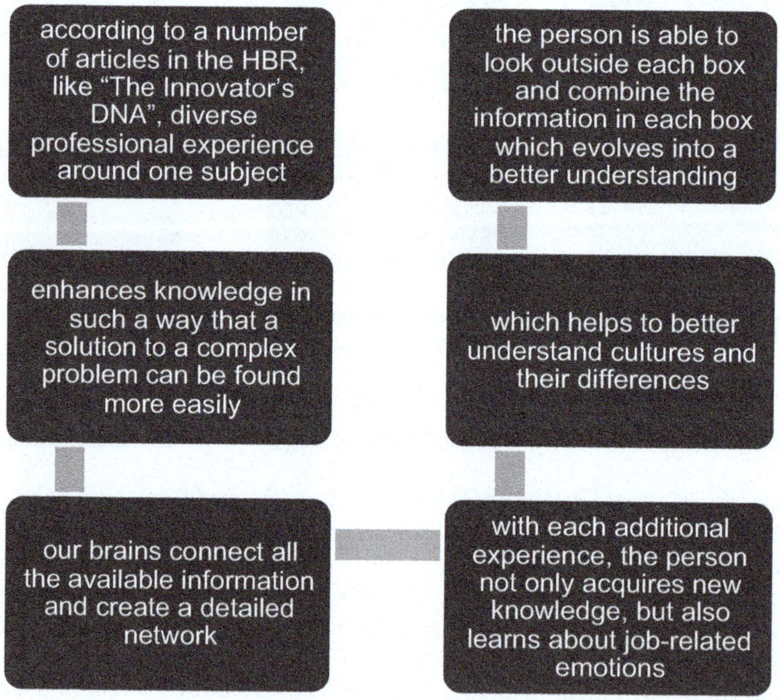

Over the past few years, financial institutions have put more attention to the topic of innovation. The term "innovation" is not that popular in the daily business of a bank, which would rather use the terms "new strategy" or "project." The management of innovations can be seen as a skill that can be trained and developed. According to a number of articles in the HBR, like "The Innovator's DNA,"

which will be discussed in more detail later, diverse professional experience around one subject enhances knowledge in such a way that a solution to a complex problem can be found more easily.

According to HBR, this can be explained by the way the brain works. It does not work like a dictionary. For example, if somebody wants to make a theater successful, information about theaters wouldn't be recalled in the format of a list. Our brains connect all the available information and create a detailed network (like the visual presentation of a text through pictures and connections in this book).

Applied to the theatre example, a person may have watched a performance, starred in a performance as an actor, been in charge of the lighting, entered the theatre as a visitor, or even directed a performance at the theatre. With each additional experience, the person not only acquires new knowledge, but also learns about job-related emotions, which helps to better understand cultures and their differences. This person is able to look outside each box and combine the information in each box which evolves into a better understanding.

I think this is the best approach for innovations to avoid hidden risks in organizations naturally and to allow experts to become professional when introducing innovations. The need for enhanced rules and regulations in order to make banks safer and to more effectively control day-to-day processes and activities in the future will therefore require people with diverse experience around key activities.

Future banks will have resources equipped with a diversified work experience around a subject in order to be able to reduce complexity, and, in case they do not have it, they will acquire it through training. This fact has not been considered so far as a potential solution to today's complexity, and the only proven way to reduce risks as well as costs.

1.4.2 Project Management

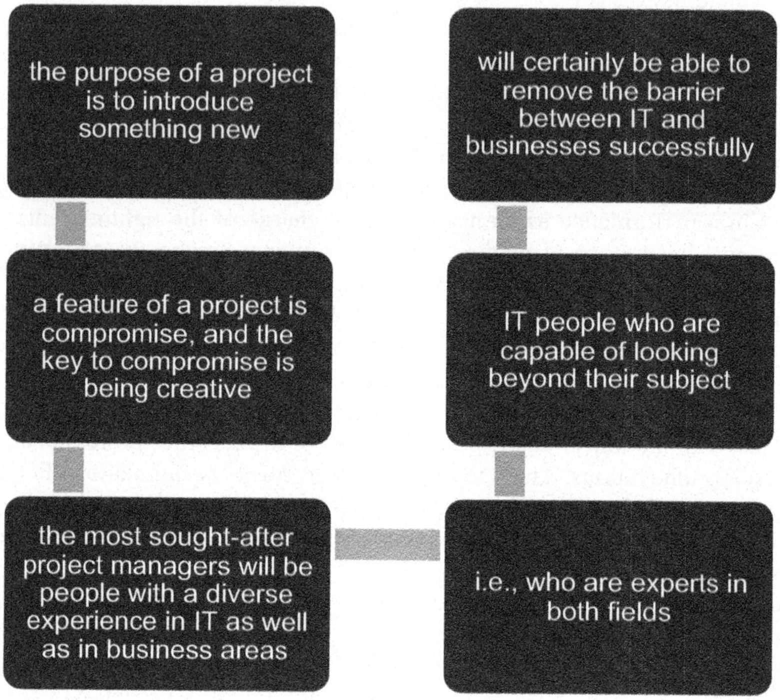

As mentioned, the purpose of a project is to introduce something new. A feature of a project is compromise, and the key to compromise is being creative. As a project manager in a bank, you will either be asked to find a new solution to a particular issue or to implement a solution that has already been found. You need to follow the bank's internal methodologies when managing a project, but in the process of searching for the best possible solution, you are free to try out new ideas within the process of finding that solution.

In the future, the most sought-after project managers will be people with a diverse experience in IT as well as in business areas, i.e., who are experts in both fields. I do not mean business experience as in having worked in a business area where IT services have been provided, although this experience can also be enriching, but IT expertise by a person who has previously worked as a business expert in the field that he is currently working in.

IT people who are capable of looking beyond their subject will certainly be able to remove the barrier between IT and businesses successfully and will equally be able to lead a project to success by understanding their project teams, by being empathic and earning their trust. The best possible solution in such a project can then be delivered in a more smooth way as a result of a perfect co-operation between IT and business.

According to Young et al. (2009), the reasons for failed projects are often a lack of management competence, wrong cost calculations, over-ambitious objectives within an unrealistic timeframe, limited availability of skills, wrong decisions, and frustrations. The established body of knowledge and guidelines around project management do provide a sound basis for running projects successfully; however, additional, well-intended guidelines around basic principles will only make the management of a project more complicated.

For instance, there is no need to develop new strategies for hiring new resources for a project, as in the majority of cases the project manager must deal with given resources. The combination of business/IT knowledge and soft skills will remain key for successful project management.

1.4.2.1 Project Management and Internal Cultures

There is no doubt that departments which perform certain activities, for instance, a trading environment, have developed unique cultures, characterized by risk taking, speed of actions, and quick profits. Thus, soft skills will become more enhanced in case a project manager has experience in dealing with different cultures in an organization. This understanding will naturally grow with work experience in as many different areas of an organization as possible.

1.4.3 Methodology

Another question that this book seeks to answer is, what is the role of methodology and guidelines on a particular subject such as project management in today's banking world, and how can we become practical and reduce complexity?

In the banking world, methods and structures are being developed to avoid chaos in a project. There are many guidelines and methodologies for running a project, like CMMI, Six Sigma, or Prince 2, that basically explain the same logic. There is no doubt that these guidelines and methodologies are useful in order that we are able to follow a road map and do not have to define the basics of running and controlling a project from scratch. The question that we come across while practicing these methodologies is: how can over-controlling or under-controlling in a project be avoided in order to deliver a successful closing of the project? How can we avoid spending too much time in managing administrative processes in our project?

Example

CMMI will be taken as an example for internal guidelines to be followed by a project manager. Can we exclude all the common sense and at the same time make the methodology itself practical? How do we find a simple way of explaining a method or an internal rule which covers many dimensions? In case you manage a project in a bank, the entire project setup will be done and run according to CMMI. The complexity of a project is based on the type of project management methodology used, such as Waterfall or Agile.

In practice there are ways to avoid too much controlling of a project, such as using Agile-based principles instead of principles based on Waterfall. Through the agile-based approach, the project consists of many small deliveries within a short period of time and has been created for activities in the field of engineering, information technology, and for product or service development projects in a highly flexible and interactive manner.

1.4.3.1 Preferred Concept

Agile project management provides an approach that enables that deliverables are completed in a pre-defined period of time. An Agile project manager will ask his team three questions every day: What have you done yesterday? What were the issues? What will be done today?

Today, Agile is a preferred approach when it comes to IT development, but it can also be used for any business-related topics, even if IT is not involved.

Example

- A business area must establish a process around clients' tax regulations.
- They decide to run this project based on the Agile approach and involve all needed areas, such as IT, client relationship management, the legal and compliance department, internal tax advisers, and the back office for updating client data.
- They agree on a project delivery in several phases and not only in one, as it is the case with the Waterfall concept. Thus the deliverables are the following: a process around forms which clients need to sign; a process around IT updates; a process for obtaining legal advice; a process for receiving tax-related information; and a process around the client relationship managers' activities.
- Each phase includes all the steps like a large waterfall project, such as the design, development, and testing in each phase.
- The Agile technique allows to correct decisions after the implementation, which is a big advantage compared to the waterfall technique. In case the relationship managers have defined and confirmed their process around form XY, the IT department can provide additional information, like about another form XYZ, which is already implemented in the relevant systems and includes all the information from form XY, which makes the change of the

confirmation process for relationship managers be considered as an advantage.

– The Agile approach provides the possibility to test findings after each phase and to prove that they are correct and can move forward. In case it is not, it adds the information and takes it to the next step.
– In the Waterfall method, once you are in the testing mode, it is not possible to move to the imitation phase of your project and evaluate again.

In many cases, business-related projects without IT involvement are not following any concept. There are also widespread applications of hybrid approaches consisting of Agile and Waterfall techniques. It would be beneficial to apply especially the Agile concept on a more widespread basis, no matter if it is an IT-related or a business-related topic.

1.4.4 Creativity

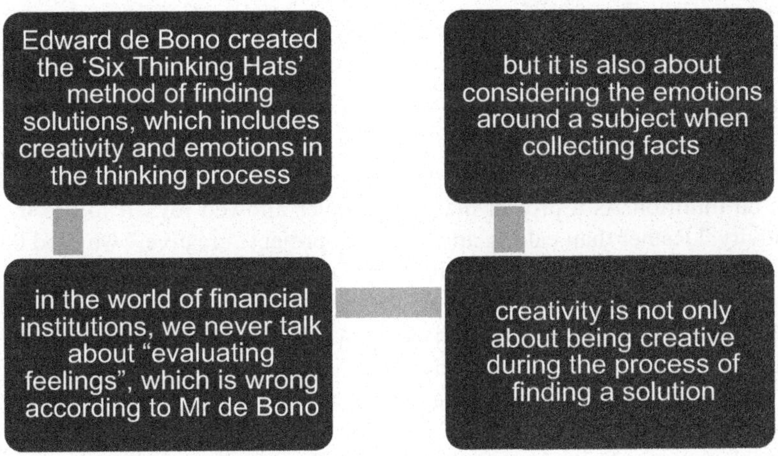

1. The Beginning

The logical structure of a solution finding process can remain logical and still be based on intuition As a project manager I never allowed myself to use the word "creativity." Rather than calling anyone in the project "creative," we used the term "thinking-outside-the-box." de Bono (1985) created the "Six Thinking Hats" method of finding solutions, which includes creativity and emotions in the thinking process. Surprisingly, this method is known and accepted by those people who normally do not allow words like creativity in their working environment. In the world of financial institutions, we never talk about "evaluating feelings," which is wrong according to Mr de Bono.

I think that creativity is not only about being creative during the process of finding a solution, but it is also about considering the emotions around a subject when collecting facts about a particular subject and going through an evaluation process regarding the collected information. The logical structure of finding solutions can remain logical and still be based on the collection, structure, and filtering of information, but it can also take emotions into account, and final decisions and outcomes can be based on all these factors. This book includes many examples from my previous experience.

Here is an example which highlights the importance of considering emotions in order to manage a particular project successfully. During the merger of two of the largest banks in Austria, a decision was made to implement the derivative system from Bank A in all branches of Bank B around the world. Tensions and emotional disagreements at Bank B ran high during the project, and only intensive education and support helped them to accept the new solution. This project took a lot of time in dealing with the employees of Bank B in order to promote the perception that their opinions were important. This decision was critical.

The project was concluded successfully, because the needs and emotions of the employees of Bank B were taken into consideration. At the same time, a good relationship with the employees of Bank A was maintained. If we had neglected our extended duty towards the employees of Bank B, the results of the project could have been a disaster.

In this instance, the requirements of the two groups of employees were very different. By balancing these differences, we were able to ensure both banks continued their daily business smoothly, after the project was completed.

1.5 Brain vs. Banking

Our brain operates more complex than the banking business does, but everything we experience seems to be very natural and easy to process for our brain. The brain is crucial for our functioning and we, as humans, are crucial for the functioning of a banking system. The main question that this book would like to find an answer to is the following: What needs to be done so that we have similar natural controlling processes over our banking day-to-day activities as we have in our brains?

When an organization strives for become more practical and less bureaucratical, it has to pay attention to the individuals involved. Studies have already confirmed that when people feel good, they work at their best, they are more aware, they make less mistakes, internal or external customers of an organization trust them more, and they are just better all round. The internal customers in organizations are the employees from those departments that pay another department to receive a particular service. The employees from the department who pays become clients (internal clients) to the department that receives a payment. In a productive organization they generate a culture where the values of the internal and external clients are the same.

1.5.1 Processes Behind the Operations in Banks

The various areas in a bank have different responsibilities; they all exist so that the bank is protected and functions well. Behind each function is at least one human, with all available brain functionalities, such as feelings, thoughts, knowledge, and creativity. There are many parts in a bank that one cannot modify for day-to-day business, such as rules, guidelines, and regulations. Is it possible for an organization to become naturally functional like a brain?

1.5.2 Processes Behind the Functions of the Brain

The different areas in a brain have different responsibilities; they all serve so that the body is protected and well-functioning. The main functions that we can directly control are the following: feelings, thoughts, memories, and creativity. We are not able to access all functions of our brain and change them for our day-to-day lives.

What is the relation between our brains and banking? Some readers might think there is no way to compare these two subjects, but I think there is, and later in the book there will be an explanation of why we believe that the brain could be a good role model for any organization, which seeks to become practical naturally.

References

de Bono E (1985) Six thinking hats. Little, Brown, Boston

Stafford P (2014) Swaps and derivatives: tougher capital rules boost traders' feelings of security. Financial Times

Tuveson M, Ruffle S (2014) Diversity is the way to avoid cyber collapse. Financial Times

Young RR, Brady SM, Nagle DC Jr (2009) How to save a failing project: chaos to control. Management Concepts, Vienna

Innovation

2

We can observe how Steve Job's inventions have changed our view of technology. Oberlander and Jones argue the following in an FT article (2011) entitled "10 years of iPod": "Since it came on the market 10 years ago, Apple's iPod has turned the recording industry on its head and revolutionized the way consumers listen to music."

Now we can give an iPad to our grandparents and they will love it, even if they were not missing such a device before. These grandparents might also be the customers of banks, have access to the latest innovations in technology, and learn how to access the latest news or knowledge via their iPad, provided they know exactly what they want to know.

Innovations either come along with changes in industries and the wider economy or constitute major changes themselves. The inventor of management, Drucker (1985), called innovation a diagnostic discipline, which systematically examines areas of change that offer opportunities. More specifically, Drucker sees seven sources of innovation. The first four sources can be found within an enterprise, an industry, or a service sector that is mostly visible to people within these areas. Despite being only symptoms, they are highly reliable indicators of changes that have already happened or can happen with little effort. These four sources are:

- The unexpected—an unexpected success, failure, or outside event;
- The incongruity—which is between reality as it is and reality as it is assumed to be or as it "ought to be";
- Innovation based on process needs;
- Changes in industry structure or market structure that catch everyone unaware.

The remaining sources for innovative opportunities, according to Drucker, involve changes outside the enterprise or industry:

- Demographics (population changes);
- Changes in perception, mood, and meaning;
- New knowledge, both scientific and non-scientific.

© Springer International Publishing Switzerland 2015
S. Thuiner, *Banks of the Future*, DOI 10.1007/978-3-319-07554-9_2

All seven sources are listed in descending order of reliability and predictability. In contrast to popular belief, Drucker continues, new knowledge—especially new scientific knowledge—is the least reliable and least predictable source of innovation, despite its visibility, glamor, and importance. Analysis of the symptoms of underlying changes, on the other hand, like an unexpected success or failure, features relatively low risk and uncertainty. Innovations arising from such symptoms take relatively little time for result generation.

2.1 Creative Solutions

Over the past years we were introduced to many new creative solutions, like mobile banking or cloud computing. According to Franklin and Andrews (2012), cloud computing will enable people to access their data from everywhere, and social networks will become a part of everybody's life. Although there are many interesting predictions in their book, I liked the ones that I think are most suitable for the content of my book.

2.1.1 Future Internet

A couple of years ago there were companies that made money only via the traffic on their website. Today, as a source of making money, the value of website traffic only has diminished. These companies need to find new ways of keeping their business going. The internet will evolve to a stage where website traffic or the number of viewers alone won't be sufficient and thus requires added value in order to stand out.

Individuals and companies will come up with new ideas for sharing information and creating virtual money, even on free platforms like YouTube, and the original idea of using the internet for free will change its direction, with less and less people sharing their services for free. It will become standard practice that participants in a particular market exchange knowledge and services among each other instead of giving it away for free.

It might also become standard market practice in the internet of the future to facilitate exchange with virtual money. The virtual money will only facilitate this kind of exchange in the virtual economy, but not in the traditional economy, to enable the exchange of knowledge. Virtual money for sharing our knowledge will also allow us in the future to pay for services from the likes of Google or Facebook. As with all developments in the internet in the past, it will happen fast, with more and more solutions around a particular idea coming to the market.

2.1.2 Creation of New Ideas

Many new solutions were implemented in banking in the wake of the financial crisis of 2008, which are largely related to processes, employees, and IT infrastructures. Each solution is supposed to meet new client needs, enhance competitiveness, increase profitability, and to serve customers better. Today, in a time of changing business models, banks are searching for ways to reduce costs, to increase productivity, and to leverage innovations in order to revive growth. New players in banking aim for creating a new customer experience, such as offering low-cost services for standard products, payment services by smart phone, and extended service hours. New stringent regulations ensure that customers' wealth is better protected than before the crisis.

2.1.3 Development of Technologies

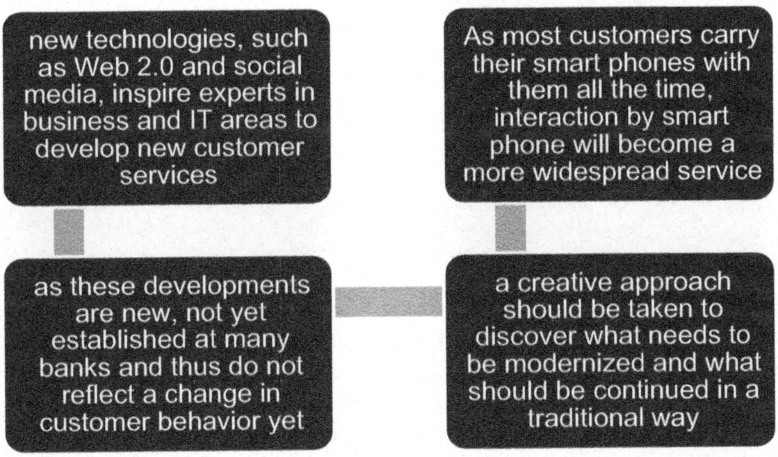

Developments of new technologies, such as Web 2.0 and social media, inspire experts in business and IT areas to develop new customer services and to ease the interaction between banks and customers. As these developments are new, not yet established at many banks, and thus do not reflect a change in customer behavior yet, a creative approach should be taken to discover what needs to be modernized and what should be continued in a traditional way.

New revolutionary bank business models have already been introduced to the market, where web 2.0 and social media have started to draw attention in the banking sector to new forms of interaction, which enable customers to share their experience and to use a smart phone for the dealings with their banks. As most customers carry their smart phones with them all the time, interaction by smart phone will become a more widespread service.

We also need to keep in mind that there will always be customers who prefer the traditional way of banking. I think that the market for this type of customers will not disappear anytime soon, at least not until they have no choice but to adapt to the changed circumstances. Until then there will always be a market for the traditional way of banking, even if the number of enthusiastic modern customers, who prefer to use their smart phones for banking, continues to increase.

2.1.4 Creativity

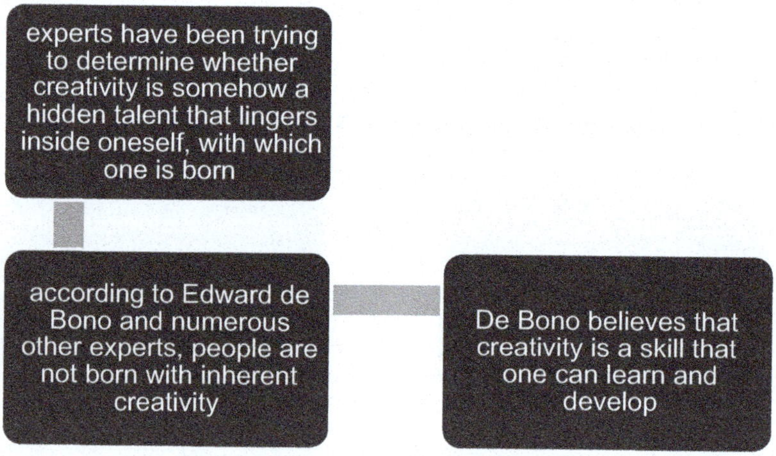

Experts have been trying to determine whether creativity is somehow a hidden talent that lingers inside oneself, with which one is born. In all my research, I didn't come across a conclusion that says one has it or not. According to Edward de Bono and numerous other experts, people are not born with inherent creativity. De Bono believes that creativity is a skill that one can learn and develop.

Charles Limb is a medical researcher who studies creativity by experimenting with what music does to our brain. Limb believes that our brain is able to learn creativity. In this chapter I want to describe different ways of becoming more creative that I have researched, understood, and tried out, and which can be beneficial for organizations in their attempts to become more innovative (Limb 2010).

2.1.4.1 Humor

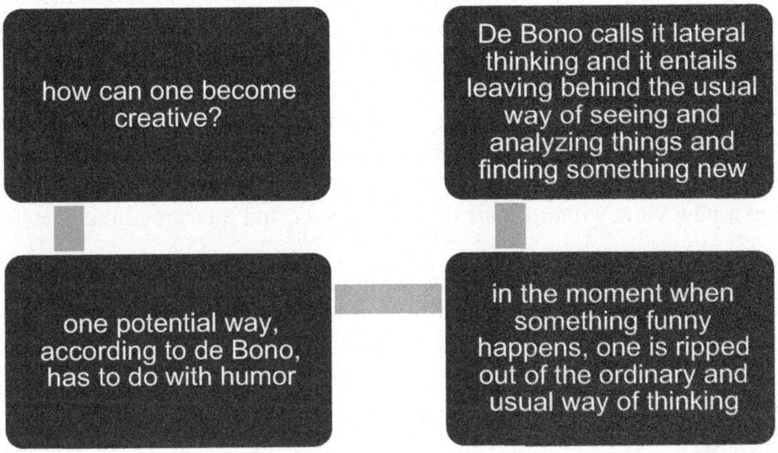

How can one become creative? One potential way, according to de Bono, has to do with humor. In the moment when something funny happens, one is ripped out of the ordinary and usual way of thinking. This means that one way to become creative is to allow humor more often to be expressed in an organization, such as a funny presentation about finding a solution to a complex subject so that the audience remains engaged. De Bono calls it lateral thinking and it entails leaving behind the usual way of seeing and analyzing things and finding something new. We look at the same things, but with different eyes, thoughts, and feelings.

2.1.4.2 Hobbies

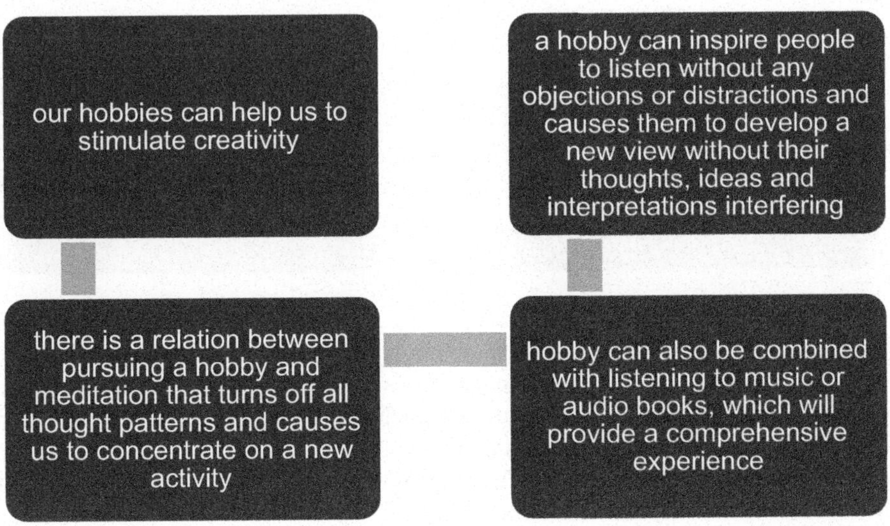

Our hobbies can help us to stimulate creativity, make us feel better, and relax. I think that there is a relation between pursuing a hobby and meditation that turns off all thought patterns and causes us to concentrate on a new activity. A hobby can also be combined with listening to music or audio books, which will provide a comprehensive experience.

I have more patience for listening to a discussion or speech about a complex and potentially boring subject while painting than at any other time. A hobby can inspire people to listen without any objections or distractions and causes them to develop a new view without their thoughts, ideas, and interpretations interfering.

2.1.4.2.1 Listen and Comprehend Complex Topics

While we are busy with an activity related to a hobby that does not engage our brain, it looks like our brain becomes hungry, because it seems to empty itself of unnecessary thoughts, which enables us to listen and comprehend complex topics and to develop a better understanding.

This is also the case with meditation since it calms our thoughts. It is the exact opposite situation when one tries to read and understand a complex subject during a break in the middle of a busy day.

2.1.4.2.2 Emotions and Creativity

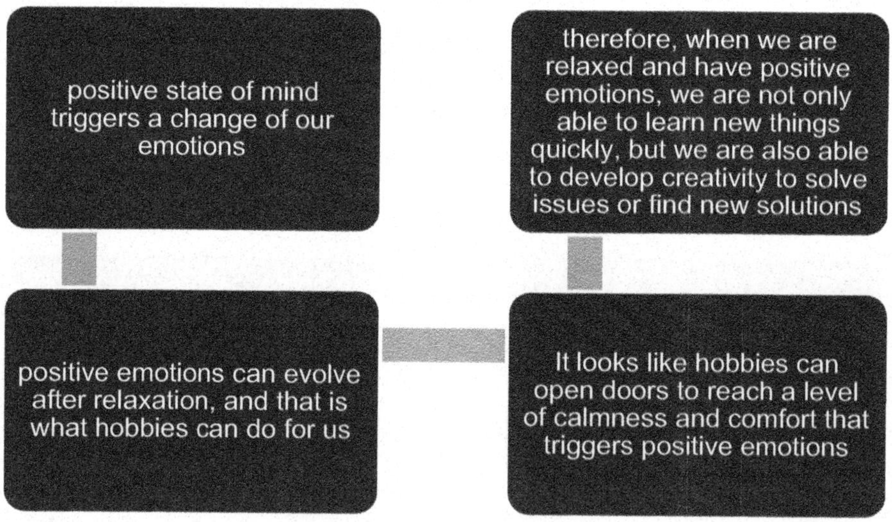

A positive state of mind triggers a change of our emotions. Positive emotions can evolve after relaxation, and that is what hobbies can do for us. It looks like hobbies can open doors to reach a level of calmness and comfort that triggers positive emotions. We can easily experiment and confirm by ourselves that our brain can memorize better when we are relaxed and calm. Therefore, if we combine a calm and relaxed moment with reading a book or listening to an audio book, we are better able to memorize the content of the book.

Therefore, when we are relaxed and have positive emotions, we are not only able to learn new things quickly, but we are also able to develop creativity to solve issues or find new solutions. A hobby makes us more productive and constructive in our thinking patterns, regardless of what hobby one has, be it building, collecting, painting or hiking, activities one enjoys to spend time on.

It does not really matter what we do as a hobby, what does matter is that we can become more creative when we feel comfortable and, at the same time, are busy doing something completely different. This might be a confirmation that working non-stop is not necessarily productive, especially if you have to find a solution to a complex IT problem.

2.1.4.2.3 Art and Other Hobbies

A break where we pursue our hobby makes us more creative while looking at an existing issue from another point of view, allowing us to come up with solutions that we were not aware of. In one of my previous projects we had a tabletop soccer game in the middle of the office of the IT department. I saw all of my colleagues playing from time to time, but could not understand their joy. In order to support the team dynamic like the others in the team did, I decided to join them and play it as well. Despite always losing, I enjoyed the game. My aim was to keep the game going as long as possible and to enjoy it. Issues that bothered me before the game were all of a sudden wiped of my memory; I could handle them more easily afterwards. It was further proof of the fact that we can become creative whenever we enjoy something. The result of a creative state of mind can be based on a combination of many factors. I was once told that listening to Bach is a kind of positive relaxation exercise, and that it is even more positive when we combine it with walking, driving, or traveling by train.

It is always a combination of several factors that produce a better result, such as the combination of physical movement and enjoyment that creates a higher awareness for an issue and adds more positive emotions to our mood.

2.1.4.3 Environment

Another way to stimulate creativity is by changing environments. During one of my assignments, when we had to deal with a difficult subject and were searching for a solution, our team occasionally met off-site for workshops in a completely different and relaxing environment. Such settings helped to become more open-minded when looking for new solutions. I think that leaving the usual environment and being dressed casually instead of formally will also help us to feel more comfortable. This change in our emotions will support us to think differently.

2.1.4.4 Bottom Line

Bottom line is that by taking time to enjoy something and stopping old patterns of looking for a solution to a problem, we might be able to find the best possible solution by applying a creative state of mind. This takes us to a state of mind in which we can leave our old thinking patterns behind and establish a good foundation to think differently and to analyze an issue or situation from different angles.

De Bono said humor leads us to lateral thinking and makes us more creative. As explained before, it seems that everything that makes us feel good will not only give us the chance to become creative in our profession, but also in our private lives.

2.2 IT Innovations

Technological progress has brought the world the internet. For example, it enables experts from around the world to share their knowledge and ideas with each other and with the rest of the world, which can be enriching to a lot of people. There is a range of innovations around technology waiting to be implemented in many traditionally run banks, which will change the interactions between financial institutions and their employees and customers. There might be only little benefits during an early implementation compared to an implementation at a later stage. Some customers might appreciate that their banks carefully consider a change, while others appreciate a quick introduction, as they prefer to use the latest technology for the interactions with their bank. There is no right and wrong, as the perception of the situation is subjective.

2.2.1 Improvements in IT

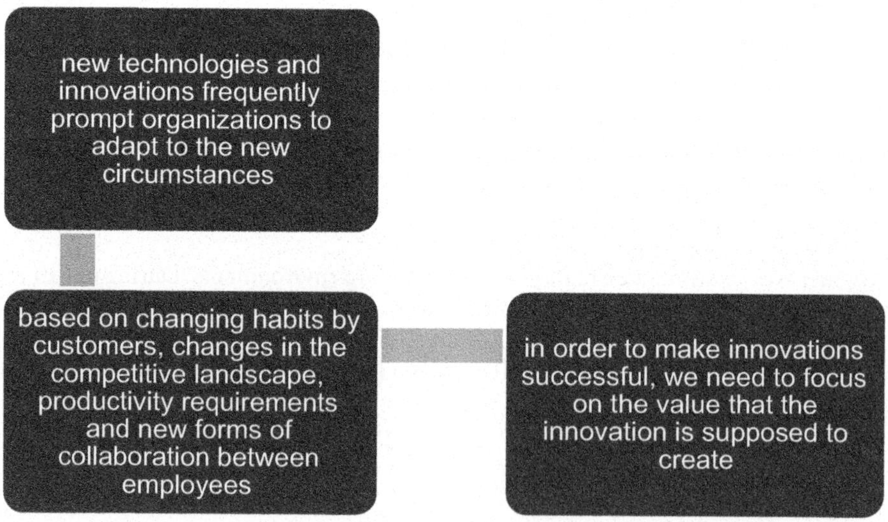

New technologies and innovations frequently prompt organizations to adapt to the new circumstances, based on changing habits by customers, changes in the competitive landscape, productivity requirements and new forms of collaboration between employees. In order to make innovations successful, we need to focus on the value that the innovation is supposed to create. This should be measured from the customer's or organizational point of view. Furthermore, process innovations, for instance, potentially bring along a change in the entire process landscape. Therefore, a sufficient risk assessment is a key factor to support the innovation process.

Although we have seen numerous innovations in banking technology over the recent years, there are further innovations on the horizon that will transform business models and customer relationships in the near future. Due to the fact that established banks have numerous legacy systems in place compared to more recently established banks, the implementation of new solutions will take a different level of effort, depending on the legacy inherent in the organizational structure of the bank. Another aspect related to the introduction of an innovation is to measure the security implications of this solution. In a large organization the security experts might be spread all over the world, and a committee in charge of approving a change might not be that easy to convince. There are potentially numerous checks and evaluations required in order to be able to measure the impact of the innovation.

2.2.2 Defining Controlling Mechanisms

Innovations can also prompt an organization to serve existing customers in a new way. It also means that new products can be invented to serve new or existing clients. The source of any innovation is creativity. A creative idea will arrive first and the innovation will then take place after the idea has been evaluated and accepted.

2.2.2.1 Simplification of Processes

If an IT company is able to simplify the process of implementation of a new technology for the banking sector, it will likely become a much sought-after IT provider. The implementation of a new solution is more challenging for an established bank than for a bank with a fairly short operating history, due to established banks having numerous, difficult to replace, systems and processes in place to deal with. Any new implementation should be aligned with existing solutions.

Banks with a short operating history have fewer concerns about security or risks regarding their infrastructure, as it is easier to establish an overview about their infrastructure and its underlying processes than in a large established bank.

2.2.2.2 Processes

The best way of controlling a complex IT solution and its underlying business processes is to set up a process to control it. The process can be created based on a number of simple solutions/processes and must always involve many experts from around the organization and encompass their knowledge. Going forward, the benefits of well-defined control processes in an organization and their impact on overall controlling will be highly regarded.

2.2.2.3 The Technology Landscape

New IT solutions for different areas of a financial institution have evolved quickly over the last two decades. Financial institutions have always invested in business ideas via technology in order to better serve their clients and to remain competitive in the market. If we look at the landscape of technology for the day-to-day business in a bank today, we will discover that many solutions that we take for granted, such as smartphones, laptops, video conferences, the Internet, email-based communication, and more were not commonplace for most of us not long ago.

2.2.3 Smarter with IT

About 20 years ago, banking started to become more sophisticated. Intelligent tools, such as search engines, started to be used more frequently in daily business in banking, but were not as important for our work as today, since there was only little information available in the internet. At its beginning, the internet was mainly used by IT specialists and less by ordinary people. The first reliable environment for banking data was a host with a very unfriendly user interface.

IT systems in the daily business of a bank were mainly used by a particular group of people, as not all employees needed to use a computer. I remember meeting a senior bank manager on the trading floor of a bank in 1996 and was surprised to hear that she refused to use a computer, as she did not need one.

In 1995 I was a member of one of the first social networks in Austria called "Magnet," where only IT people chatted and exchanged IT-related issues and solutions with each other. This was a pure IT-related information exchange among members of the IT network. It felt like being part of a small community where it was easy to remain in touch with one another and to occasionally meet people to initiate professional relationships.

Since then, the ways in which we think about professional networking and about IT have changed. Today, many other solutions support us in our day-to-day professional and social lives. In order to remain in touch with colleagues, friends, and family members, we sometimes need to join several social networks, as there is not just one platform where everyone is a member of.

2.2.3.1 Hosts

After decades of revolutionary developments in technology, I wonder how hosts with unfriendly user interfaces could survive for such a long time, as they still exist and are important for all kinds of sensitive information in almost all large, established organizations.

2.2.3.2 IT Could Go Haywire

Most of the IT experts remember how scary the turn to the year 2000 was for many organizations. We were told that the IT experts in the past have developed technology in a way that only the last two digits of a year are considered and that IT could go haywire if the two digits suddenly became "00." We performed every check and considered new services to ensure that our banks' systems would work well after 2000. I am not aware of a single case of proof that all the fuss regarding the year 2000 was worth it. There is no doubt about the intelligence of IT specialists; maybe this is also additional proof of it. Does it also mean that Michio Kaku's (Kaku 2009) prediction about intelligent robots, which might see humans as their pets, is a nice fantasy and that in reality people who created them have also increased their intelligence to solve ever more complex problems?

2.2.4 Freedom of Developers in Banking

In fact, the freedom of developers can sometimes harm a business. During my work for a large organization, I was a member of a project where data was needed to be sent to a data warehouse. As the data were based on derivative transactions, we needed to ensure that the right information was stored in the right table of many databases of the data warehouse. Our project plan suddenly could not cope with the deliveries on time, as we discovered that the same information was called differently in different tables of the same data warehouse. There was no unique naming convention and even the new databases did not use unique naming. This meant that every change in this environment would need more effort and would cost more. Our project reported this issue, but I am not sure if unique naming was implemented or if the developers are still using their creativity to make it a bit more complicated than necessary.

2.2.5 IT Standards

We are now in a time where we use many IT standards in order to ease interaction within IT landscapes and to increase the quality of what we do. As IT becomes increasingly more sophisticated, there will be many questions around these IT standards in the future, and there will also be new proposals for a change from the existing standards to simpler solutions. The new IT standards will be based on new principles to serve more complex IT infrastructures of a future financial world. This IT standard will be based on common sense in a modern form of Artificial Intelligence (AI) and makes it easier for the banking industry to exchange pre-defined information automatically on similar levels of authority.

2.2.6 Artificial Intelligence

Going forward, different areas in organizations with common subjects like tax issues, will apply AI solutions with inherent common sense in order to exchange information between each other. Making technology understand common sense will be one of the innovative solutions of the future that will be used to cope with today's complexity and to reduce risks.

2.2.6.1 Tax Regulation

AI-inherent common sense applied to the internal handling of tax issues will make automated decisions based on available knowledge, such as a client's account type, domicile, citizenship, and allocation ratio on the one side, and about the exchange of information between relevant parties on the other side, possible. All information which has been exchanged in the process will be recorded.

2.2.6.2 Future Change Management

In the future, changes in IT will be performed in a more natural way by modern technologies, which will be able to understand common sense. New technologies will be able to simplify change with the creation of an overview of that change. The new technology will be able to communicate all the dependencies clearly and to produce documentation automatically of what will be changed and by when. It will even create educational videos and audio books for training sessions automatically, which can be run on the intranet of the organization at any time for training purposes. Upcoming new technologies will be able to use an updated best practice every time a change takes place.

The system will update best practice of the organization by enhancing it with new experience if necessary. This system might be called "AI Change Management" and is a new way of running a change. It will be very powerful and will even be able to assist anybody at any level during the entire change process. For instance, an intelligent change management system can coach a manager through the change and will support him in becoming an even more effective leader.

2.2.6.3 Future Controlling/Monitoring

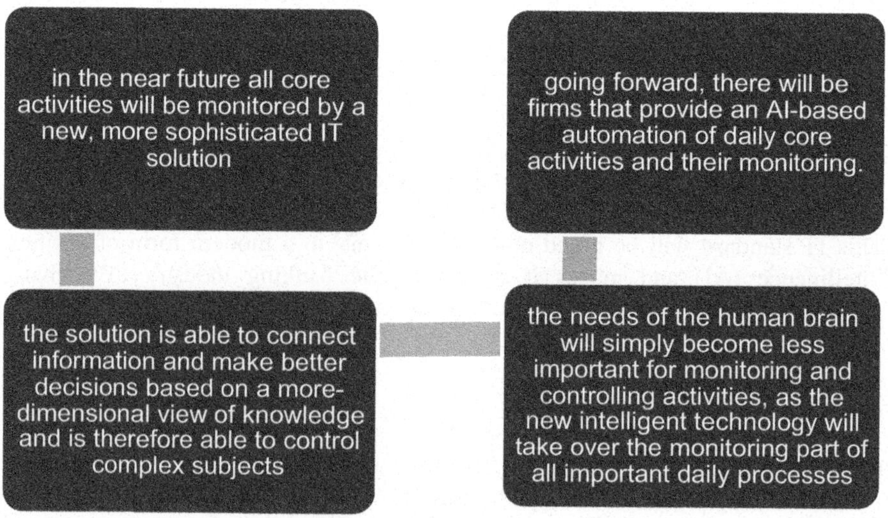

In the near future all core activities will be monitored by a new, more sophisticated IT solution. The solution is able to connect information and make better decisions based on a more-dimensional view of knowledge and is therefore able to control complex subjects. The needs of the human brain will simply become less important for monitoring and controlling activities, as the new intelligent technology will take over the monitoring part of all important daily processes. For instance, daily activities around the IT service life cycle will be monitored and managed by a new intelligent system, which will cover all steps, such as service design, service transition, and service operation almost effortlessly. Going forward, there will be many new procedures to monitor solutions based on the logic of AI.

Today, there are already a number of intelligent solutions available on the market, which enable the review of day-to-day processes so that hidden risks are avoided. Going forward, there will be firms that provide an AI-based automation of daily core activities and their monitoring. As technology continues to grow rapidly, there will be even more advanced IT solutions available for a wide range of applications. We will have institutions similar to our universities that measure the available IT solutions on the market in terms of the appropriateness for the world of finance and can then facilitate the selection of the best solutions.

They might be called "Software Measurement Institutions" and will also have the duty of providing the best knowledge for building an intelligent system. IT firms and individuals can obtain a certificate for having the right solution, based on the highest standards. These firms or individuals are authorized to receive a certificate for their solutions after passing a number of tests. As controlling and monitoring can be complex tasks with a high priority in banking, banks will entrust this kind of service only to those firms who are specialized in providing monitoring services for daily processes. These service companies will need to demonstrate that they already have satisfied clients, but they will also need a certificate from a future software measurement institute to confirm their expertise and that they are able to act practically.

In the aftermath of the financial crisis, controlling and compliance procedures in banking became more and more important. There is a huge desire to monitor every process and activity in order to discover issues, risks, or weaknesses as soon as they evolve.

2.2.7 Handling of a Project

I think that the task of managing a project requires a broad view and that the value of a successfully concluded project tends to be underestimated. During a project, project managers regularly discover that the project plan cannot be implemented as envisaged. This is the reason why a project manager must use the project plan as a road map, but needs to remain flexible and make compromises. The basic means for compromise and solution finding is creativity. It is difficult to compromise if a project manager is not able to understand the business implications as well as potential IT implications. In financial institutions we are used to being constructive or able to think out-side-of the box. Although I avoid using the word creativity in my projects, I use the term in this book, as it is more precise.

2.2.7.1 Initiation Phase and Emotions

We can define innovation processes as projects. The best way of running a project is to leave no room for interpretation. The entire preparation and initiation of a project is based on clear communication with all key experts related to the project. For project managers it causes frustration if they are responsible for the evaluation of a topic that will never leave the initiation phase. The best idea will suffer if the initiation phase is too long, if there are too many people involved and if the decision-making executives are missing. In case the efforts of the initiation phase are higher than in the actual implementation phase, the outcome of the project will not have the desired level of success. Such projects have an expensive initiation phase and will cause frustrations before they are even started.

2.2.7.1.1 Smooth Initiation Phase

I think that a project with a smooth initiation phase will have a good chance of being successful. We have to cope with increasing complexity in business and IT, which is the reason why in the future there will be a strong demand for a highly specialized expertise in a single subject, such as process management or management of the evaluation phase of a project. While a combined expertise from experts of different fields around one particular subject will be in high demand, these experts will still be specialized on particular solutions, such as process management. A large number of consulting firms offer a range of services and competences in different industries and are able to offer solutions to a range of different requests, but the future will require more narrow specializations as a core competence.

This is the reason why there will be companies in the future that exclusively offer the management of the initiation phase of a project. They will have intelligent systems and tools to support only this kind of project and, at the same time, are experts for running clear processes to cover all steps of the initiation phase.

2.2.7.1.2 Emotions

2. The Intense Landscape

There is no need to understand a particular subject during the initiation phase of the project, but it requires soft skills to deal with the emotions during the project and the involvement of the right group of people to discuss the facts and emotions related to a particular subject. In addition, agreements made during discussions need to be recorded and the relevant stakeholders need to be involved in order to communicate the agreements and to collect their objections.

The objections should be dealt with in the core group of the project. Following an agreement, the stakeholder group must be invited again in order to enable the core team to present the new agreement, collect any objections, and to get back to the stakeholder group after they have come up with new solutions. This process must be structured and repeated as often as necessary until a solution is found. Note that the core team of a project is always included in the conversation with the stakeholder group. Stakeholders and senior managers only provide information or ask questions, but do not try to find solutions to problems, as this is clearly the core team's responsibility. You have to understand that the key to success and the containment of emotions and conflicts is to assign clear responsibilities to each of your project team members and to focus on results during the entire project. As simple as it sounds, and though it is a guiding principle in all project-related internal guidelines, many project managers still fail to follow it. The initiation phase of a project becomes expensive and is sometimes never finished, because there is no clear separation based on the context and no clear responsibilities assigned in the core team of the project.

Example

One of my previous employers was a medium-sized bank which decided to change the trading system on the entire trading floor. We looked for a system that can cover front-to-end activities. We found several suitable solutions that covered trading, controlling, back office functions, accounting as well as risk management. Due to internal politics it was challenging to bring the evaluation phase to an end. Although the responsibilities of the involved project team members were clearly assigned, it was impossible to finish it, as internal politics stirred up emotions and conflicts which was damaging for the project. At the end, a senior manager came out on top and made the final selection for the bank, but as the decision was not taken by the group, he lost support and eventually left the bank after helping to finish the entire implementation properly. Even the newly appointed senior manager did not manage to get support for the implemented solution. The emotions and controversies involved made it difficult for the departments to start using the application properly, which made the usage of the application becoming a pain for the whole organization. The application is still in use at the bank and is now based on a solid understanding of the application. The application was able to increase the organization's productivity and to enhance its risk management, but the history made it difficult for the application to be fully accepted right from the beginning.

2.2.7.2 Bottom Line

I think that the most important aspect in any evaluation project is to carefully listen to the opinions of the project team members and to never allow any person or area to dominate. It is important that the group takes joint decisions in order to provide for an eventual smooth implementation of the solution. The initiation phase is all about collecting ideas, facts, making decisions and includes the following steps:

- Definition of scope
- Organization of kick-off meeting
- Composition of a core team of the project, based on the needed expertise in the project
- Definition of a means of communication, confirmed by the core team members and stakeholders
- Stick to the agreed means of communication and use it to control your project as well as for reporting
- Hold each team member accountable and let them discuss their suggestions within a larger group, but make sure that they remain responsible for their assignments
- Following major agreements, organize a meeting with stakeholders to discuss the findings and agreements in a large group
- Always consider that your core team members come from different areas of the organization; listen to their ideas, concerns, objections, and emotions
- Ensure that all core team members are satisfied with the progress of their tasks and the agreed decisions before meeting with stakeholders and senior managers; this is the key to ensure progress in your evaluation project, as the project members will promote the solution in their areas afterwards

As a project manager, I have learned that a clear process helps to earn the trust of the experts and keeps emotions in check in order to avoid distractions of the team and wasting productive energy. If the collected ideas and facts and the decisions taken are not satisfactory to the stakeholders, new ideas and facts need to be collected and decisions made, based on these collected ideas and facts. They need to be presented to the stakeholders to ensure that no aspects have been missed. Processes around the initiation phase need to be kept simple and well established in the organization.

2.2.8 Procedures vs. Processes

In every project we come across procedures and practice related to the topic of the project. A procedure explains how a task is done in a particular area, while a process explains all the steps that need to be taken and who the involved experts are for these steps. In today's banking business, procedures and processes are critical for the productivity of the organization. They can be set up in a way so that the day-to-day business can be run smoothly and avoids hidden risks. Although procedures and processes play an important role in every aspect of the day-to-day business of banks, they tend to disappear from our minds once they have been defined and implemented.

Despite being considered an annoying topic at times, it is important to keep in mind that well designed processes and procedures prevent organizations from facing troubles, but at the same time they tend to not being always clearly understood. I think that in an organizational environment, processes and procedures need to be transparent and understandable for everybody, have to be documented clearly, and must be updated regularly. Documentation of processes and procedures in an organization should include graphics and be written in a clear and understandable language, with no room for mis-interpretation. It should also be kept as practical as possible, with no science behind it.

2.2.8.1 Processes in a Project

As mentioned, managing a project in a bank is based on pre-defined guidelines on reporting, documentation, communication, change management, etc. which must be followed by every member in a project. The guidelines should be seen as a tool to run a project efficiently, based on a pre-defined processes, with the responsibility for following the guidelines being with the project manager.

In practice, guidelines and methods should be designed in a way that leaves room for a practical approach. Studying the entire documentation of CMMI creates the impression that this documentation, due to its scope, could be the foundation for a university lecture, and that it is not very helpful for good practice. Going forward, financial institutions will need to keep documentation around guidelines and methods as practical as possible in order to provide simple access to essential information. The important information, for instance, around the topic of CMMI, could potentially be provided at the following three levels:

1. One page with high level information on CMMI
2. Two pages with explanations on the content of the high level information
3. Three pages with further details and links on where to find specific information

All detailed information is only available to those who are assigned to explore the subject without applying common sense and therefore they need to go through the entire CMMI documentation. CMMI is one of the best methods available on the subject of successful project management, but I think that, going forward, banks will implement this guideline in a more practical way.

2.2.8.2 Projects and Creativity

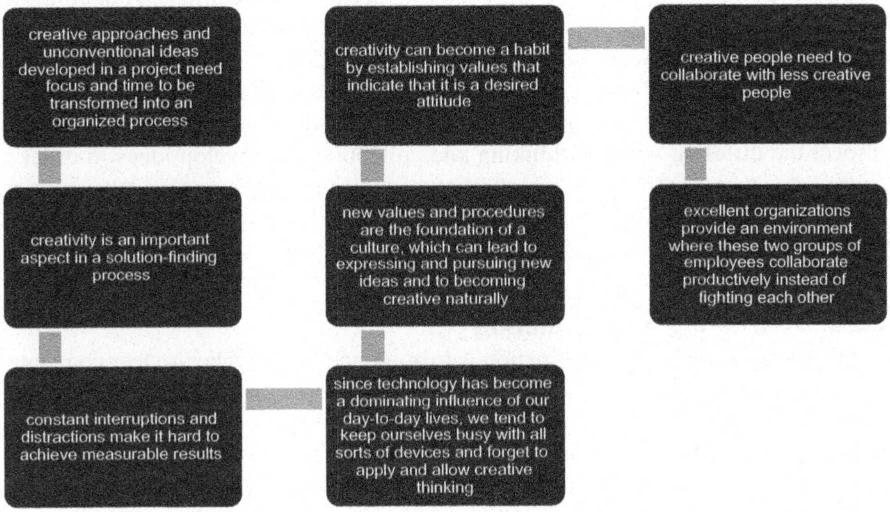

Creative approaches and unconventional ideas developed in a project need focus and time to be transformed into an organized process. In order to let creativity flourish, a project manager needs to provide a setting that allows reflection and intellectual engagement. Creativity is an important aspect in a solution-finding process. Constant interruptions and distractions make it hard to achieve measurable results. Since technology has become a dominating influence of our day-to-day lives, we tend to keep ourselves busy with all sorts of devices and forget to apply and allow creative thinking. It helps organizations in the context of innovations and in coming up with out-of-the-box solutions for competitive advantages.

New values and procedures are the foundation of a culture, which can lead to expressing and pursuing new ideas and to becoming creative naturally. Creativity can become a habit by establishing values that indicate that it is a desired attitude. For instance, if action orientation is more highly valued than endless discussions in meetings with no outcome or if meetings are conducted while standing as opposed to sitting, it is a reflection of the importance of professional meetings for managerial efficiency.

Creative people need to collaborate with less creative people. In many cases, less creative people tend to be the ones who are good at implementing things and who are usually happy if nothing changes. Projects need a good mix of doers and dreamers. Doers and dreamers in an organization need each other in order to realize the full potential of an organization. An organization with many doers and only a few dreamers will be able to create a highly productive environment, but it will more slowly adapt to change and potentially loose out against competition in its attempts to defend market share.

I think there are ways of finding the right balance between doers and dreamers in an organization, for instance, by only looking at their presentations. A doer argues based on facts only, while a creative mind wants to convince not only rationally, but also with emotion, which is why they tend to influence us more strongly, by aiming at our emotions. Excellent organizations provide an environment where these two groups of employees collaborate productively instead of fighting each other. They respect the different ways of thinking and collaborate to develop ideas in order to better serve their customers. The intention of senior management must be to create a culture of respect which allows both types of personalities to co-exist productively.

2.2.8.3 Gathering of Information

A quick way of gathering information is to approach people who are less concerned about their power, influence, or popularity, as these people will be most happy to share information. Less popular or less valued people can sometimes also play an important role for the information and knowledge transfer in an organization. An organization that has placed them strategically will not only ensure that an area is communicative internally, but it will also ensure that the lack of knowledge transfer will not cause any risks.

2.2.8.4 Solving Issues

An important rule for solving issues that I have experienced is to keep things fact-based and simple. Simple also means keeping them visual and keeping a sense of humor as a means to ensure that all parties are engaged in the entire problem solving process. Another important point in the process of solving issues is to always keep a top–down approach and never to blend a bottom–up with a top–down approach once you have started to solve an issue.

2.2.8.5 Speed of a Project

In order to keep all parties engaged, a project manager needs to keep an eye on speed so that everyone is aware of approaching deadlines and decisions to be made to keep the project on schedule. Running a project is like in an endurance activity—maintaining a good balance between burning calories and not losing breath.

It is also the speed of a project that contributes to a productive collaboration between all involved experts and helps to keep emotions and conflicts under control. The speed of a project is supposed to be such that the project plan is set up in a way that everybody is able to cope with it, with administrative procedures being kept low and performance in daily, weekly, or monthly sessions being kept high.

The project manager defines the balance between speed and quality of performance. I think that a project manager must be a bit of a doer as well as a dreamer and should create a culture of "why not" thinking. We live in a time where change in organizations is constant and therefore organizations need to create a culture to act and adapt to change quickly.

2.2.8.6 Visibility and Transparency

A project manager must keep a focus on practicality, no matter if he plans, manages, or reports. He needs to use the customer's expectations as his road map and provide visibility and transparency to all involved experts and stakeholders. An effective project manager is able to ensure that his project is transparent to the entire organization. He uses the organization's best practice in a practical way, based on personal experience.

The meaning of best practice is to apply established ways of doing things in order to remain practical and avoid failure. Best practice has become knowledge, since it has enabled organizations to become more efficient in their attempts to introduce change and innovations. As every organization has its own definition of best practice, they have discovered where the best practice was applied, classified existing solutions, developed a body of knowledge and shared it with each area of the organization. The best managers are those who are able to identify best practice and take responsibility for its re-validation and enhancement when necessary. Outdated practice should be retired and new best practice be published. Best practice is the application of tools, methods, and processes that have been validated, like specific templates that a PMO of a project can adapt and re-use. One of the important tasks of a PMO is to audit whether the entire project applies best practice.

2.2.8.7 Complexity of Projects

Managing a project means, depending on its scope and complexity, considering rules and control mechanisms that project managers need to apply in order to be finished on time and within budget.

In one of my projects we once decided to use the Agile methodology instead of Waterfall in order to avoid being on the bank's big projects radar. Through this decision, we avoided the requirement of producing numerous documents and the need to involve many different areas and people, which would have slowed down the project significantly. Instead, the budget was split into small amounts (sprint), with each amount looking insignificant on the bank's project radar. Therefore we had a better control of what we did and could provide a higher quality by correcting the outcome of the latest sprint.

2.2.8.8 Intuitions and Emotions

A project is supposed to be managed based on facts only and is not set up to allow intuitions or emotions playing a role. The connection between intellect and emotions is largely ignored in the context of today's working life. Successful projects, however, encourage an interplay between intellect and emotions to facilitate the best possible outcome. In the future, projects will remain method-based, but practicality will be seen as the guiding principle.

The latest insights into the connection between brain and emotions will influence what will emerge as new best practice in project management, with tools being available to leverage the effect of a combination of both aspects of a project. Newly advanced methods of managing a project will become more refined and sophisticated and incorporate intellect, creativity, and emotions, something which is not adequately considered today, but will be seen as an additional strength tomorrow.

2.2.8.9 Project Management Tools

Instead of using several different systems and numerous process steps to manage a project, future project management practice will be based on a single piece of software, which provides the possibility to combine brain and emotions. In the near future the main objective will be to handle a project naturally and to avoid risks almost effortlessly. A future intelligent software will act as your PMO and will adjust all templates and daily processes to ease the administration of your project.

The software will send out reports, invitations to meetings, or advise what the solution to a particular issue is. In the end the software will ease the administration and will ensure that your project is following internal guidelines without noticing. There will be no need to take a decision on which method to apply or what the best means of communication should be. The software is able to make suggestions, like organizing conference calls for update meetings at a particular date and time. The software is able to make this decision, due to the information you have entered, like core team members' domiciles and locations. The underlying guideline of your project will be a method-based combination of brain and emotions as best practice.

By using a tool to support a project, the entire view of running your project will be changed and it will no longer require an explanation at every step of the way when instead a computer can follow the process and advise a project manager what to do next. Therefore reporting and documentation during a project can become automatic, with the project manager answering the system's questions and clarifying the common sense of the information so that it's entered into the system correctly.

Running a project with the support of such a system will make life easier, as it enables the project manager to remain focused on the critical aspects of the task and to spend less time on administration.

2.3 Internal Audit

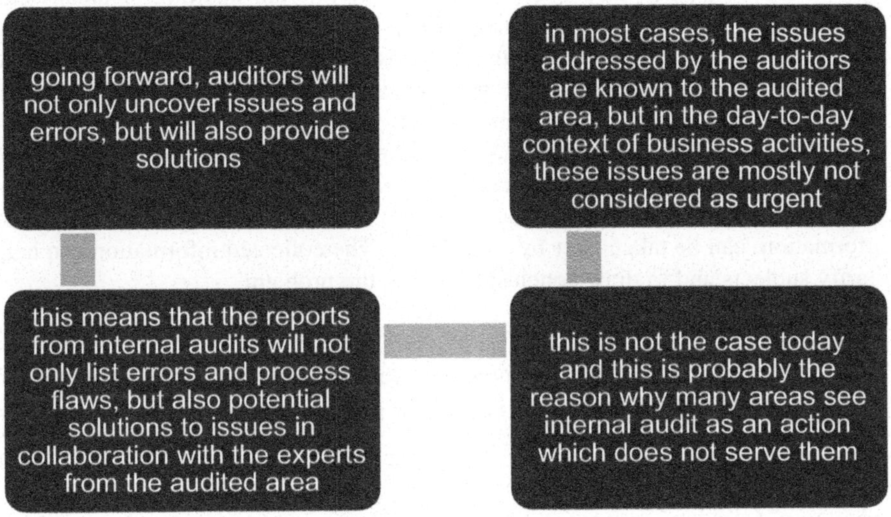

Auditing is about analyzing, being able to collect information around the audited subject, and understanding its connections to other relevant subjects or areas. Going forward, auditors will not only uncover issues and errors, but will also provide solutions. This means that the reports from internal audits will not only list errors and process flaws, but also potential solutions to issues in collaboration with the experts from the audited area. This is not the case today and this is probably the reason why many areas see internal audit as an action which does not serve them.

In most cases, the issues addressed by the auditors are known to the audited area, but in the day-to-day context of business activities, these issues are mostly not considered as urgent. In the future audit needs to adopt its approach to generate a benefit for the audited area too. The most important task of an internal auditor is to be able to analyze the collected information, while the question part of an audit can be done by a junior auditor. By repeatedly asking "why?," an auditor can collect large amounts of information which helps to understand the entire landscape around a subject. It enables the auditor to evaluate the facts and make assessments.

When I was working as an internal auditor, I was involved in a project that was searching for an early warning system using available technology. We were tasked to ask simple questions and to evaluate the collected facts about a particular subject. In contrast to Eliza which became famous decades ago for being a revolutionary IT solution, the operating system featured in the movie "HER" did not provide a revolutionary new insight into the latest AI technology.

2.3.1 Eliza as Internal Auditor

Can AI such as Eliza take over the activity of internal auditing? Humans can differentiate between a conversation with a human and a conversation with a robot. Furthermore, they are able to make jokes, write poetry, or recognize a lie by a person's voice or mimic. As mentioned, by asking the simplest questions, almost everybody can access information. How intelligent must AI become in order to be able to act as an internal auditing system, and what would be the role of humans in this process? I think that by even having simple artificial interaction software in place, the interview part, as well as the structuring of the collected information, can be taken over by a computer. The collected information can help clarify subjects and to draw conclusions about the problem.

Example

Here is an example of how a simple question can be asked to collect all needed information about a particular issue: The issue is that I get up early in the morning.

AI Why? **Answer:** Because I like the early morning energy and silence.

AI Why do you like silence? **Answer:** Because, if it's quiet, I get into a different state of mind with little effort.

AI Why do you need a different state of mind? **Answer:** Because in a different state of mind I can see ordinary things from a new perspective.

AI Why do you need a new perspective? **Answer:** Because different perspectives can reveal new solutions to problems.

AI Why? **Answer:** Because new solutions will give me the ability to better solve outstanding issues.

AI Why? **Answer:** Because by better solving my issues I have a better day.

AI Why do you have a better day? **Answer:** Because a good day starts with no issues.

AI Why? **Answer:** Because a good day should include fun.

AI Why do you need fun? **Answer:** Because with fun, life is much more enjoyable. . ..

In practice, questions can be chosen in a way that the person being interviewed does not discover that the questions are asked without the answers being listened to.

2.3.2 AI and Internal Audit

After the financial crisis, the area that would benefit the most from the introduction of AI into its processes is internal audit. This way, existing resources can be used in a more efficient way and it would be possible to audit more areas in shorter period of time. In the future, internal audit will use software like Eliza to interview experts from all areas almost monthly and will be able to collect information by setting up an early warning system for reporting by searching for critical words.

Areas with the most critical words will be audited with the most urgency. The interview can also include hidden checks to ensure that the person understands the answers being given and validates the truth. This will help to control more efficiently, without any additional resources. Furthermore, issues can be found more quickly, and potential losses can be detected much earlier before they cause damage to the organization.

2.4 Intelligent Solutions

Can AI cover more sophisticated tasks in the future? In terms of logical evaluations, the creation of a memory and the valuation of information, IT software beats human abilities. In the near future, computers will become a thousand times faster and will need less power than the IT solutions available today.

2.4.1 Daily Business and New Solutions

Today, financial institutions are able, for instance, to scan a cheque with a machine, with the machine being able to read the exact amount on the cheque. There is a lot of intelligent online support available for software applications, although the intelligence behind the support is not very sophisticated. These solutions are useful and can help saving time. In the near future more AI solutions will be used in banking which will be able to do all the things that humans are capable of, with less risks involved and with incredible accuracy.

The question regarding the development of AI today is whether it can have a consciousness or synthetic "emotions"? Can we go even further and develop AI with a sub-consciousness? Another key question is why would we want to build an IT solution that is similar to humans? I think in the future we will all come to the conclusion that there is no need to have an exact copy of humans. We should rather focus on avoiding it, because human feelings and the sub-consciousness tend to make things more complex and therefore allows hidden risks to evolve.

We already know how to develop AI that trains itself. In terms of controlling and auditing, this knowledge and the introduction of such systems can help to reduce risks and costs in organizations, but until today I did not come across a solution that is suitable for the banking business.

According to Markram (2009), it is important to have a human brain in a computer, as it helps science to experience and understand the brain's ability for social interactions and complex cognitive functions.

An interesting process in the brain is decision making. Once we understand the human brain in all its facets, we could incorporate human emotions in a computer and make the computer having all kinds of emotions, such as love, fear, or excitement. It took a long time for scientists to develop AI that is able to understand emotions to some extent, but the question is what is the benefit of adding emotions to technology?

Example

An AI solution is introduced to employees in order that each employee can speak to it and verbally transfer its knowledge to the system. This knowledge will be available via intranet for all employees throughout the organization. In the near future such a solution will be capable of recording emotions and measuring them.

According to Edward De Bono, it is important to evaluate feelings in the same way we evaluate facts. Therefore, the emotions of the speaker must be recorded in a way that the correct application of knowledge is possible. In such a scenario, AI solutions will also support ethical behavior, and the smarter they become, the more controls an organization can implement in its business activities.

2.4.2 Organizational Networks

Each business area is connected to the rest of the organization, which means that an issue can sometimes affect several areas. This issue can not only harm an organization, but also its employees and clients. The conclusion here is that if a financial institution is able to implement AI in an area like internal audit, it will not only better control an organization, but it can also avoid risks which come along with innovative IT solutions. AI is currently either not embedded in day-to-day banking processes or it is minimized in its abilities.

Example

Historical data about financial products are important to enable predictions about the future. If a product is new, it can be synthetically created based on pre-defined rules. The calculation of the overall risk, for instance, would not make a difference between real historical data and synthetic data; thus, decisions taken are less precise. In the future, intelligent solutions will enable the reader of the report to differentiate between real historical data and synthetic data, which will facilitate decision making.

2.5 Documentation

Documentation is key and is the foundation of any control mechanism in an organization. In a project, depending on the method applied, a document can be given many different names, related to user stories or requirements, user guides, compliance documentation, use cases, process flow diagrams or business requirement documents, change requests, etc. Records of meetings or emails, formal as well as informal, are also considered documentation in a project. Whether a project has been finished or a task been accomplished can only be determined based on proper documentation.

2.5.1 Projects and Documentation

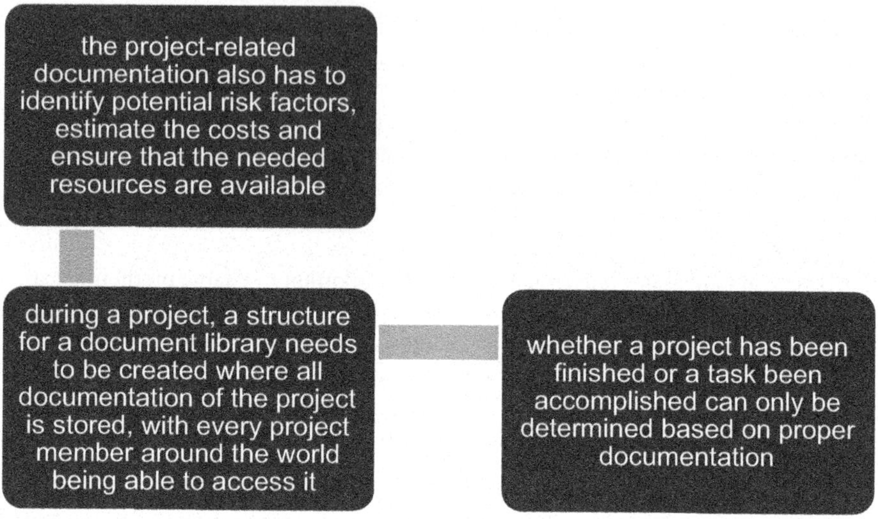

A project normally starts with a detailed, well documented business case, with a project charter following afterwards when the project team members are determined. A project plan as a crucial document encompasses purpose, scope, people involved, time of delivery, and potential risks. Only after production of all initial documentation is the project team able to start and close the initiation phase of the project.

The project plan is the main tool to manage a project and to support the monitoring and measurement of the project progress. The project plan and other project-related documentation provide overall documentation about the ways the project decisions were taken. The project plan, once developed and executed, is also the basis for change requests at the end. Careful planning helps to clearly analyze, specify, design, develop, test, and finally implement the result of the project. A well-conceived plan is crucial for finishing the project on time, within budget and for delivering all addressed requests with accuracy. Perfect project plan documentation will also provide a clear understanding of the scope, the list of activities within the scope and a clear time and action table for all involved project team members and their assignments. The project-related documentation also has to identify potential risk factors, estimate the costs, and ensure that the needed resources are available. Every major topic, such as development, quality, risk management, performance reporting, change management, and project roll-out should also be documented in a project plan.

During a project, a structure for a document library needs to be created where all documentation of the project is stored, with every project member around the world being able to access it. This has the benefit that the information can be shared quickly and audits performed by reviewing the documents if needed.

2.5.1.1 Practical Ways of Documenting

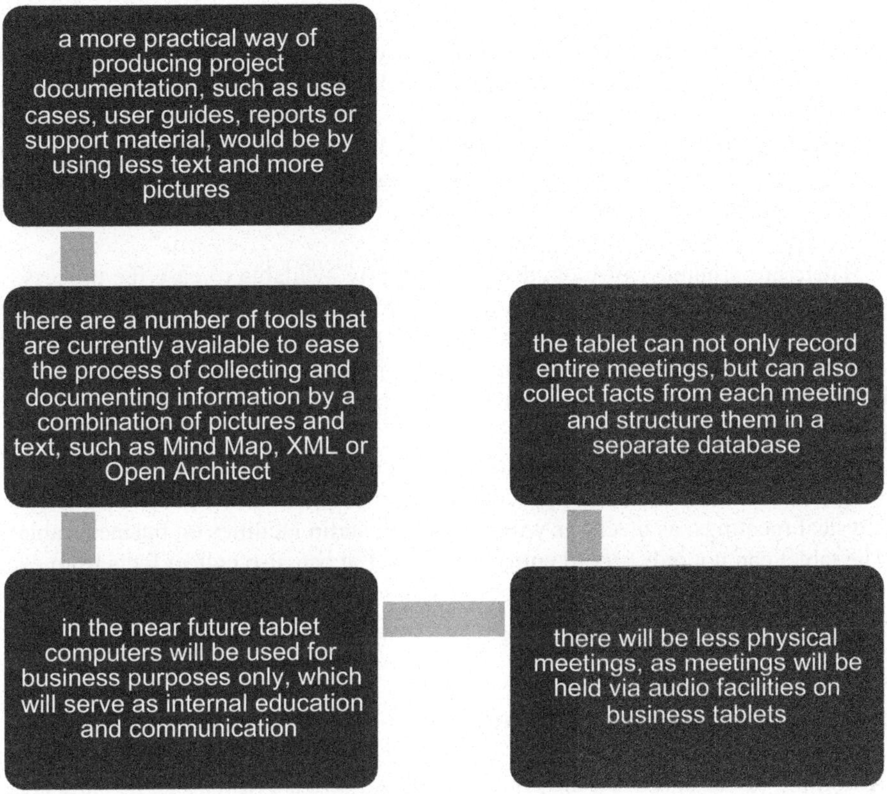

A more practical way of producing project documentation, such as use cases, user guides, reports, or support material, would be by using less text and more pictures. Based on the reason why the document is created, its scope or the group of users, the content of the documentation should only include the information in such detail that it serves the addressed stakeholders.

When creating a document, no matter how simple or complex it is, a list of tasks must be defined regarding the creation of such documentation, like what needs to be done, whose input is needed, by when we need to be finished, and who is going to sign it off as being approved.

This process is simple and should be documented more often than not, but in today's day-to-day business we are not aware that we should follow this process as our road map for documenting different topics.

Knowing the process will make sure that we follow every step and that the date of delivery and the involved people are already defined and considered in our work. The implementation of this process for the creation of documentation will ensure a basic quality that can be delivered almost effortlessly.

In a project, especially in terms of developing a solution, the documentation of what needs to be done is important to avoid a misunderstanding of the request. In this case, one person creates the documentation, such as a business analyst with available tools like Microsoft Word, XML, or Visio, another person reviews it, such as the person who has requested a solution, and a third person will obtain it, such as a designer or developer to realize the next steps. In most cases the project team has a prototype of each type of document that is needed. This can be used and maintained for any subject at any time. In the ideal case, the prototype is part of the best practice in the organization and is adjusted by an intelligent software when necessary.

There are a number of tools that are currently available to ease the process of collecting and documenting information by a combination of pictures and text, such as Mind Map, XML, or Open Architect. I use Open Architect for the creation of my documents, as I can create a blend of text and pictures in a structured way so that the creation of a document based on the created picture is easy to accomplish and to maintain afterwards.

In the near future tablet computers will be used for business purposes only, which will serve as internal education and communication. There will be less physical meetings, as meetings will be held via audio facilities on business tablets. The tablet can not only record entire meetings, but can also collect facts from each meeting and structure them in a separate database.

2.5.2 Documentation and Intranet

According to Stibel (2013), the principle that the sum is greater than its parts is not new. Wikipedia could not have been created by one person. There are 22 million articles in 285 languages as of 2012. In order to learn about breakpoints, we need to watch examples like ants and how they work together to accomplish an extraordinary task.

Today, there is no central structure that has been defined for the archiving of existing key documentation. Internal documentation is put together in a similar way like content on Wikipedia. The knowledge available on Wikipedia has been provided by many experts and is available for everybody. This is how the future will look like for the knowledge management systems of banks. It is much easier to mobilize experts from all areas to participate in the creation of a central knowledge management system, which will later be used by everybody. The knowledge is based on key subjects of the daily business in a bank, like the daily activities of employees in a particular department of a bank.

Going forward, all employees will be asked to document their daily processes and to upload it to the intranet so that everybody throughout the organization can see what the process around a particular role is and therefore what the tasks and duties are. Future requests can be addressed clearly, as one can start a search on the intranet to check, for instance, who communicates with external publishers in the organization. This kind of information can be delivered because of the process documentation for each activity in the organization.

2.5.3 Documentation and Brain

At some point in the future, documentation will be structured according to the way our brains works, which means a move away from text-only documentation. According to Tony Buzan, our brain thinks in images and associations and is designed to follow emotions (Buzan and Buzan 1996).

This will also change the way how we document our problems and solutions in the future, as we will use more pictures in order to be able to easily remember them and learn. In today's business processes, we tend to avoid using too many colors in our presentations and documentation, as we are concerned of being taken less seriously. According to Tony Buzan, our brain likes colors that make it easier to structure information. I think that a mixture of text, color, and pictures will be the only way to document in the future, as we will use our brains in a more effective way by using colors and pictures to ease the process of reading and understanding.

2.6 Communication

According to Smith (2005), internal communication supports the communication between management and staff and includes employee communication, change management, management communication, etc. Today's experts on internal communication have the following backgrounds in order to be able to communicate a particular subject to the entire organization: senior experts (67 %), human resources (22 %), and marketing (10 %). They have to bring along certain skills, such as diplomacy and numeracy, with the culture of an organization defining internal communication. Going forward, internal communication will become shorter and more colorful, even including emotions such as funny cartoon figures. The more open-minded an organization is, the more color, cartoons, and even videos will be included in internal communication.

Sometimes we are swamped with emails from internal communication, consisting of long text, loaded with facts, that in most instances we just ignore it, due to the heavy workflow during the day. I think that internal communication in the future will be either much shorter than today and include bullet points and colors in order to highlight the content or it will be produced with colors, pictures, and potentially music and maybe cartoons in order to encourage employees to go through internal information during their lunch breaks or weekends. Why should we be afraid to receive less credit if we are able to provide our message in a more attractive way? In the end our aim should be to influence others to pay attention in our organization with the content of our communication and not to impress with writing skills that could win a prize in literature competitions. A boring document or interview will not win-over employees to work extra hours in support for their managers to achieve the department's objectives.

Going forward it will be all about engaging employee's emotions, and in case an organization develops the culture to engage their employees' emotions with their internal communication, they will create a new organizational identity, which is shared by all employees and is an incredible powerful tool to increase competitiveness. In case an organization is able to make their employee's hearts to beat for the organization, it will certainly have a big influence on the performance of the organization and the satisfaction of employees for being able to work for this particular organization.

2.6.1 Communication and Project Management

Communication has many facets and depends on the context in which it is used. In case we would like to develop a supporting communication method for a project, we need more skills than only perfectly written emails. According to Dignen and Mcmaster (2013), excellent interpersonal skills not only require the understanding of cultures and the individuality of team members, but also an understanding of the business environment. A person with excellent interpersonal skills is good in building relationships and in purpose-based networking and is able to deal with difficult people, to manage conflicts, build trust, exert influence, exchange feedback, and feels comfortable to participate in virtual team group meetings.

Although the entire book is focused on communication between a native English speaker and a non-native speaker, I think that we could use some of the ideas in projects. In projects we mainly deal with people who are mostly fluent in their expertise. Implementing a clear communication between different areas of expertise is sometimes a challenge for a project manager. Project managers cannot expect that all project team members bring along strong interpersonal skills.

A project manager must be able to help team members understanding each other and to communicate in a productive way so that the best possible solution can be achieved with the project. A key factor of success for a project manager is to be pro-active, on top of all the interpersonal skills mentioned above. A project manager who is not pro-active or too afraid of potential, inconvenient interactions with other people will become a risk for his project. The project is all about interacting with other people, challenging the team with objections, remaining authentic, and being able to argue with the team and having lunch afterwards. In order for a project manager to be able to successfully manage a project with all needed skills, it requires a supportive principal.

The key to a successful project will always be excellent communication. Efficient communication must be planned, agreed with the project stakeholders and used during the entire project. Although internal guidelines can provide a road map for the best way to communicate in a project, the available road map should be adjusted for your project needs. The planning of the communication must explain what needs to be communicated to whom and in what ways. The aim is to avoid using only one channel of communication, such as using only emails instead of communicating via phone or face-to-ace.

A lot of projects either fail or will be cancelled after they have started because of poor communication or other reasons. The reasons can vary, but the way we communicate within a project can be a big support in avoiding failure or frustration. A communication plan is like holding a map which helps to avoid getting lost in the demands of the project.

2.6.1.1 Projects and Common Sense

Clear communication will support the stakeholders and project team members to be informed and focused on relevant topics, based on recently communicated information. Common sense is needed by every project manager in order to be able make decisions, for instance, about which members of the project team need new information immediately, while others can wait until the next regular project meeting.

The entire communication must be done in a practical way, and common sense is useful to immediately do the right things. A mix-up will confuse the project members, for example by either involving too many people, with no decisions being made or work done or due to too many discussions and explanations or by not involving certain responsible people, which hinders the completion of their assignments.

As you see, communication can cause project failures and frustration, but can also make a project run smoothly and successfully.

Communication with stakeholders is mainly pre-defined or is done at an event where a decision must be made. In the process of communication we need to keep the professionalism in our job in mind, but we could occasionally allow ourselves to add humor in informal day-to-day communication with the core team of the project, so that the process of coping with issues can be eased.

2.6.1.2 Complicated Circumstances

I think that clear communication will even serve to deal with challenging circumstances and helps to maintain the cohesion of the project team. If an issue appears, the chance that the issue is tolerated is extremely high in case the issue was not communicated clearly. Communication is the foundation for good collaboration. Communication between the project manager and stakeholders must consider all possible facilities, such as formal meetings, informal conversations, online chats, email exchanges, phone conversations, workshops, etc. As we see, a crucial skill that a project manager should have is communication and linking that interaction with people.

A project manager who is open, communicative, and can convince people to work for the project because of their own interest is probably the most successful project manager.

2.6.1.3 Project Rules

The golden rule of communication for a project manager is to avoid sending too much information or to avoid providing all the details to every expert. Stakeholders, management, and all other non-related experts and relevant core team members must receive different levels of information in order to make a decision or to complete their deliverables. As mentioned a project manager should have a common sense of who needs this information and at what level of detail the information is needed. The information that needs to be communicated are related to the news of projects and includes status reports, deployments dates, etc.

A useful approach is when a project manager defines the way of communication during a kick-off meeting and lets everyone agree. Once the means of communication for a project is approved and becomes part of your project's guidelines, there will be no confusion about the way the project communicates with all parties. As important as the subject of communication is, it is not always discussed with the project team members what the best way of communication is for this particular project in order to support it successfully.

Even if the communication is structured and defined, it is the project manager's responsibility to make sure that the communication agreement is followed. The project manager ensures that all details, progress, and outstanding decisions, etc. are documented and communicated.

Clear communication can keep stakeholders satisfied and by communicating with them regularly about budget restrictions and timeline updates they will support your project to an even greater extent than otherwise expected. It is insufficient to only communicate issues or when a project needs decisions as a project must continuously communicate with all involved parties to avoid misunderstandings, risks, or frustrations.

2.7 Education

According to Hobert (2013), a global IQ is based on communication, comprehension, compromise, compassion, and creativity and learning can increase our brain's cognitive functions.

Banks as well as other corporations are interested in new ideas and want to introduce new forms of education so that hidden risks are avoided effortlessly. The world has become more and more connected through technology and this has changed our knowledge about education. Today, we can access knowledge at any time through many available devices, such as smart phones or iPads. Because of easy access to knowledge, we can educate ourselves almost everywhere. No matter whether we are at work, at home, on holiday, in a restaurant, at the gym, or in the train, we can collect information about any subject that we have in mind. We can correct our knowledge and extend it and are therefore able to make better decisions. The question is what have big multinational organizations such as Google changed in terms of their education culture?

2.7.1 The Process of Education

In the day-to-day banking business the process of education has hardly been changed. The progress that the world made in education and access to knowledge through new technology has only just started to be considered in educational institutions like schools and universities or other organizations. Using new technologies is key for the future of the education system. Outdated educational practice like sitting in classrooms will disappear not only for internal or external education in organizations in the future, but also in schools and universities.

According to Sheryl Nussbaum-Beach, in the future teachers will not be replaced by technology but teachers who don't use technology will be replaced by teachers who do use it. One reason for using technology in the process of education is that we like engagement with the modern technology and already use it daily. In the preparation of this book, I mainly used new technologies and was able to listen to many interviews with the best experts of our time. Instead of only reading text in a book, by using technology, we learn to use a number of other senses, such as our audio and visual abilities.

2.8 Modern teamwork

Everyone who works in an organization probably knows that a team is able to achieve a level of performance that an individual is never able to achieve. This is the reason why teamwork in an organization is valued highly when it comes to tackling complex tasks. According to Tom Wujec (YouTube), there is a marshmallow challenge in every piece of teamwork. The marshmallow challenge will force a group to collaborate quickly. He experimented with the nature of collaboration and what a marshmallow challenge does is help to avoid hidden assumptions. The modern way of teamwork is doing it naturally and it is like we did it as kids. Nobody showed off at the age of four and everybody was naturally trying to make something work, even if it was a simple game like putting a puzzle together.

Team work will continue to remain important, but the tools will change in the future. We will use virtual facilities in order to socialize in the context of internal communication and for collaboration with people in the organization around the world. This means that organizations will remove the currently implemented island solutions of available tools for making a more efficient team work possible and to centralize a new facility for working in a team.

Here is some guidance for project managers in terms of establishing a well-functioning team work:

- Adjust internal guidelines in terms of meetings and communication in the way you think would serve your team the most
- Remain informal and always make it possible that experts from you project are in the spotlight with their strength

- Avoid micro-management, but have a clear grasp of ongoing activities and next deliverables
- Recognize that a project manager is not a line manager and has no power: in order to have the team's support and to achieve project success, you need to win your project team's trust by giving them clear responsibilities and by understanding their culture and by being authentic
- Listen carefully in a way that you also recognize the emotions in conversations with team members, as it will provide you with a clearer message without the need for interpretation
- Support your project's team members to become a star in the project, based on their expertise, which makes them feel being appreciated and willing to put in the extra effort when needed. Avoiding conflicts in your projects also means avoiding hidden risks.
- The guiding principle of a successful project team must be enjoying being a valuable expert among other valuable experts. Your role as a project manager is to make it possible by taking away any potential obstacles.

References

Buzan T, Buzan B (1996) The mind map book: how to use radiant thinking to maximize your brain's untapped potential. Plume

Dignen B, Mcmaster I (2013) Communication for international business: the secrets of excellent interpersonal skills. Collins, London

Drucker PF (1985) Innovation and entrepreneurship. HarperCollins Publishers, Inc, New York

Franklin D, Andrews J (2012) Megachange: the world in 2050. Profile Books, London

Hobert CF (2013) Raising global IQ: preparing our students for a shrinking planet. Beacon Press, Boston

Kaku M (2009) "The world in 2030: how science will affect computers, medicine, jobs, our lifestyles and the wealth of our nations" by Kaku on his speech at Queensborough Community College NY (on YouTube)

Limb C (2010) Your brain on improve. TEDx Mid Atlantic, November 2010

Markram H (2009) A brain in a supercomputer. TEDGlobal

Oberlander M, Jones C (2011) 10 years of iPod. Financial Times, 3 November 2011

Smith L (2005) Effective internal communication. Kogan Page, London

Stibel J (2013) Breakpoint. Why the web will implode, search will be obsolete, and everything else you need to know about technology is in your brain. Palgrave Macmillan, New York

Banking Culture

3

The culture of an organization and its values are the foundation for the successful execution of a strategy. The determining components of an organizational culture, like attitudes and beliefs, should be transparent and known to everybody in all involved areas. A strategy which is not aligned with the culture, the guidelines, and the procedures in an organization is not going to realize the defined objectives.

I think that an organization with an ambivalent culture that sends mixed messages will have difficulties attracting the talent that the organization needs in order to achieve their goals. Only a clear strategy and goal as well as a performance-oriented culture will support the hiring of qualified and motivated personnel and keeping them for a longer period of time.

According to Schein (1999), the culture of an organization must be considered when management makes a decision. It is dangerous to over-simplify the culture, as cultures exist on many levels. It can be based on what one can observe in the organization or the internal guidelines and the core values or beliefs of the organization. A new manager will lose their organizations' and their team's trust, in case he/she makes a decision without considering the internal culture.

© Springer International Publishing Switzerland 2015

S. Thuiner, *Banks of the Future*, DOI 10.1007/978-3-319-07554-9_3

3.1 Meaning of Culture

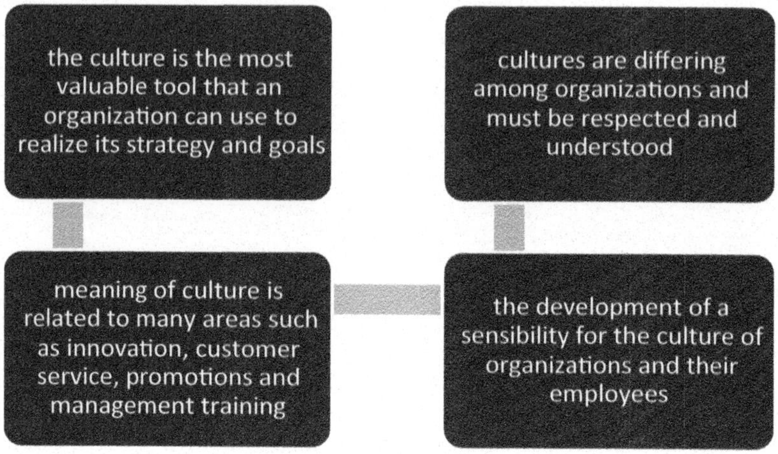

A company's culture should be aligned with the values and visions already in place. Organizations should not change their cultures, but rather ask themselves what the obstacles are which need to be removed in order to establish an alignment between a company's values, its visions, and strategy. This is an eminent task for corporate management and a prerequisite in order to achieve superior and sustainable results. The importance of culture obviously affects other areas as well, like innovation and change management.

The culture is the most valuable tool that an organization can use to realize its strategy and goals. The meaning of culture is related to many areas such as innovation, customer service, promotions, and management training.

Living in several countries and working for a number of different financial institutions made me to appreciate the development of a sensibility for the culture of organizations and their employees. As consultants, people move from one project to the next, from one specific area to another, and from one bank to the next discovering that cultures are differing among organizations and must be respected and understood if consultants want to be effective, but not for the employees who worked there already for a long time.

3.1.1 Promote Change

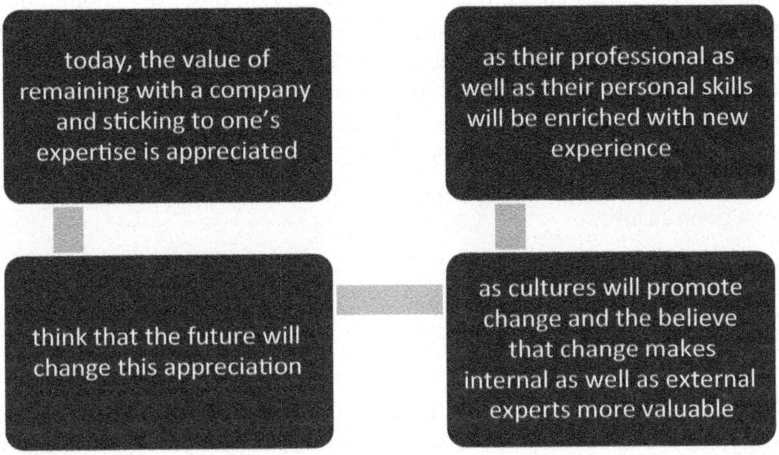

Today, the value of remaining with a company and sticking to one's expertise is appreciated, but I think that the future will change this appreciation, as cultures will promote change and believe that change makes internal as well as external experts more valuable, as their professional as well as their personal skills will be enriched with new experience.

Example

The skills and mindset needed to work as an employee are different from the ones of an entrepreneur. As an employee, you need to support your manager in achieving the overall objectives of the department. The more you contribute to your manager's achievements, the more freedom you tend to have to deal with your tasks, based on your own style of work. It is an efficient way of working and you will never worry about money, as your salary will be paid at the end of each month, and the better your results are, the easier it becomes for you to succeed. Your focus is on supporting the department in its goals and to socialize with colleagues during lunch breaks and with family and friends after work. After years, one becomes an expert in understanding the culture of being an employee and nothing can really bother you, no matter how often you go through re-organizations and changes.

If employees decide to become an entrepreneur, they have to realize that the work experience and competence of an employee do not necessarily match with the requirements for being a successful entrepreneur. There is a big difference between the employee culture and the entrepreneur culture. As an entrepreneur you are forced to work alone and trying to find a partner to share the goals might not be as successful as one expects. The attitude and skills needed for an entrepreneur are being pro-active, building a business network, and investing in marketing of your services. At a later stage the entrepreneur begins to understand that the size of the network does not matter, but the quality, and therefore it is essential to keep the business network rather small, but of a high quality, in order to maintain the focus on the project and work itself. An entrepreneur also needs to learn that even though his or her company's contribution was beneficial for an organization, they forget about it, as you are just one of many consultants. The close relationships which you had as an employee in your former organization will be of little use, while the only benefit you keep after a successful collaboration with an organization is to remain focused on the outcome of your work and to only accept assignments where you can predict a good result.

3.1.2 Experts

The future organization will not support the traditional way of promoting competent experts to management positions. People in expert roles will be as much appreciated as people in a management role. I think that there is a fundamental difference between the skills needed for being an excellent expert and the skills needed to be an excellent manager. Although both roles are essential for a successful organization, the skills required for each role are completely different. It is like the wish to make a quite introvert all of the sudden an entertaining extrovert. It is like trying to transform an extrovert person to an introvert person overnight. Their ability of being extrovert or introvert was a winning skill in one role, but a pain in another role.

3.1.3 Internal Departments

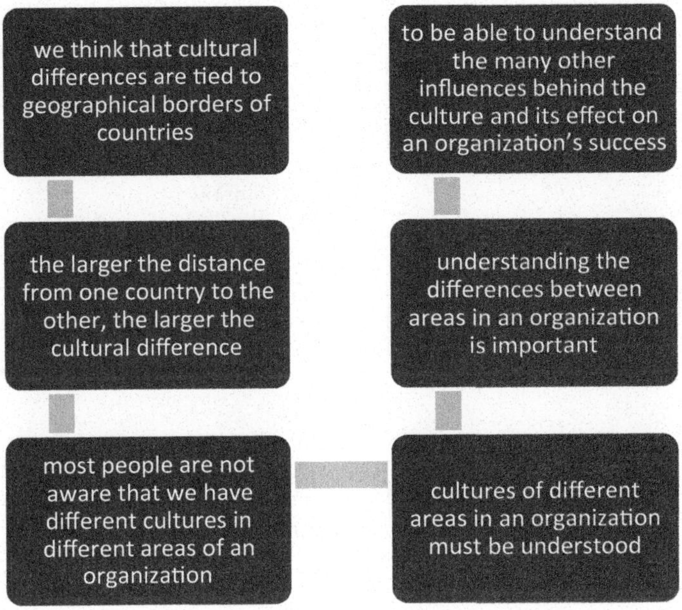

After outsourcing IT solutions to emerging markets, organizations have started to develop a strategy to educate their employees about cultural differences in order to facilitate collaboration. We think that cultural differences are tied to geographical borders of countries. The larger the distance from one country to the other, the larger the cultural difference. Most people are not aware that we have different cultures in different areas of an organization.

We have forgotten to look at already existing cultures internally. The cultures of different areas in an organization must be understood so that innovations or new solutions can be implemented via an internal project without hidden risks and so that the culture of collaboration is in harmony with existing culture as well as solutions and accepted by all involved areas. As mentioned, understanding the differences between areas in an organization is important in order to be able to understand the many other influences behind the culture and its effect on an organization's success.

3.2 Future Culture

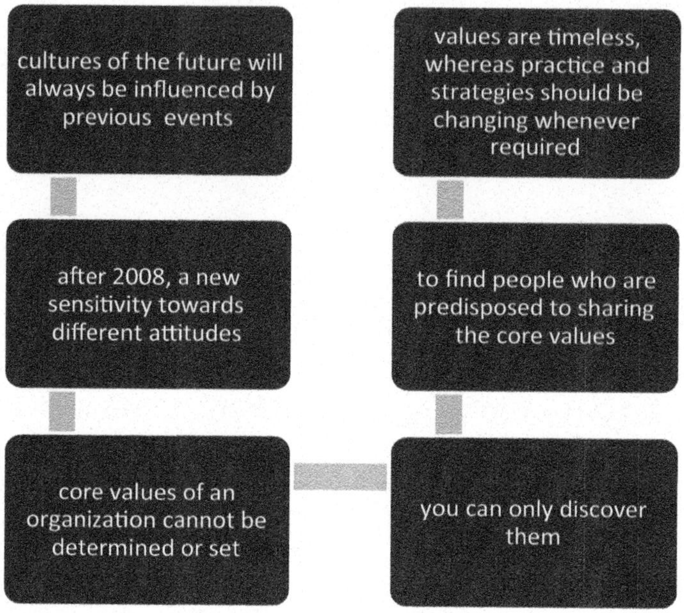

The cultures in banks have undergone significant changes in the aftermath of the financial crisis in 2008. Widespread regulatory changes which resulted in stronger oversight of the sector, newly emerging business models as well as rapid technological developments have been determining factors for cultural change. Cultures of the future will always be influenced by previous events. After 2008, a new sensitivity towards different attitudes, values, and practice has evolved, arising from public hostility towards the banking sector and the burden it put on public finances and taxpayers.

The core values of an organization cannot be determined or set, you can only discover them. Once discovered, organizations need to find people who are predisposed to sharing the core values. These values are timeless, whereas practice and strategies should be changing whenever required. And that is what's needed in banking—a change in practice, and business models, not only because of regulatory requirements, but also due to changing market dynamics and customer behaviors.

3.2.1 Values

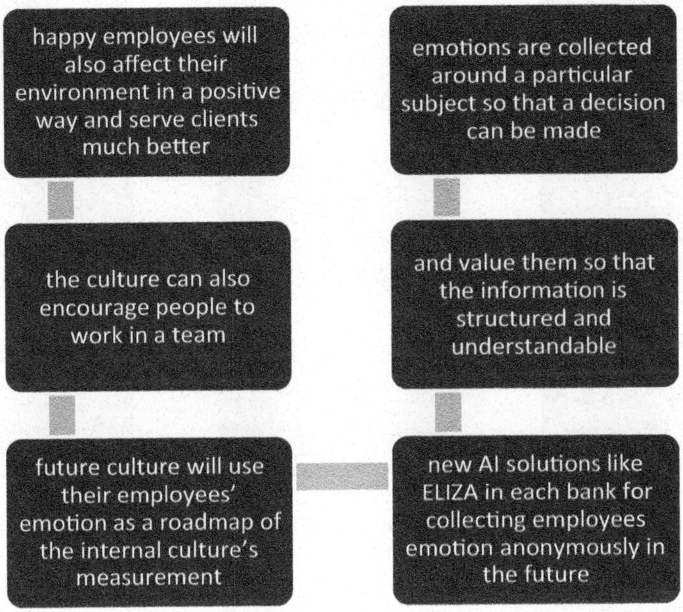

According to Ken Wilcox, CEO of Silicon Valley Bank, in a presentation for Stanford Technology on March 5, 2008 entitled "The culture of a bank trumps its strategy," with the right culture, people will develop a strategy. Ken Wilcox believes that culture will motivate. The culture is supposed to make people feel valued and respected and cause them to think that it is a good organization to work for, one which is motivating and productive. He thinks that it is possible to have both a happy and productive environment. Unhappy people will work only with a part of their brain, as the rest will be busy thinking about how nice it would be if they could work somewhere else.

Happy employees will also affect their environment in a positive way and serve clients much better. Ken Wilcox tries to hire smart people that are as diverse as possible and does not request the exact experience in potential employees required for the open position. The main required skill is being able to work in a team, but the culture can also encourage people to work in a team.

The future culture will use their employees' emotion as a roadmap of the internal culture's measurement. There will be new AI solutions like ELIZA in each bank for collecting employees emotion anonymously in the future and value them so that the information is structured and understandable. The emotions are collected around a particular subject so that a decision can be made by the management.

3.2.1.1 Measuring the Culture

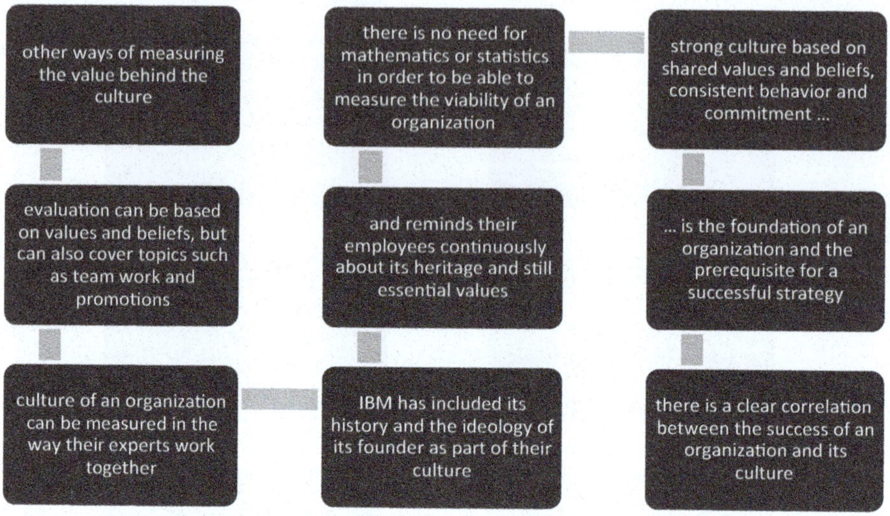

There are other ways of measuring the value behind the culture of an organization and its effect on the success of the company. The evaluation can be based on values and beliefs, but can also cover topics such as team work and promotions. In this case the culture of an organization can be measured in the way their experts work together.

The history or the size of the organization also matters in the creation of a success-promoting culture. A small company will sometimes provide a sense of being part of a family, helping people to care more about and work closer with each other. A change of daily processes, a change of a service offering, or business tools is often easier to achieve successfully in this kind of organizations. IBM has included its history and the ideology of its founder as part of their culture and reminds their employees continuously about its heritage and still essential values.

In fact there is no need for mathematics or statistics in order to be able to measure the viability of an organization. A strong culture based on shared values and beliefs, consistent behavior, and commitment is the foundation of an organization and the prerequisite for a successful strategy. Therefore there is a clear correlation between the success of an organization and its culture. A supporting culture can be identified by continued success in the marketplace.

3.2.1.2 Internal Culture

Over the last 20 years I worked in IT areas as a programmer, an analyst, a project manager, a trader, and an auditor for a bank. In each environment I was introduced to another working culture. While in the IT department, the beauty of a program was how short and complex it is and in the audit department an environment with no risks and no weaknesses was considered perfect. In trading areas, high volatilities in the markets combined with high trading profits are considered a perfect business.

A change of culture in IT areas was a challenging task and needed to be implemented in the context of a project, with many departments involved to ensure that all dependencies are considered. The final change was either completed, postponed or stopped for a reason. A change in the culture of internal audit never became a topic because of the negative attitude towards change. A change in the trading areas was highly appreciated and employees were permanently asked to share their ideas for improvements. Although the core values of an organization like ethics and transparency must remain unchanged, but there are other unwritten rules and practice which need to be adjusted from time to time. Change becomes more and more a fundamental characteristic of an organization in order to maintain competitiveness in the marketplace.

If an organization has difficulties changing internally, it can only react slowly to the changes in the market, which also means that the organization will have difficulties competing and will therefore risk its viability in contrast to competitors who are quicker in implementing change.

3.2.2 Innovation and Culture

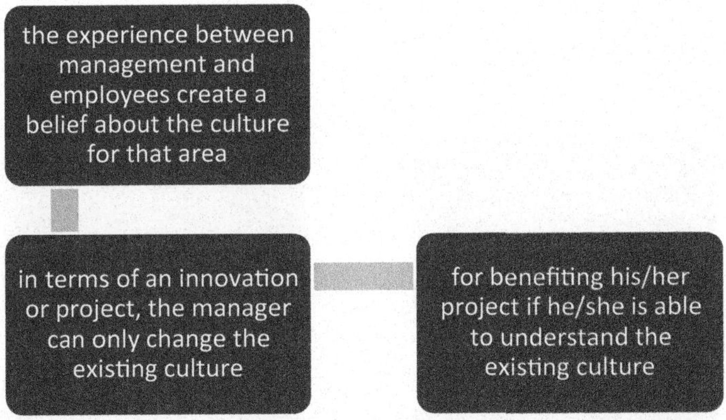

According to Connors and Smith (2012), we should cultivate a culture within employees/management to see an issue, solve it, and do it and not to cultivate a blame culture. The experience between management and employees creates a belief about the culture for that area.

This belief can also be used to changes the existing culture by planning an experience and asking for feedback. The following behavior could also help a manager to change a culture: setting up the right group of people and ensure that everybody is involved in the subject, respect their decision, and be consistent with your values.

Being aware of the possible creation of the blame culture in our daily work and continuously measure our behavior in order to avoid supporting the blaming culture in what we do, will help us to enjoy our work and the collaboration with our colleagues. This is an important fact of causing risks for ongoing innovations or projects. A project is all about a change and means that a change can only be implemented if the manager appreciates change. It is a risk to give the responsibility of a change to a manager for instance who was managing a team with PL1 programmer since 10 years. As a project manager we introduce a change to an organization and this can only be done properly when we also are able to change the culture of different experts from different areas of an organization.

In terms of an innovation or project, the manager can only change the existing culture for benefiting his/her project if he/she is able to understand the existing culture and also the change needed to make his project team successful in his project no matter what each team member's background is and what their current level of success is.

Example

My experience is that a project manager can only change the culture for a project if he/she is comfortable to change by himself or herself if it is needed. If a manager is too afraid to change anything or is radically changing too much, both will make it difficult for him/her to win the team member's trust.

3.2.3 Culture of Change

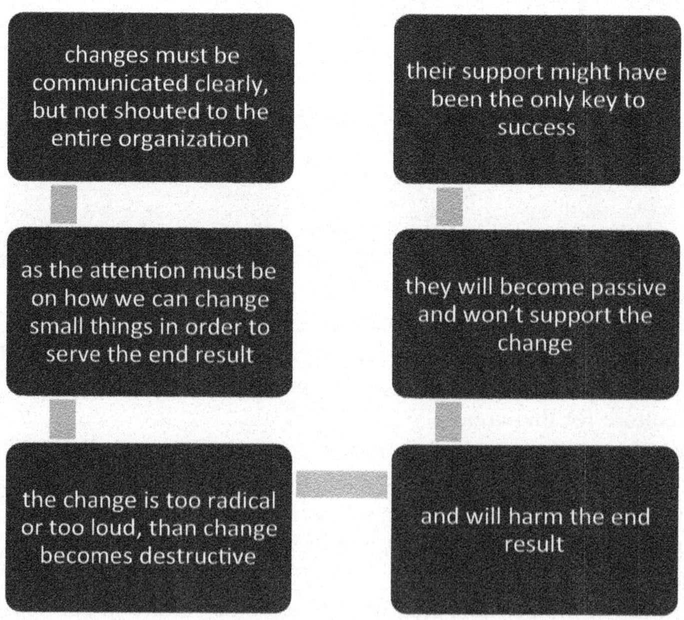

Changes must be implemented gently and communicated clearly, but not shouted to the entire organization, as the attention must be on how we can change small things in order to serve the end result. If the change is too radical or too loud, then change becomes destructive and will harm the end result. A radical change will be seen as aggressive and hurt some team member's basic principles. Eventually they will become passive and won't support the change. Their support might have been the only key to success.

3.2.4 Internal Rules

There are principles and values of an organization that are introduced to employees in the context of the overall strategy. They become culture when internal rules, processes, and decisions are made based on them. A culture might change over time, due to events inside and outside the organization.

It might establish itself on a permanent basis if certain individual behaviors and actions are rewarded for their results.

3.2.4.1 Regulations

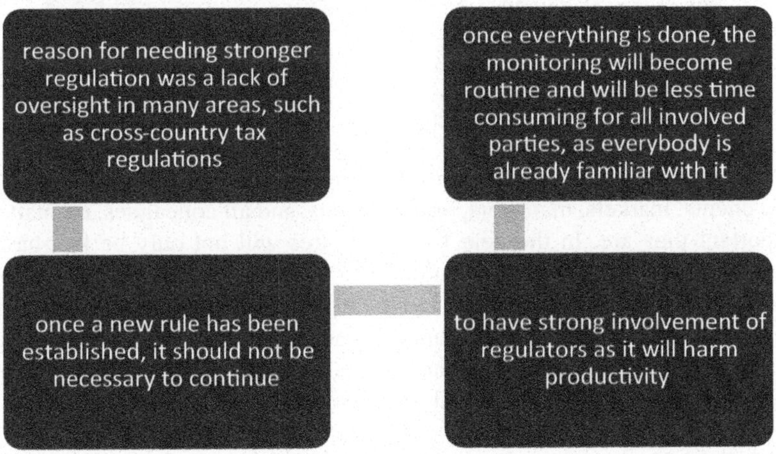

In the aftermath of the financial crisis, regulation played a much larger role than before. The reason for needing stronger regulation was a lack of oversight in many areas, such as cross-country tax regulations. I think that the involvement of the regulation must be reduced or at least changed after many years of crisis. Once a new rule has been established, it should not be necessary to continue to have strong involvement of regulators as it will harm productivity.

For many topics we had not clear regulations in the past. It is like not getting a penalty for avoiding a payment for wrong parking. If there is no law to regulate this action, there is no penalty for violating the law. It will be hard to convince a person to respect it by appealing to their good nature. It is like driving to Italy and constantly parking wrong and never getting a penalty since it is not regulated for cars from other countries. If there is a decision to regulate and control it, there will be a phase of intensive solution finding processes and monitoring. Once everything is done and all are informed about the higher price they will pay in case of a violation, the monitoring will become routine and will be less time consuming for all involved parties, as everybody is already familiar with it.

This is the reason why we should be able to move away from the heavy involvement of regulators to a routine phase, once everything is set and the monitoring of the implemented solutions can start.

3.2.4.2 Service and Soft Skills

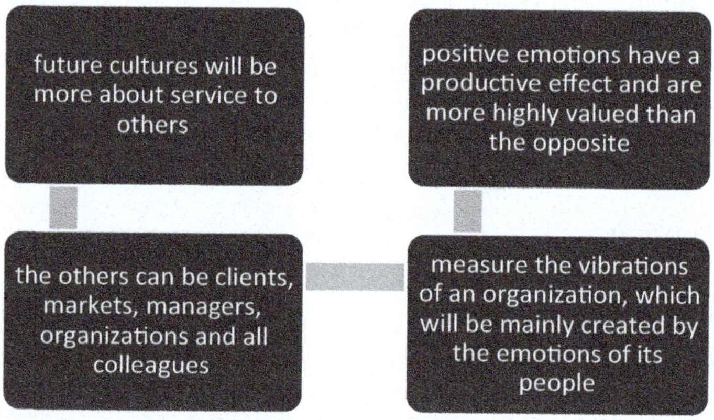

Future cultures for employees will be more about service to others. The others can be clients, markets, managers, organizations, and all colleagues, no matter how unimportant they are. In the near future cultures will not only be fact-based but emotions will also be appreciated in order to measure the vibrations of an organization, which will be mainly created by the emotions of its people. Positive emotions have a productive effect and are more highly valued than the opposite. This means positive emotions because of successful collaboration will make it possible for us to find the best possible solutions almost effortlessly.

3.2.4.3 Test Management

I would like to add here examples from my previous experience and explain how supportive the understanding of cultural differences within an organization can be. I think in a project the understanding of different internal cultures is quite helpful. ***Example:*** During the implementation of a new FX-trading system, I needed to manage the testing session of the project and to ensure that the issues are fixed as quickly as possible.

As a new person in an old group, I had a quiet time during the first days of the preparation of the test. No one seemed to have any news for me on what they did during the day. I started to visit test members on their desk and have casual small talks with colleagues and received an update from some of the IT experts. I started to report their daily work related to testing progress to the senior managers and stakeholders of my project.

Very soon all test members came to my table to give their updates as they did not want to look like they did not do anything. Later they also appreciated that senior managers and stakeholders around the world knew what their expertise was and what they accomplished daily for the success of the project.

3.2.4.3.1 Meetings

We could use the understanding of culture to avoid frustrations in the project team. Let me explain this with a simple tool for running our projects such as the setup of a meeting:

Legal Department

Did we need to set up a meeting, for instance, with the legal department of a bank? I used my understanding from the culture in the audit department as the internal audit could also be seen as internal authority like legal department. Formal meetings with an internal authority should be set up for between 1 h and 1 h and 30 min. There must be a clear agenda for the meeting as usual. I need to include experts from the project team and experts from the legal department as well as two managers with the same seniority. One manager is from our side and one manager is from the legal department.

In order to lead the meeting and the collaboration with the internal legal department to success, a project manager needs to follow the following procedure, for instance, related to the subject "client data" to come to an agreement:

- Contact the legal department via email and ask them to provide all internal guidelines related to the legal aspect of client data.
- Go through all guidelines and understand them in a way that their dependencies to each other are clear (use Enterprise Architect or Mind Map or other tools to document the dependencies between the rules visually).
- Set up an informal meeting first and meet the senior manager or the responsible expert alone to ask some questions.
- Set up an email with a summary of what you think is related to the client data and ask them to change the information they think is wrong.
- Do not be frustrated in case it is still not clear what needs to be considered.
- Set up a formal meeting as mentioned above and invite internal experts and managers.
- Let experts in the project and legal people talk and as you already understand the dependencies, lead the subject in the meeting to ensure that your team members have all needed information.
- Sit with experts from your project team and put together a formal document of what the project is planning to do based on the discussions and highlight in the meeting.
- Ask the experts from the legal department via email (with "cc" to the managers) to feel free to change the documents, sending them back to you by the end of the week. The authorities of banks hate to be pushed and therefore you need to have patience.

- You can be sure that you will receive a final document with all their corrections.
- Take their input and make a decision for how the solution must look in order to be compliant with internal guidelines.

Front Area

The process around meetings would not look the same in case you involve the front areas. In case a project manager is responsible for the collaboration with front areas, the following rules must be followed:

- Convince them that your project will help them and explain the reasons.
- Never set a formal meeting for 1 h or 1 h and 30 min. Rather walk to their desk and ask when they think they would have time to answer some questions.
- Never set the meeting for longer than 20 min but remain longer if they have more time.
- Send your conversation to them as bullet points and keep them fact oriented and short and ask them to confirm or change if there is need.
- Never ask the same questions, always improve your knowledge after meeting them.

After following the steps above, you will have the front areas' support at any time you need.

IT Department

In case a business project manager is responsible to ease the collaboration between IT and business areas, the following rules must be considered:

- In order to win them for your project you have to win their trust and they must know that their work will be recognized by different areas in business. The reason here is that in most cases IT experts are too busy with technology that they forget to promote their skills in their business areas where their support is considered a big value. If the project manager supports them in presenting their strengths to the stakeholders or other involved internal business areas, they will enjoy working in the project, as you have helped them to remove the wall between business and IT.
- IT areas are sometimes underestimated in the project plan when it comes to their work, their time effort, and responsibilities. Thus projects tend to be more challenging than necessary, due to not involving them right from the beginning. In case a project involves all related areas already in the planning phase and the plan is well structured and responsibilities clearly defined, all IT employees will probably support you and work for your project more than in other ongoing projects in their areas.

– IT people are intelligent and do not appreciate if their project managers are sitting in their necks. By understanding their subject, respecting their expertise for details and opening conversations with other areas for them if needed, they will appreciate your approach of leading the subject and the collaboration becomes easy.

3.2.4.3.2 Bottom Line

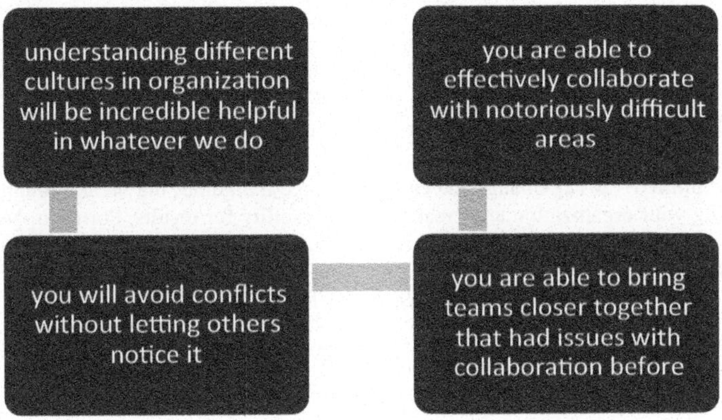

The rules above explain that understanding different cultures in organization will be incredible helpful in whatever we do. As a project manager you will avoid conflicts without letting others notice it. You are able to bring teams closer together that had issues with collaboration before, or you are able to effectively collaborate with notoriously difficult areas in your project.

I think that all project managers and team members are looking to be a part of a project where there are no issues related to cultures involved and where everybody has a clear expertise and can participate with his strengths and knowledge.

3.2.5 New Role: New Culture

Many years ago at an interview for a new role, I was told that the company expects their employees to work long hours. My first thought was that the organization values hours more than results. If an employee has a family, the person might prefer to take the unfinished work home and avoid long hours in the office.

Does it mean that the employee is unable to deliver results? It is also important to understand that everybody can work efficiently and productively over a period of 8–12 h and still deliver. By constantly expecting employees to work more hours week-in and week-out, the errors and failures resulting from overwork will affect the daily work in an organization. Solving these failures might be more expensive than the cost of using more resources.

Example

Here is a better example to validate this fact: Do we want to be treated by a doctor who is constantly overloaded with work and who is close to a burnout because they have no time to rest or for family and friends? A healthy banking industry for a healthy economy is as important as our health to our body.

References

Connors R, Smith T (2012) Change the culture, change the game: the breakthrough strategy for energizing your organization and creating accountability for results. Portfolio, New York

Schein EH (1999) The corporate culture survival guide: sense and nonsense about culture change. Jossey-Bass, San Francisco

Wilcox K (2008) Culture trumps strategy. Stanford Technology Ventures Program

4 Education

As technology will continue to change business processes and practice, it will also become more important to educate ourselves before or as soon as a change takes place. A successful change will require education and the change in combination with education will also affect employees' level of expertise. This makes employees more valuable for organizations so that organizations can improve and adapt more quickly to a changing environment.

A fast-changing organization will also affect all types of areas/experts, as this organization will require employees with an understanding that change is necessary in order to remain competitive in the market. Employees have to be more interested in changing themselves in order to improve and not expecting that the organization must change to suit them.

© Springer International Publishing Switzerland 2015

S. Thuiner, *Banks of the Future*, DOI 10.1007/978-3-319-07554-9_4

4.1 Education Yesterday

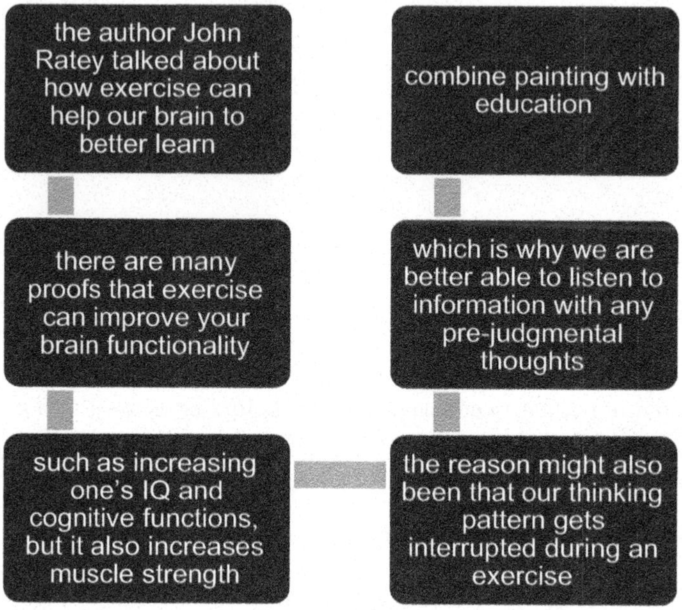

Education is no longer solely based on books as in the past. Audio books have been considered as a tool for education in the past, but not many organizations were available in the market that also provided audio books as a method of learning. Tracy (2006), author of numerous books, encourages his fans to listen to the audio format of his books as they will access information during time that they can't use for anything else such as driving to the office or taking public transport. Later during my research I have discovered the book Spark. In this book, the author Ratey (2010) talked about how exercise can help our brain to better learn. This is why he is suggesting changing our education system for kids with shorter lessons and a short exercise break afterwards, as they will be better be able to learn. According to John Ratey there are many proofs that exercise can improve your brain functionality, such as increasing one's IQ and cognitive functions, but it also increases muscle strength. I think the reason might also be that our thinking pattern gets interrupted during an exercise.

The most enjoyable way of collecting information for me was to listen to audio formats, as I was able to combine painting with education. I was listening to audio books and also discovered many interesting HBR articles which I liked listening to again and again. I think, while painting or during any other hobbies that we enjoy and that include physical movement, our thinking pattern gets interrupted which is why we are better able to listen to information with any pre-judgmental thoughts.

4.2 Education Today

Although the internet is maturing, education has only recently started to adapt. At the begging we did not know how to navigate ourselves successfully online so that we do not waste time with less relevant documentation, but after a while we have developed a good sense of selecting the most relevant documentation.

Today in large organizations employees have a number of different sources available to access new knowledge and educate themselves. There is mandatory education which is monitored automatically and where all need to participate, but there is also other education provided where employees decide whether to make use of it or not. Today in most cases, participation in the mandatory education sessions for instance about governance is online and the time can be chosen by the employee.

There is a strong separation between internal, organizational education and external online education. In each organization, there is an unwritten rule to use internal systems to educate yourself. In case other sources are available in the internet and are relevant for work, use them in your spare time. Organization do not consider internet as an education tool today as an employee can easily be distracted.

4.2.1 Issue Today

The issue is that the latest education methodologies and topics are not widely implemented internally. As education institutions like universities and schools are changing slowly, there is also a change needed in the corporate education systems. We assume that the change in the banking industry in terms of education happens quicker than in other organizations, but the opposite is true.

4.2.1.1 Education and Vitality

Following the last crisis, banking cultures have changed and processes became slower, due to regulatory demands, with other topics being put on the backburners. In terms of education we have the possibility to make an organization more vital and more qualified and therefore anything related to education must become urgent, as it is related to the vitality and productivity of an organization.

4.2.2 Saturated Markets and Developing Growth Markets

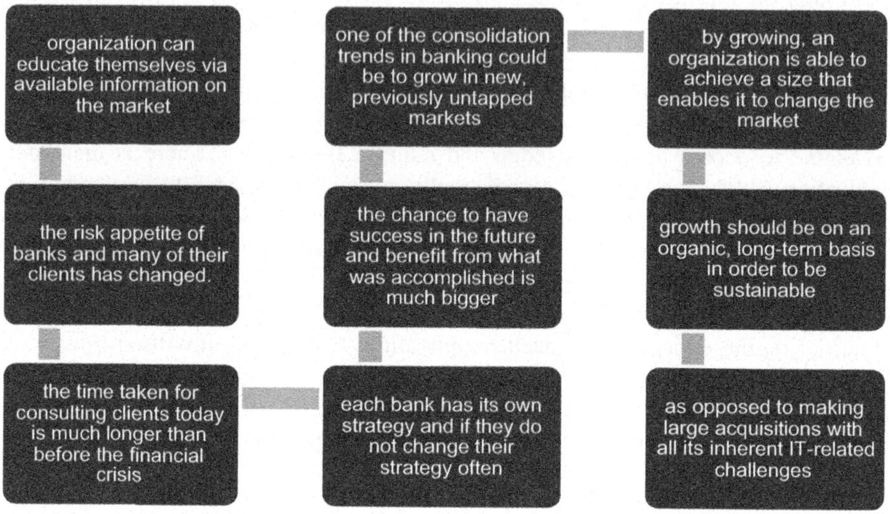

New technology opens a huge amount of information for almost every business and organization can educate themselves via available information on the market. After 2007 there has been a change in accessing new markets and clients. There are clients in traditional, saturated markets, but in much larger numbers in developing growth markets. We can also observe that the risk appetite of banks and many of their clients has changed. Many banks do not want to take the risk they used to take anymore, for instance, due to regulatory reasons. The volume of trades for clients has changed as well. In fact, clients today want to take smaller risks with smaller volumes. The time taken for consulting clients today is much longer than before the financial crisis.

Based on available knowledge and news online the existing strategy can be run more effectively. Each bank has its own strategy and if they do not change their strategy often, the chance to have success in the future and benefit from what was accomplished is much bigger. One of the consolidation trends in banking could be to grow in new, previously untapped markets. By growing, an organization is able to achieve a size that enables it to change the market. Growth should be on an organic, long-term basis in order to be sustainable, as opposed to making large acquisitions with all its inherent IT-related challenges.

The strategy can be based, for instance, on available knowledge about market segmentation and technological capabilities. Strategy-related decisions need to be based on a solid, strategic understanding and on realistic timeframes for implementation. Modern technology can play an important role in educating the management team and in supporting it to make sound decisions.

4.2.3 Knowledge Management

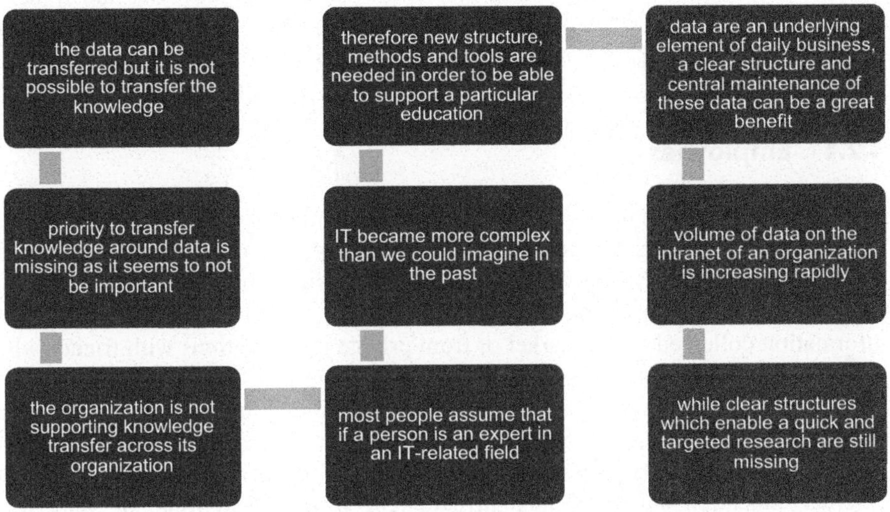

According to Leistner (2010), many organizations have issue dealing with information and data. One of the reasons can be that the data can be transferred but it is not possible to transfer the knowledge. The priority to transfer knowledge around data is missing as it seems to not be important and there could be many reasons behind it such as the organization is not supporting knowledge transfer across its organization. In terms of IT, most people assume that if a person is an expert in an IT-related field, this person should know everything around IT, be it hardware or operating systems, security, etc. This is like going to a doctor expecting expertise in optometry, cardiology, orthopedics, etc. We have to understand that IT became more complex than we could imagine in the past and therefore new structure, methods, and tools are needed in order to be able to support a particular education.

According to Atwood (2009), knowledge management is based on collected information around employees, IT, and the underlying process of the entire organization. The intranet is frequently used to provide access to the knowledge management systems of an organization. Knowledge management systems tend to be fragmented, not designed centrally and not connected to each other. Data or information based on different software is available on the intranet of an organization, but there is no central maintenance of all data and no information about the data quality.

As data are an underlying element of daily business, a clear structure and central maintenance of these data can be a great benefit for the banking business, due to the improved quality of the day-to-day work and of the decision-making processes. The volume of data on the intranet of an organization is increasing rapidly, while clear structures which enable a quick and targeted research are still missing.

After data, the sound important factor for a successful bank is its business model, which needs to be changed because of today's technology. According to Croxford et al. (2005), employees today use all their attention for their processes and systems instead of being focus on their core business. It is not that easy, especially for big organizations, to change their processes and implement the latest news.

4.2.4 Employees

Education is an important factor when it comes to employees' market value and is also sometimes a driver for motivating employees. As employees we make up our minds quickly as to whether we would like to work for a particular organization or not, and this is mainly because of internal experience and perceptions as well as information collected in the market or from private conversations with friends who have the experience of working for this particular organization. In case an organization has the reputation of highly prizing motivated employees with high interest in educating themselves in their spare time, it will attract those people. Likewise, if an organization has the reputation of taking care of their employees' internal/external education and providing an excellent working environment, they will also attract employees who value these benefits.

4.3 Future Educational Methods

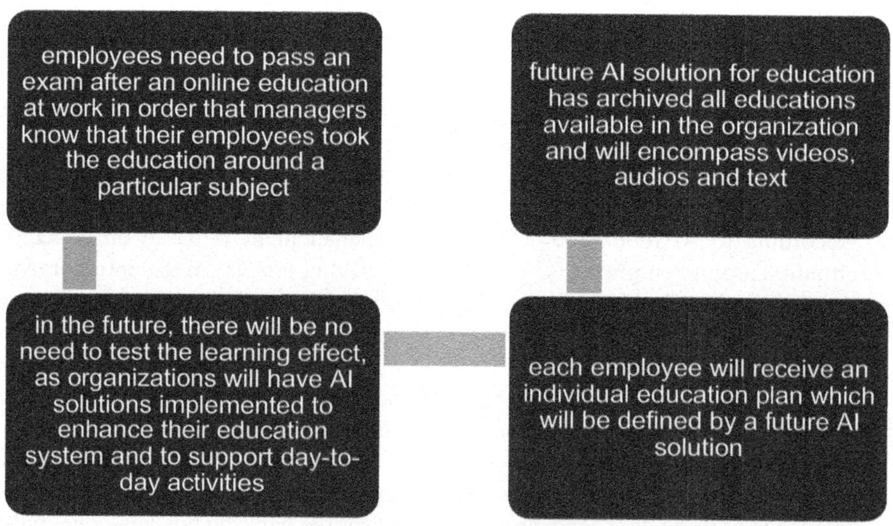

In the future, education will be largely based on tailored online learning in virtual environments, which incorporates recent insights about brain functions and how to enhance human's cognitive abilities, for instance to deal with large quantities of information or to solve complex problems. Today, employees need to pass an exam after an online education at work in order that managers know that their employees took the education around a particular mandatory subject. In the future, there will be no need to test the learning effect, as organizations will have AI solutions implemented to enhance their education system and to support day-to-day activities. In this case, employees are aware that their knowledge will be tested after finishing an online education, for instance, about a company's mission, strategy, and its related goals, without noticing, so that the organization can establish a broad understanding about these subjects among employees. Each employee will receive an individual education plan which will be defined by a future AI solution. The future AI solution for education has archived all educations available in the organization and will encompass videos, audios, and text.

4.3.1 Internal Education Through Movies

The employees are asked to explore the possibilities with technology, but they must also take the responsibility of controlling their activities, as there is zero tolerance for mistakes around key areas after they have already attended and accomplished their virtual education. The future virtual education is a movie where information is presented partly as an act between actors or where it is spoken like a documentary with the right music in order to engage the students by connecting with their emotions. Because of the entertaining factor of the future education, employees are happy to educate themselves during their spare time only.

4.3.2 Future Internal Presentation

The future presentation style of organizations will include colors and sometimes replaced with small cartoons that every employee is able to do individually, which are related to a particular subject. In the future an engaging presentation will trigger emotions and raise attention around a particular subject.

4.3.3 The Logic of the Free Software

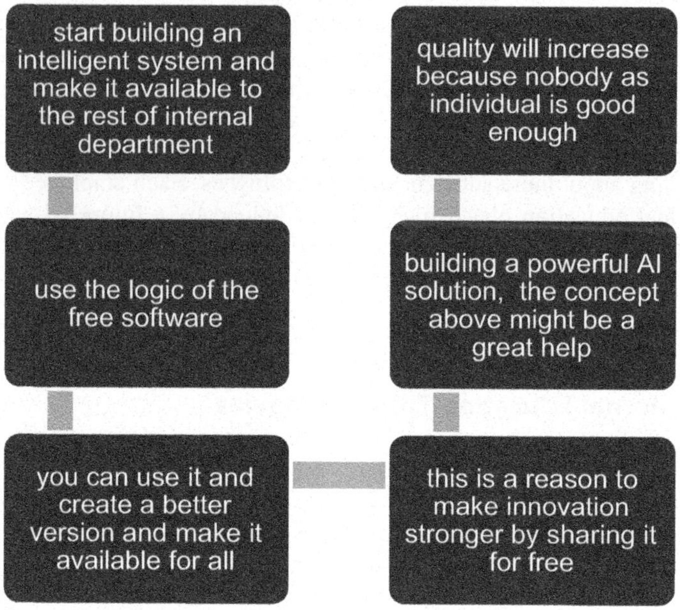

Building an AI system internally to support the internal education is not that difficult as it looks like. Organizations could ask their departments to start building an intelligent system and make it available to the rest of internal department. They basically should use the logic of the free software. You can use it and create a better version and make it available for all.

Linux is an open source solution, which means that everybody can use it. Anyone can use it, but only if the change is for the better and they have to share it. Can a concept like this have a benefit for large organization? This is a reason to make innovation stronger by sharing it for free. For example, a lot of free software available for the iPhone ease the collaboration with other services such Facebook, etc.

In term of building a powerful AI solution as soon as possible, the concept above might be a great help. The quality will increase because nobody as individual is good enough. This kind of the future solution is enriching you and at the same time enriches others.

4.3.4 Net Generation

IT kids from the past are already employees of financial institutions and the number of them is growing. What did banking industry change in term of education because of these group of employees? Are they engaged with all their strengths?

Topscott (2008) is the author of “Grown Up Digital” where he explains the people who had an internet for their whole life and are addicted to technology. The kids of the net generation are born between 1977 and 1997 and are the first generation to grow up with technology. The book looks at how their brains have changed with technology and how the brain becomes well in most cases.

4.3.5 Online Universities

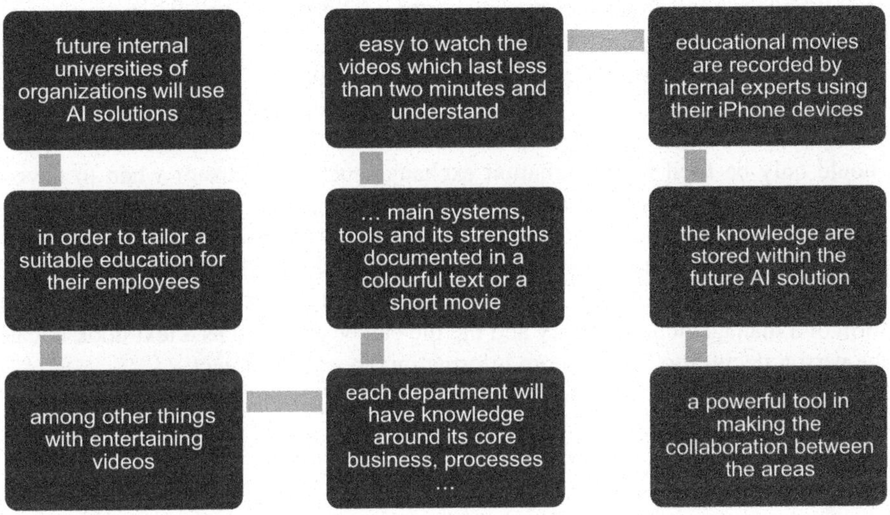

According to Christensen and Eyring (2011), universities do well in a number of areas, like supporting research and providing knowledge to students. I think that the most important change has already started to take place with online universities. Professors will work on a part-time basis as professors, occupied with research, and on a part-time basis working in large organizations where they run the entire education system for these organizations, based on a variety of subjects, such as trainings in the area of finance, human resources, management, creativity, organizational values, combined IT education, etc.

The future internal universities of organizations will use AI solutions in order to tailor a suitable education for their employees, among other things with entertaining videos. Each department will have knowledge around its core business, processes, main systems, tools, and its strengths documented in a colorful text or a short movie. It will be easy to watch the videos which last less than 2 min and understand how the organization is functioning. The educational movies are recorded by internal experts using their iPhone devices. All the knowledge is stored within the future AI solution. This solution is a powerful tool in making the collaboration between the areas easy. An example: in the future in a short period of time, a new project manager can understand what each area involved in his project is mainly doing for the organization. For instance, the change management department and its dependencies, the business analysts and their business areas, deployments and their usual schedules, the test teams and the process behind their testing, the business areas and their core activities, such as payment transactions, management reporting, accounting, portfolio management or treasury.

4.3.6 Education: Clear Thinking

Dobelli (2013) is the author of "The Art of Thinking Clearly." This book explains the mistakes in our thinking process with what we do without being aware of. One mistake was missing in this book that could help the banking industry to not only reduce costs but also avoid conflicts, which is the use of emails in day-to-day business.

Today, emails are used to solve or explain an issue. This is a mistake as emails should only be used for information exchange such as where or when to have a meeting or the agenda of a meeting or other similar information. The discussion of a business related subject should be regulated in the internal guidelines and employees will have to either set up a meeting conference call or have a video conference. All business related documentation will be provided as a video in the form of a management summary and the file can be provided as a text book in case the person decides to access more information about the subject.

4.3.7 Modern Education

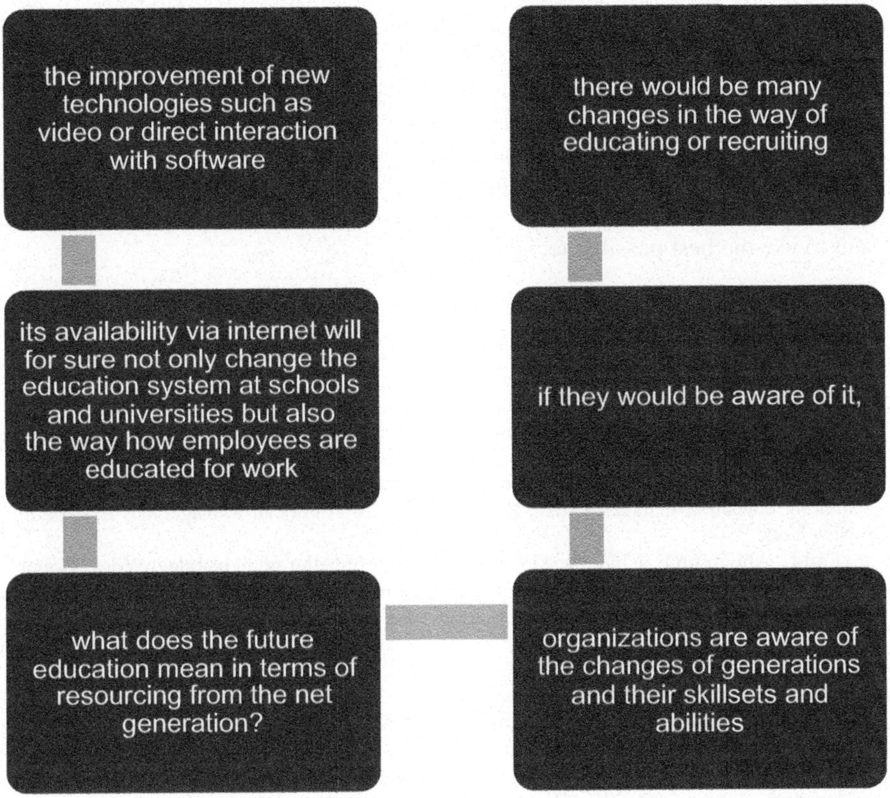

According to Cobb (2013) employees are responsible for expanding their skills and developing their level of expertise and technology now more than ever. As mentioned, the improvement of new technologies such as video or direct interaction with software and its availability via internet will for sure not only change the education system at schools and universities, but also the way how employees are educated for work.

What does the future education mean in terms of resourcing from the net generation? I doubt that organizations are aware of the changes of generations and their skill sets and abilities. If they would be aware of it, then there would be many changes in the way of educating or recruiting.

In the future job description needs to become shorter than it is today. Flexible working hours will be offered or the possibility of having regular breaks, for instance, for online games which companies like Google offer their employees already. The changes above and more will be needed if we agree with Topscott's findings.

According to Topscott, around 80 % of the net generation read interactive blogs daily, add information to it, and use their smart phone for almost everything. They prefer social media to the physical world to interact with others. They like freedom and prefer to find the right job and work when they want to work. They also prefer to customize a new product rather than having a standard one. According to Topscott, you have to be open and honest if you want to sell anything to the net generation. They see collaboration as natural and have created a solution with a higher level of teamwork and social collaboration, such as the creation of Wikipedia. They love to be entertained and want to enjoy work. They use technology instantly and expect everything to happen quickly. They expect change and want to use the best possible technology.

References

Atwood CG (2009) Knowledge management basics. ASTD Press, Alexandria

Christensen CM, Eyring HJ (2011) The innovative University. Changing the DNA of higher education from the inside out. Jossey-Bass, San Francisco

Cobb J (2013) Leading the learning revolution: the expert's guide to capitalizing on the exploding lifelong education market. AMACOM (a division of American Management Association), New York

Croxford H, Abramson F, Jablonowski A (2005) The art of better retail banking. Wiley, Hoboken

Dobelli R (2013) The art of thinking clearly: better thinking, better decisions. Hodder & Stoughton, London

Leistner F (2010) Mastering organizational knowledge flow: how to make knowledge sharing work. Wiley, Hoboken

Ratey J (2010) Spark! Quercus Publishing, UK

Tapscott D (2008) Grown up digital: how the net generation is changing your world. McGraw-Hill, New York

Tracy B (2006) The power of charm: how to win anyone over in any situation. American Management Association, New York

5 Measuring the Health of an Organization

The most important aspect of an organization is its people. If they have a good overall feeling about the organization, then you can be sure that the organization is in good shape.

According to Lucas (1999), organizations must learn to harness their employees' positive passion for achievements. The reason for a new strategy is to move towards the future in a more effective way. An organization's health can be measured based on its finances, emotions, education, socialization, and ethics of their employees.

According to Cora (2010), employees with work-life balance defiantly avoid an increase in the number of employees with burnout in an organization. The author sees a perfect world when we divide our day into three parts, which are the following: 8 h of work, 8 h of spare time, and 8 h of sleep. We are balanced when the following elements of our individual wellbeing are in balance: physical wellbeing, expression of strong emotions, development of cognitive abilities such as a visions of the future, socially by having a good connection to the community and spiritually based on values, religion, etc.

5.1 Meaning of Values

According to Kelly (2010), technology's development is based on a schedule whose path can be compared to the path of development of our personality. Technology as well as the people behind it likes a new solution based on complexity, diversity, specialization, accessibility, freedom, beauty, structure, etc. A new technology can benefit societies, but can also create conflicts or a new range of problems. Today every financial institution is following the latest technology trends, but I think that their approach will change. In the future a financial institute will have a clearer understanding about which development will never be part of the organization, as it would conflict with their believes, values, strategies, and cultures.

© Springer International Publishing Switzerland 2015

S. Thuiner, *Banks of the Future*, DOI 10.1007/978-3-319-07554-9_5

5.1.1 Due Diligence

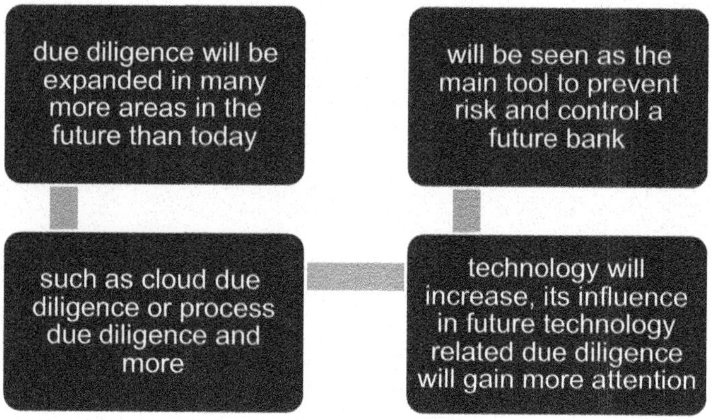

According to Grebey (2011), there are many ways of running due diligence such as financial due diligence, legal due diligence, and operations due diligence. I think that due diligence will be expanded in many more areas in the future than today, such as cloud due diligence, process due diligence or internet provider due diligence and more. As technology will increase, its influence in future technology related due diligence will gain more attention and will be seen as the main tool to prevent risk and control a future bank.

5.1.1.1 Hedge Fund Manager and Credibility

Below is an example of the hedge fund business and today's view: How could a Hedge Fund Manager gain more credibility in terms of robust IT infrastructure and transparency from investors?

5.1.1.1.1 Current Situation

We have seen over the past few years how issues like Madoff, MF Global could have been avoided through robust transparent IT due diligence and therefore could have saved billions to investors. The past issues made it also difficult for the hedge fund market to grow. IT due diligence can be and should be seen as a step to negate the effects of catastrophe failures in businesses.

5.1.1.1.2 Our Tunnel Vision

The ongoing financial crisis since 2008 has forced all to start looking at existing procedures with a fresh pair of eyes to reduce risks/costs and hence increasing productivity. As the existing solutions are based on traditional patterns of thinking, which lead us to form a tunnel vision, it makes it harder to discover the desired outside-the-box ways of reducing risks, cutting costs, and increasing productivity. In addition to the usually investigated risk factors there are a number of other sources of risks such as IT that may be significant in amount and at the same time go past unnoticed.

5.1.1.1.3 State of the Art IT Solutions

As the financial processes became more IT reliant the improvements in technology are never ending. Financial institutions have always implemented new adjustments to the existing solutions and this is why IT is continuously working on finding a new more intelligent way in order to increase productivity and reduce risks/costs. What if the state of the art IT solutions complicate your infrastructure so that mistakes are easily made without being noticed? Can IT be more simplified so that technology chaos for business is avoided?

5.1.1.1.4 Meaning of IT Due Diligence

A robust IT system means that the implemented solutions (even if it is outsourced) and the daily procedures around it are reviewed by risk reduction analysts (RRA) on a regular basis to ensure that after a change related to IT or business the interest of certain investment strategy and the guidelines/regulations complement each other.

Don't bring three to ten experts from business, IT, and audit to talk as we all know what the hidden risks on collaborations and communications are. RRA is a person who has working experience in IT as well as working experience in various business areas and understands the weaknesses of the areas and in addition the person has worked in the legal, audit or compliance department and is therefore more sensitive to risk. There is a huge need in the financial markets for these people as in financial institutions IT is seen as a back office function for managers of business who don't always see the importance of it.

RRAs are able to see the dependencies around a particular solution, its related risk, and can therefore ensure there will not be any risk either with the investment itself or with outsourced areas such as custody banks, administrators, brokers, etc. They understand the risks and know the investors as well as the regulations in the investor's country and the required reporting.

5.1.1.1.5 Growing by Receiving Credibility

The investors today would want to trust a Hedge Fund Manager who is able to ensure him the transparent service which also includes automatically reports of IT Due Diligent based on daily activities around their investments. By this a lot of investors who have taken out their money and stored it in their pillow will start to invest again as they have more control over the procedure around their investment via regular reports.

5.1.1.1.6 Trading Activities

Even if trading is based on a traditional or non-traditional trading strategies are outsourced; Hedge Fund Managers need to ensure that the outsourced area is functioning in the interest of their investors and ensure that, e.g., the right asset valuation practice is in place or all activities around the invested money are on a properly setups.

5.1.1.1.7 Investment Strategy

Note that in case the product investment strategy involves options, convertible bonds, swaps, or structure products, then the trading part needs more detailed monitoring to avoid the hidden risks such as:

1. The system is not able to block a trading step, if the limit is achieved. Where and how is the limit set up on the system?
2. The system is not able to generate automatically a report if a certain amount of investment is achieved (rules/regulation of trading hedge funds).
3. The system hasn't implemented a proper procedure to inform the Hedge Fund Manager about every change related to trading and the market.
4. Etc.

5.1.1.1.8 Hedge Fund Manager

A Hedge Fund Manager should also show IT Due Diligence from a RRA's perspective for their overall infrastructure to their investors, no matter which part of the solution is outsourced such as trading, settlement, audit regulation/taxation, etc.

5.1.1.1.9 Investors

An automatic reporting solution which has IT Due Diligence via a RRA has more value for an investor than something is passed to the investors via a Hedge Fund Manager's team. This will be one important step for Hedge Fund Managers to receive enormous credibility from the market and therefore changes the investors' outlook towards hedge funds.

5.1.2 Future's Values

According to Hubbard (2010), measurement is not about getting a precise correct answer; it's much more about reducing uncertainty. We have to understand the uncertainty and risk before starting measuring anything.

5.1.2.1 Sarbanes-Oxley

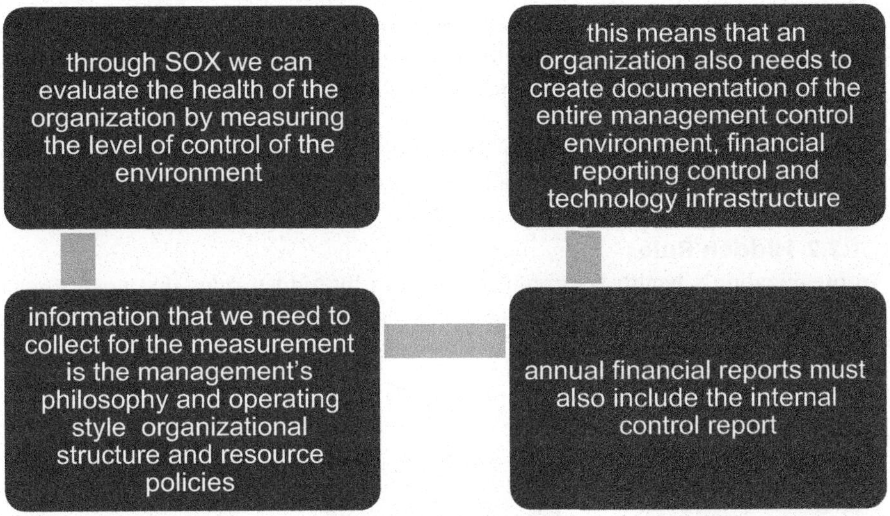

In 2002, the Sarbanes-Oxley (SOX) act was introduced, following the discovery of accounting scandals at Enron, WorldCom, and Tyco, in order to better control internal procedures. SOX did not create any new internal control procedures, but it gave them a higher priority around the subject of organizations' assets, governance guidelines, business information, and employee behavior.

Through SOX we can evaluate the health of the organization by measuring the level of control of the environment. The information that we need to collect for the measurement is the management's philosophy and operating style (e.g., free or more controlled), organizational structure (e.g., hierarchy or flat), and resource policies (e.g., responsibility-driven or controlled). Based on the facts we collect after the valuation of the environment, we can make suggestions in terms of the risk assessment and finally set up the needed control procedures. An important aspect is to check if the duties of internal experts are separated. An example is a trading floor in a bank that makes numerous trades in a day with counterparties in the market. The recording of the confirmation of the deal will be sent to the back office. This way it is ensured that not only one person is covering all the steps of a process. The main request from SOX is the availability of extended documentation for all areas, as mentioned above.

Annual financial reports must also include the internal control report. This means that an organization also needs to create documentation of the entire management control environment, financial reporting control, and technology infrastructure. If there is any gap in controlling, the organization also needs to document it. After the setup of a control mechanism and its documentation, the organization needs to test and monitor it. Being SOX compliant is also useful for insurance companies who are protecting banks from fraud by employees.

In the near future, the entire regulation, SOX, and other control mechanisms will be performed in a more practical way by educating internal employees about the law, ethics, and internal guidelines so, no matter if they are experts or managers, they will avoid risks, for their own interest. They will be trained so that they act as an internal auditor for their environment and report any doubts to their managers or compliance offices.

Future corporate values will support healthy internal environments by educating and training people extensively in all aspects of acceptable behavior.

5.1.2.2 Hidden Rules

An organization's health is strongly influenced by hidden rules that govern what people view as positive or negative or ethical or unethical behavior in the context of a business' daily processes.

5.1.2.3 Implementing a Swiss Model

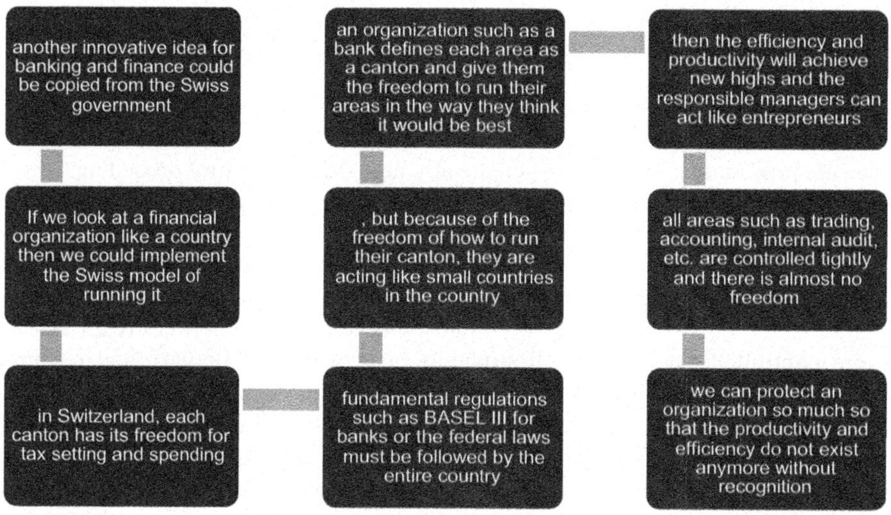

Another innovative idea for banking and finance could be copied from the Swiss government. If we look at a financial organization like a country then we could implement the Swiss model of running it. In Switzerland, each canton has its freedom for tax setting and spending. Fundamental regulations such as BASEL III for banks or the federal laws must be followed by the entire country, but because of the freedom of how to run their canton, they are acting like small countries in the country. If an organization such as a bank defines each area as a canton and give them the freedom to run their areas in the way they think it would be best, then the efficiency and productivity will achieve new highs and the responsible managers can act like entrepreneurs. Today, all areas such as trading, accounting, internal audit, etc. are controlled tightly and there is almost no freedom. One senior manager told me that there is almost nothing left for him to decide. He cannot set a strategy for his area, cannot choose the consulting firms that he wants to work with, and cannot decide how to spend his budget. In case he saves on the budget, his budget for next year might be reduced and he cannot take the savings to the next year. I think that it is not really easy for managers to act as entrepreneurs, as all management books are advising managers to do. I think that we can protect an organization so much so that the productivity and efficiency do not exist anymore without recognition. In order to demonstrate how today's organizations would look like in the future, I would like to use the Swiss model of running their company for one of large banks that I was working with:

1. The general internal as well as external guidelines must be followed.
2. Ensure that all employees are informed and know the consequences of violating the rules. Develop your area's strategy around internal guidelines.
3. Based on your overall budget you are free to strategically plan the upcoming year for your area.
4. Become creative and educate your team in the best effective way so that they are aware of your strategy and its synergy to the organization.
5. The budgets will be the same as you had last year, starting with the Swiss model. For all other years the budget will either be adjusted, due to satisfaction of all your involved internal clients, as they will anonymously provide a note. Only the worst note and the name of the area of your easement will be openly communicated.
6. Select on the market all kinds of support in the way you want and by when you need it.
7. Celebrate as much as you think that would support the team building mentality in your area or ongoing project to serve your strategy.
8. You have complete freedom with your budget of your area and use it in the way that you think it would support your strategy and if it is, for instance, the provision of daily apples for your employees for the entire year.
9. Define the education of your employee in the way you think it would serve your area.
10. If external IT support is better than the internal, you must not take the internal support as far you can to ensure that your support is following the internal IT guidelines. By this way, internal IT will not feel as a monopoly for all IT-related decisions in the organization.

The points above are a creative view of how it could be organized in order to introduce a new level of energy in the organization, but it can be changed in many other ways. Fact is that the old fashioned way of organizational cultures was good, but not good enough for the current fast changing environment and must be changed in the way that it is suitable for our time. I think the Swiss model could become a successful model for large financial organizations which can help the organization to simplify complex multinational financial institutions.

We are more competent in solving issues through creativity. When intelligence is combined with creativity, does it lead to the idea that creative people are more intelligent? I have met many intelligent artists, but they were only able to act intelligently if they controlled their emotions. Most artists are driven by strong emotions throughout their entire life and think that if they let their emotions control their life, they become a better artist. The question is whether an artist can only be productive and creative in an intelligent way if they have no control over their emotions, especially over the negative ones. I think that positive or negative emotions can open doors to creativity but they might also make us become blind by emotions and cause us to not act intelligently. The best emotional state to be in to remain creative as well as intelligent is to keep a balance so that positive and negative emotions longer exist within us. Emotion makes us human and likeable and it is important to allow them but it even more important to allow them to leave.

Sometimes we will allow ourselves to become a slave to our feelings and make mistakes or control our emotions so strongly that no one will collaborate or interact with us. As humans are social, we need to develop a strategy that avoids the hotness of emotions as well as the coldness of loneliness. Here is an example: It can be like losing a close friend and forgetting everything else for a long period of time. It is okay to hold on to the sad feeling for a while but we also have to allow it to become smaller. If we don't do this, we will become destructive and might forget important tasks or start annoying others with our behavior. We will also likely hurt ourselves, as we will miss opportunities to balance our feelings.

References

Cora G (2010) ExecutiveHealth.com's leading under pressure. Strategies to avoid burnout, increase energy, and improve your well-being. Career Press, Pompton Plains

Grebey JF (2011) Operations due diligence: an M&A guide for investors and business. McGraw-Hill, New York

Hubbard DW (2010) How to measure anything. Finding the value of intangibles in business. Wiley, Hoboken

Kelly K (2010) What technology wants. Viking Press, New York

Lucas JR (1999) The passionate organization. Igniting the fire of employee commitment. AMACOM, New York

Internet & Socializing 6

How could internet and socializing serve financial institutions to get closer to their clients and rebuild their old reputation again? According to Goleman (2006), we are wired to connect and our brain is isolated and operates like a computer. Our social intelligence gives us the ability to understand others and act more intelligently. The key skills for social intelligence are the following: understanding feelings, listening fully, understanding the reactions, and finding it easy to interact with others.

Today's game world brings video games to the real world. Are games going to be adjusted for banking in order to simulate a newly launched product within the real world with no consequences so that a financial institute is able to expose on a fictive market before really implementing it in the organization and using it internally as well using it for clients? Is this going to be promoted by regulators? Each issue should be positioned, which will help to understand what is happening and the reasoning why is it happening and the result. Or is it possible to ease the online banking or interaction with clients via an application like an intelligent game for clients' iPad? Could we develop an online intelligent IT solution for clients providing advisors, market behavior, etc?

Experts in the field of AI are concentrating their efforts in order to understand our brains' operations from an intelligence point of view, but also to take the emotional side into consideration in order to apply the knowledge to AI-based systems and processes.

6.1 Digital Information Transformation

The innovator with the most far-reaching impact of the last decades was probably Steve Jobs, who had the vision to change the world years before the iPad and iPod have been launched. He was the first person in the world of IT who used his connection to art in everything he did. Being creative and imagining things in his mind that no one has realized yet was his mission throughout his whole life.

© Springer International Publishing Switzerland 2015

S. Thuiner, *Banks of the Future*, DOI 10.1007/978-3-319-07554-9_6

Not long ago we used to carry a number of our favorite songs with us on a large music player, but Jobs' invention allowed us to enjoy the luxury to carry our entire music collection as well as audio books on a small device. With a small device, thanks to Jobs and his team, we are able to entertain and educate ourselves at any time in any place.

6.1.1 Possibilities of Future Technology

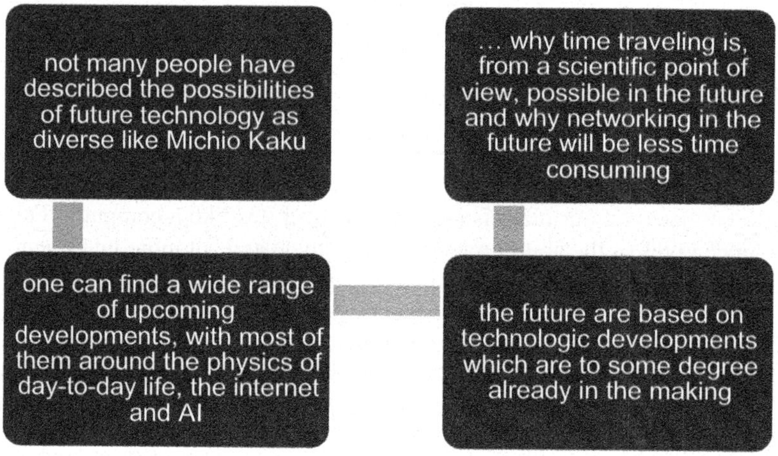

Not many people have described the possibilities of future technology as diverse like Michio Kaku. In his projections about the future, one can find a wide range of upcoming developments, with most of them around the physics of day-to-day life, the internet, and AI. As his predictions of the future are based on technologic developments which are to some degree already in the making, it is almost a pity that his version of the future is not already available to all of us today. It is insightful to learn from Michio Kaku why time traveling is, from a scientific point of view, possible in the future, why we will soon have self-driving cars, and why networking in the future will be less time consuming, but more effective than it is today.

6.1.2 Information and Transformation

According to Hart (2009), author of "From Information to Transformation," education today is not in good shape. The surface of information (discrete facts and basic skills) is often skimmed at the expense of knowledge (systems of information), understanding (based on empathy, listening, service, appreciation, accommodation), wisdom (among other aspects, expanding and integrating perspectives, seeing beyond what is visible from a stance of fear and self-interest), and transformation (a process which incorporates decomposing data, breaking its code, moving through layers of knowledge, intelligence, understanding, and wisdom). Education for transformation does not try to impose, force, or even teach liberation, but provides liberating (transformative) habits and tools that include the strengths of clear and compassionate critical dialogue. Is technology ever going to be able to create its own imagination? What benefit could it be for an innovative bank?

Hart defines education in a more comprehensive way by taking into consideration aspects such as imagination. He thinks that imagination should be applied for building bridges between the known and unknown.

6.1.3 Technology Connects

Bobby Gruenewald is the founder of a successful internet company who thinks that we need to take responsibility for technology. Today, technology connects grandparents to their grandchildren, makes one wealthy through an online business, or makes another one poor from the same technology by gambling all of his money online. We use technology for pursuing interesting activities and he believes that we should use it for significant things, too. In the future, innovative technology will come along great responsibility and technology needs to be used for good purposes. Everybody can participate in the world with his technology.

Technology provides shared platforms for banks where its employees can talk to each other about work-related subjects without sharing their company's confidential information. This will happen naturally, as their natural senses have been activated to judge what to say and what not. Each employee receives the education today which will be different in the future.

6.2 The Value

I think that in the near future the internet will become a role model for our society. It will represent all good values and ethics. Daily, an overnight cleaning process will remove all information that might violate these values. Search engine, providers governments, and large institutions will provide support and sponsoring for cleaning the internet. In the near future, a user of the internet will be able to talk to the internet instead of entering text via keyboard. Communication will be largely verbal in nature and will have the option to turn off advertisements and access only the valuable resources.

It's like the old-fashioned way of buying a book or newspaper—we can decide which search engine offers the best quality and what we would like to see and will not get annoyed by the rest. Today we use search engines with the highest number of links, but the desire for quantity will change to quality in the near future.

According to Michio Kaku, the internet today is what physicists wanted it to be when it was invented and it should not be controlled by anybody. I think that freedom can be preserved even if we decide to avoid all information that might not be a value at all. The internet remains enriching and free, even if we decide to run a cleaning service so that ethics and good principals as originally intended by the creators are upheld.

6.2.1 Intelligent IT Solution

The success of smart technology has moved our lives for good. In the near future the internet will also provide more new AI solutions to us, with IT competing with other human abilities, such as vision and recognition of the uniqueness of voice and manipulation of objects by additional devices which we do not have the ability to buy yet. As of today, we have still not developed software that is able to compete with humans in all its facets. One of the most complex and unique ability of humans is common sense, which will also be embedded in future IT solutions.

6.2.1.1 Robots

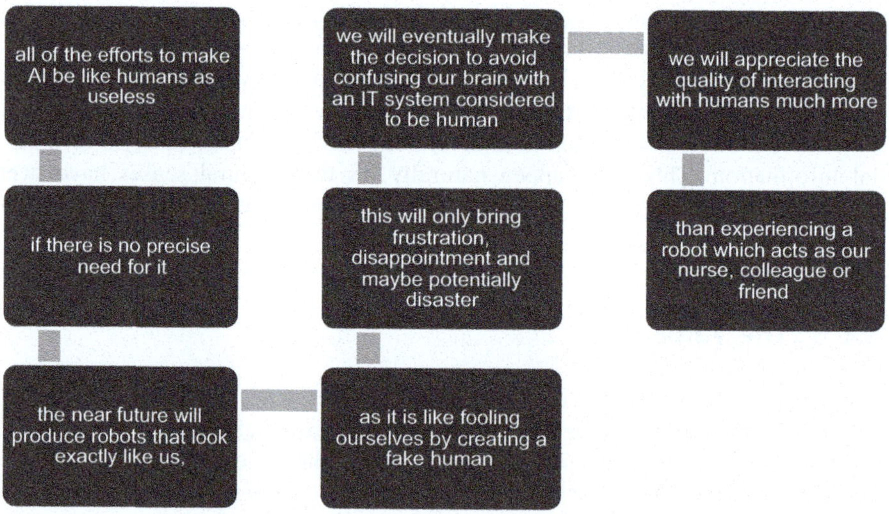

We see all of the efforts to make AI be like humans as useless if there is no precise need for it. I do not believe that the near future will produce robots that look exactly like us, as it is like fooling ourselves by creating a fake human and trying hard to make us feel that they are like us. This is like fooling ourselves and will only bring frustration, disappointment, and may be potentially disaster. We will collect sufficient experience so that we will eventually make the decision to avoid confusing our brain with an IT system considered to be human. Instead we will work on developing a new culture to increase our ability to better understand how to collect the right group of people which suit us best and make our work-life balance stronger by getting closer to the people around us. There is no need to buy a robot to program him in a way that he does what we want. We will appreciate the quality of interacting with humans much more than experiencing a robot which acts as our nurse, colleague, or friend.

6.2.2 Regulation in the Internet

We are going in a direction where technology will organize and control all cross-border collaborations based on rules and hierarchies. Today we already have companies and authorities that are specialized in acting like police officers on the internet. In the near future there will be companies like this, but with a more complex ability of reporting and auditing as well as directly collaborating with law enforcement agencies and police institutions around the world.

6.2.2.1 Future Guidelines for Using Internet

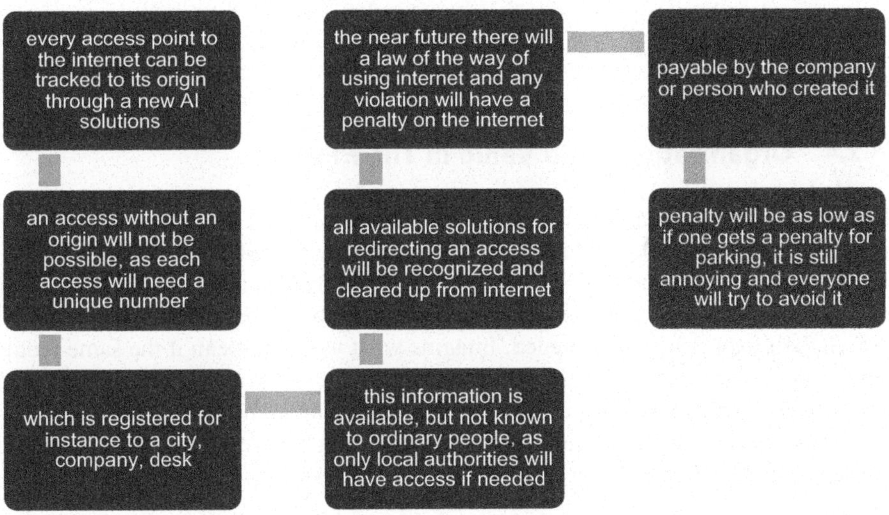

In the near future there will be evaluations of internet providers by local authorities. Every access point to the internet can be tracked to its origin through a new AI solution. An access without an origin will not be possible, as each access will need a unique number which is registered for instance to a city, company, desk, etc. This information is available, but not known to ordinary people, as only local authorities will have access if needed.

All available solutions for redirecting an access will be recognized and cleared up from internet. In the near future there will be a law of the way of using internet and any violation will have a penalty on the internet, payable by the company or person who created it. Although the penalty will be as low as if one gets a penalty for parking, it is still annoying and everyone will try to avoid it.

6.2.3 Offshoring or Outsourcing

What would be the worth of offshoring solutions or outsourcing solutions without the existence of the internet? Today they use remote access to solve issues through providing outsourcing solutions or providing other services from other countries, such as offshoring solutions for financial services.

6.2.3.1 Online Banking

Even online banking would not be possible without internet access for everybody. The security for access to each page, no matter if it is for banking or any other financial purpose, can be assured via "https." The given security is the reason that more and more people are interested in using online solutions to manage their private or business-related finances.

E-banking became a desirable option, as it not only saves time for clients, but serves banks too. Instead of having branches full of people to serve clients, they are asked to use e-banking in order to improve the profitability of retail banking. The value of online banking solutions for clients is that banks can communicate as well as collaborate with their clients in a more efficient way.

6.2.4 Organizations Add Value in Their Future

Technology might be a threat to many existing jobs, but it also creates many new ones. In many cases the first level support for a newly implemented IT solution is performed by employees whose job was no longer needed and was replaced by an IT solution. These employees have been trained for taking over a new task for which their experience was needed. Imagine what would it mean if the same would apply for all employees with business experience who are no longer needed, because of a crisis and are placed in the IT department and trained as one of the IT experts in roles such as business analyst or testing, where business knowledge is a big advantage for IT.

6.2.4.1 Interconnectedness

Over the past years, online communication and interaction has increased rapidly. Interconnectedness via mobile communication devices raised the need for the development of appropriate communication strategies for targeting specific client segments. Experts in organizations are involved in developing strategies of how they would need to communicate online, which information should be available online for their clients and which information should be kept for one-to-one conversations.

There are cross-border regulations that need to be considered in terms of banking solutions, no matter if it is, for instance, for investment banking or private banking activities. Whatever the online solution looks like, the need for transparency is much higher today than before the crisis.

6.2.4.2 Collaboration with Customers

The internet has already changed banks' collaboration with their customers. They use social media to market their products and services. Banks use internet to communicate their messages to the market, to influence the market, and to hire personnel.

6.2.4.3 Deep Understanding

Information available on the internet today can be seen as fragmented, the problem being that we have access to too much diverse information which makes it challenging if we would like to gain a deep understanding of a topic. I think that in the near future, the internet will be an ideal environment to provide information, but in a structured and enjoyable way to clients around the world so that the transformation of information is possible.

6.2.4.4 Investment Decision

The internet can be a useful tool to make an investment or trading decision. Alternative banking could be based on new technological solutions where the need for a physically existing bank is no longer required.

6.2.4.5 Growing of Data

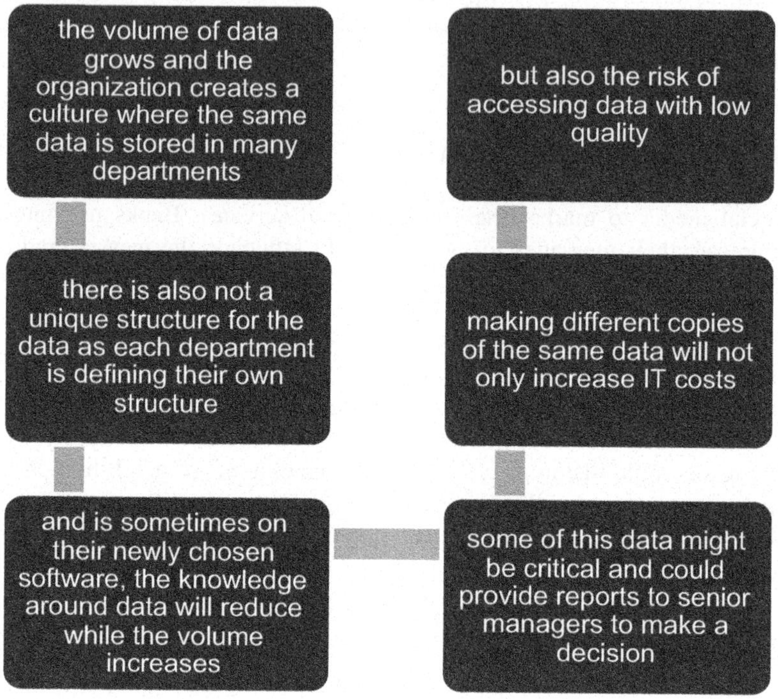

As the volume of data grows and the organization creates a culture where the same data is stored in many departments and there is also not a unique structure for the data as each department is defining their own structure and is sometimes on their newly chosen software, the knowledge around data will reduce while the volume increases.

Some of this data might be critical and could provide reports to senior managers to make a decision. It is not very often the case that a senior manager asks how you got the data for a report, especially when the data is growing and if there could be hidden risks involved. Making different copies of the same data will not only increase IT costs, but also the risk of accessing data with low quality.

For instance, I never understood why we receive basic data of a transaction from a back office system which has received the data from a front system. Why do we not have an internal guideline which says that the basic data should be taken from the original source to avoid coping the copy? This already causes high maintenance, as more reconciliation work will always be involved when we copy too often. The reconciliation will also bring along risk of low quality and hidden errors.

Example

There is also the case that the same data which has been copied from a copy gets a new name with each copy so that the mapping is being kept complicated. Data from the front area is transferred to many other areas of an organization for different reasons. The same data is transferred to different databases or data warehouses. In many cases the same information will be stored with different names and sometimes the data that is delivered to a back office environment is sent to another back office environment and so on. A report for the board might have the 16th copy of some of the data from a chain of copies. There is no doubt that the quality is poor and decisions based on this quality might harm the organization. There are hardly any clear guidelines for handling data in organizations today. This simple fact is based on a lack of internal regulations, which not only creates higher maintenance costs, but also hidden risks.

6.2.4.6 Attitude Around Data

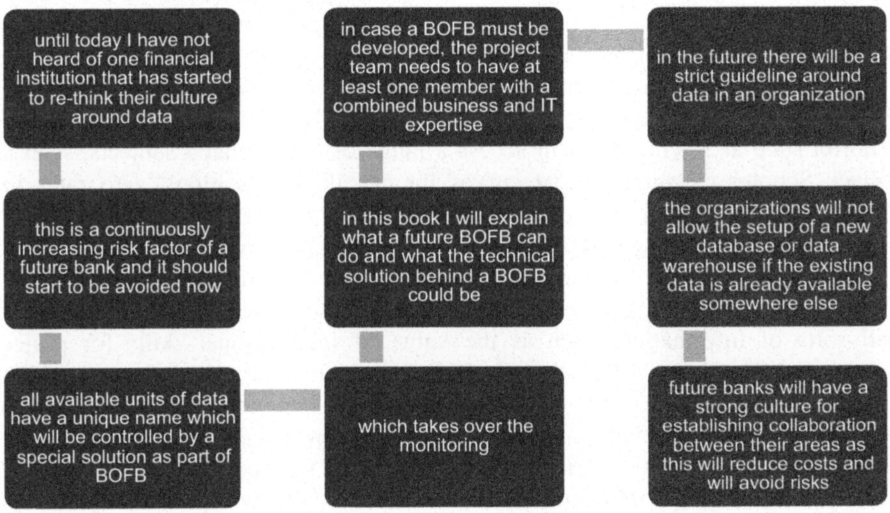

Until today I have not heard of one financial institution that has started to re-think their culture around data. This is a continuously increasing risk factor of a future bank and it should start to be avoided now.

All available units of data have a unique name which will be controlled by a special solution as part of BOFB (Brain of the Future Bank), which takes over the monitoring. In this book I will explain what a future BOFB can do and what the technical solution behind a BOFB could be. In case a BOFB must be developed or re-programmed, the project team needs to have at least one member with a combined business and IT expertise.

In the future there will be a strict guideline around data in an organization and the organizations will not allow the setup of a new database or data warehouse if the existing data is already available somewhere else and can be reused. There will be a penalty if the same data is taken from a source and is called completely different from what it was called originally. Unfortunately this is not the case today and if a project is under pressure, developers become creative with naming the new attributes, which will confuse many experts for many years after implementing. Future banks will have a strong culture for establishing collaboration between their areas as this will lead to better knowledge management, will reduce costs, and will avoid risks.

6.2.4.7 Research Online

The benefit of using an online knowledge system is that once we have started to search for a particular subject such as the trading of derivatives, all documentation related to the topic trading of complex financial instruments will be displayed, giving us the possibility to navigate through all related documentation, such as risks in trading, setting up of a structured product, using modern applications to hedge positions in a portfolio with derivative products, control the limits for trading derivatives, reporting of derivative products, pricing of a derivative trade, understanding the Monte Carlo simulation method for derivative instruments, calculation of VaR for a derivative, separation of MtM or accrued interest calculation for PnL reporting, calculation of the outstanding position, and more. By choosing one subject such as pricing, we will access a range of other related subjects, such as Black Scholes calculations, par curves for calculating positions, zero rates for calculating PnL, and more.

I have started to research project management methodologies; online IT-related hidden risks, innovations, and creativity. Because of accessing many other information, I had access to many other related topics and was reading and listening to all sorts of information, such as the value of interpersonal skills for project managers, Six Sigma, Lean, Kaizen, CMMI, hidden risks in investment banking, creativity the most expensive art of our time, many innovative solutions available on the market and the dilemma of innovation, brain functionality and its ability, changing habits, practical life advice, education, IT-related security issues, and biographies of many interesting individuals, such as Michio Kaku, Steve Jobs and Oprah Winfrey.

6.2.4.8 IT Movies

According to the guardian, with a Christopher Nolan space odyssey and Darren Aronofsky's biblical epic coming out, there's still plenty to get excited about science fiction and fantasy. Recent movies such as HER, Transcendence, Interstellar, Jupiter Ascending, The Hunger Game, The Hobbit, *Sin* City, and more are all fantasizing a world outside our today's real world, where technology and rules are different as we do know them. In case the movie is done excellently, we will leave the cinemas and be stoked about what a possible future could be. I have used the word shook as all of the movies of technology and future have negative side effect and I wonder if we would not be all more constructively inspire if the movie would present a better world. Maybe the human nature has to be constantly shocked with drama in order to appreciate the smoothness in life and seek for the right values in life. Technology so far made our life more comfortable, why should this not be the case in the future?

6.2.4.9 Innovations in the Banking

Many new innovations in the banking sector made it clear that the right values in banking are servicing the customers. New innovative services have been already implemented and the heavily engagement of customer is a good proof of their appreciation for the new solutions.

6.2.4.9.1 Cutting Edge Banks

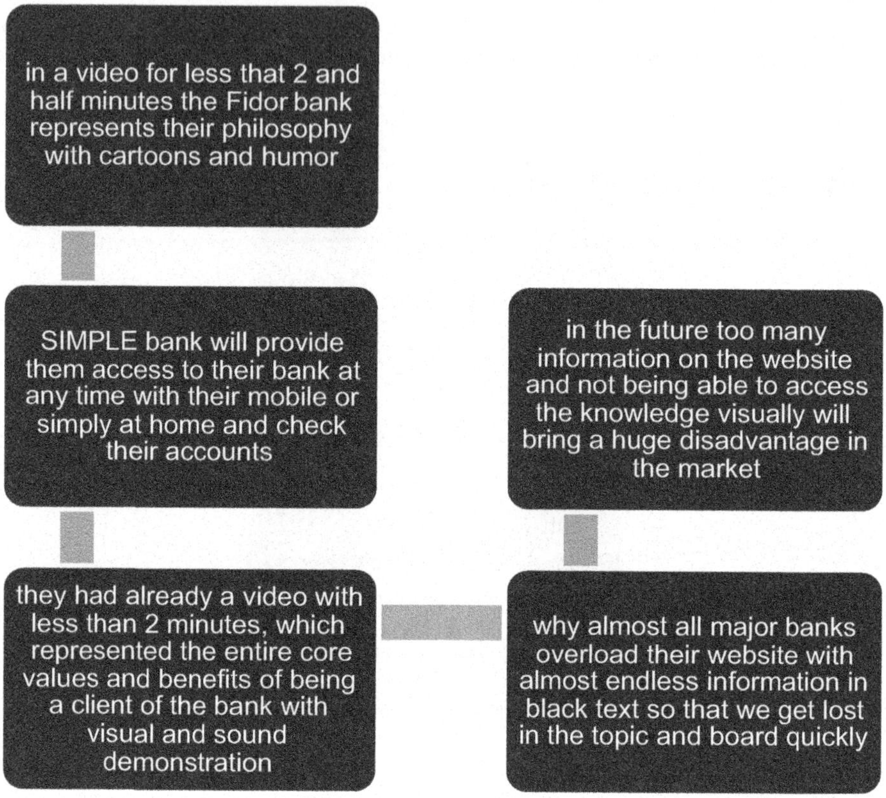

As an example we can refer to Fidor Bank that is one of the first innovative banking on the market with a lot of attention and their website on April 2014 was overloaded with images and color. Cutting edge banks have a market presentation which were seen as not trust worthy in the old tradition, but are known today for their incredible efficiency and are therefore highly recommended by experts. In a video for less than two and half minutes the Fidor bank represents their philosophy with cartoons and humor. The Fidor bank community can exchange their information between each other and make a suggestion about where to invest or share the opinion about a finance adviser or give each other ideas of new ways of saving. A client can share ideas with the bank and let the bank know what he is missing. They can anonymously share their portfolio information with others and get access to other opinions. The active clients have not only had more knowledge but also have a better financial statement. You can use mobiles and transfer money by using the email address of your contacts or other information such mobile or as twitter account. The client can also use a Fidor prepaid online account so that online shopping is safe and gives a new level of security and freedom. The Fidor bank wants to be perceived as "making banking with friends."

SIMPLE bank welcomes the clients to a better banking through an online application that helps clients to run their banking but also keep record of their expending and give them an access to a better overview of their finances and spending habits during a longer period of time. Using the online system of this bank represents fun and entertainment. This bank has defiantly all the attention of young people who like to use their smart phone for everything. SIMPLE bank will provide them access to their bank at any time with their mobile and simply at home to check their accounts. On April 2014 they had already a video with less than 2 min, which represented the entire core values and benefits of being a client of the bank with visual and sound demonstration. After watching this short video I was asking myself are they only based in New York or can everybody around the world become a client. The next question will be why almost all major banks overload their website with almost endless information in black text so that we get lost in the topic and board quickly. Unfortunately it is still the case that using colors and video will be seen as not serious and is avoided in daily business in most cases. I think that this culture will be changed very quickly as they will adapt to avoid losing clients to banks such as FIDOR or SIMPLE bank. I think that in the future too many information on the website and not being able to access the knowledge visually will bring a huge disadvantage in the market.

6.3 Future of the Internet

According to Snyder (2009), we will have a networked life in the future. We have around four billion individuals utilizing wireless solutions already affecting our behavior. There are also many developments in the area of technology disruption which will make people to become critical in term of wireless networks of the future.

6.4 Online Security

With the internet we come across many new ways of interacting with each other, such as Smart Mobs or GPS or other useful software.

6.4.1 Smart Mobs

Alongside traditional socializing in the internet, there are also other ways of meeting through new technology, such as “Smart Mobs.” These are used to organize a group of people to come together for a particular subject such, like an exhibition. All what we need is to communicate to our network and let them know where and when (location and time) the gathering takes place.

6.4.2 GPS

Another dimension of looking at new technologies is the usage of GPS. Although being a very useful tool, it also opens a door to harm our privacy, as we create a digital footprint of us which is stored as data and is available. For instance each photo taken with our phones and posted in the internet has all the GPS data attached to it.

Having a GPS application on the phone might be useful sometimes, but for private persons it is also a violation of their right to privacy.

6.4.3 New Software

Text messages or current locations can be easily recorded by a software on your phone that has been installed after you gave your phone to a friend to enter his/her contact details and there are also many other possibilities.

The issue today is that we miss a central knowledge management system for cyber security where everybody can enter their knowledge. This should also be created like Wikipedia by many people with experience in the field of private security, but also for organizational or government security. We also have to understand that, as a private person, if we wish for privacy, it is not a crime. The question that the future will answer for sure as well is that is it okay to leave our digital foot print.

6.4.4 The Old Culture of IT

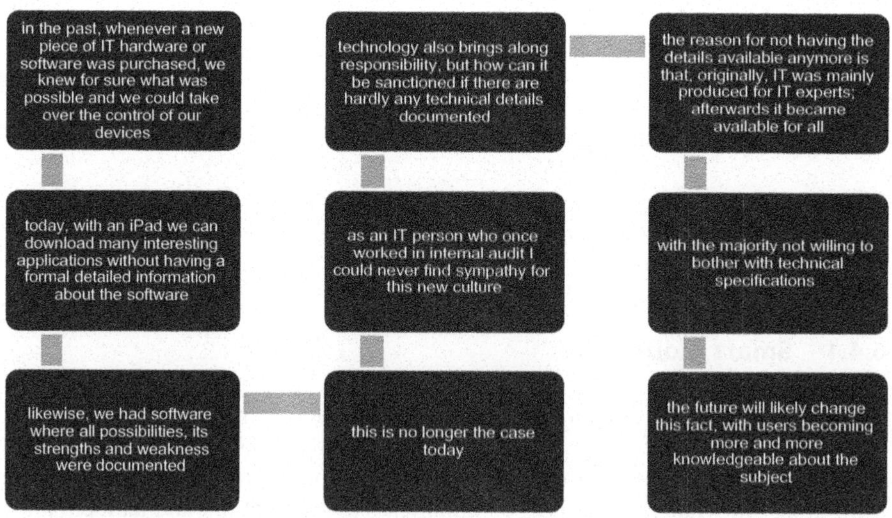

In the past, whenever a new piece of IT hardware or software was purchased, we knew for sure what was possible and we could take over the control of our devices. Today, with an iPad we can download many interesting applications without having a formal detailed information about the software which is binding the producer like in the past. Likewise, we had software where all possibilities, its strengths, and weakness were documented. This is no longer the case today. As an IT person who once worked in internal audit I could never find sympathy for this new culture of using technology and being crazy about it.

I think that technology also brings along responsibility, but how can it be sanctioned if there are hardly any technical details documented. The reason for not having the details available anymore is that, originally, IT was mainly produced for IT experts; afterwards it became available for all, with the majority not willing to bother with technical specifications. The future will likely change this fact, with users becoming more and more knowledgeable about the subject. Users will be informed about the capabilities and about the possibility of turning off technical features and removing or extending them.

6.4.5 Smart Usage of the Internet

However, the usage of the internet will become much smarter than it is today, and users will be more educated than they are now. I think that the availability of APP will also be regulated in the future so that it will become either a rating of very secure, partly secure with a list of weaknesses, or not secure at all so that when users want to install a new APP, the person has all information and can then freely decide.

6.4.6 Future Cyber security

Kuchler (2014) argues in an FT article titled "Technology groups take need for investment in security to heart" that "...Google, Microsoft and Intel have come together to fund an important encryption project, after a lack of money contributed to one of the most significant cyber security flaws yet."

6.4.6.1 Serious Concerns Today

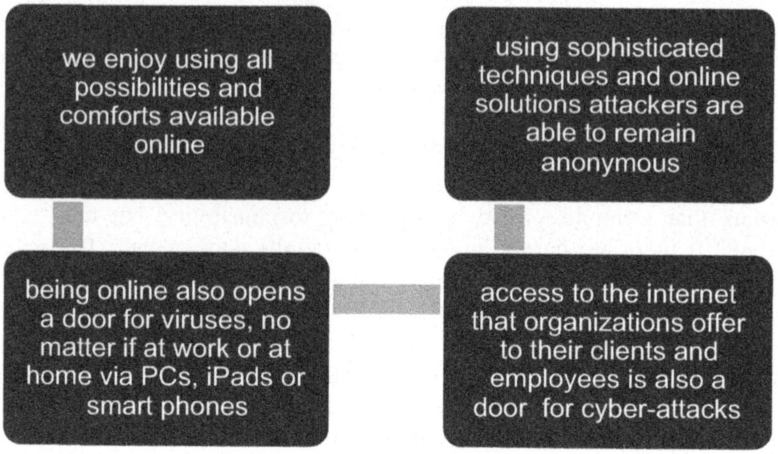

The internet was created with no security concept or regulations in mind. This is the reason why cyber security became a big concern for organizations and governments alike. Although we enjoy using all possibilities and comforts available online, being online also opens a door for viruses, no matter if at work or at home via PCs, iPads or smart phones.

For instance, access to the internet that organizations offer to their clients and employees is also a door for cyber-attacks on particular applications that are used by clients and employees. By using sophisticated techniques and online solutions attackers are able to remain anonymous.

6.4.6.2 Possible Solutions

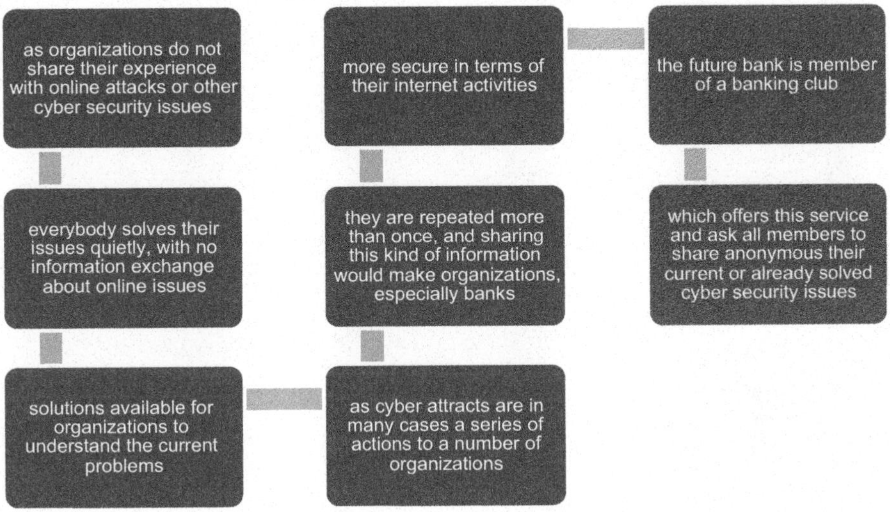

As organizations do not share their experience with online attacks or other cyber security issues, everybody solves their issues quietly, with no information exchange about online issues and solutions available for organizations to understand the current problems. As cyber attracts are in many cases a series of actions to a number of organizations, they are repeated more than once, and sharing this kind of information would make organizations, especially banks, more secure in terms of their internet activities. I think that the future bank is member of a banking club which offers this service and ask all members to share anonymous their current or already solved cyber security issues.

6.4.6.3 Cyber Stalkers

Privacy and security is also an issue with social media platforms. Cyber stalkers are not a rare incident in social networks. GPS, social media, new cutting-edge software solutions, and many other activities create a digital footprint which will be part of big data.

From today's point of view, everybody is involved, there is no privacy and nobody really bothers with this fact, but I think this will become a subject sooner or later, and regulations and maybe new devices will neutralize such violations will be available in the future. This subject might look like there is no relation to the banking industry, but such a view would miss the fact that these private users are also employees/clients of banks who might use their smart phones for their finances. We need to ask ourselves if this generation of phones has weaknesses that we do not know yet, but we run our finances on it; who is covering the risk—the phone provider, the internet provider, or our bank?

6.4.6.4 Big Data

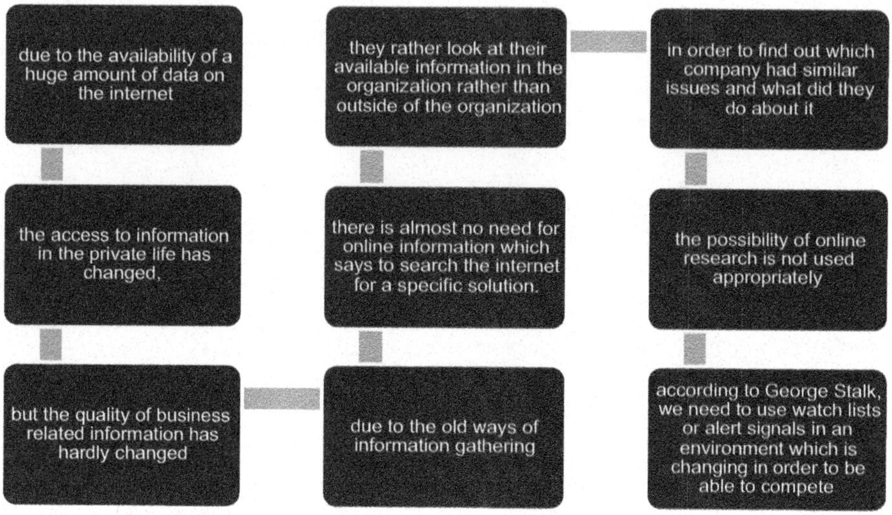

Due to the availability of a huge amount of data on the internet, the access to information in the private life has changed, but the quality of business-related information has hardly changed, due to the old ways of information gathering. There is almost no need for online information which says to search the internet for a specific solution. They rather look at their available information in the organization rather than outside of the organization in order to find out which company had similar issues and what did they do about it. Intense research outside the company also requires a clear milestone dedicated to this task. Sometimes it is necessary to call some of the competitors and ask for information about what they did.

Example

- A new IT solution is needed to trade FX, as the old system became inadequate and must be replaced.
- The project manager will define all necessary milestones which are needed for the project in order to identify the best possible system.
- In the current evaluation process we underestimate the benefit of available information in the internet.
- We need to search for successful FX trading organizations.
- We need to contact the IT department of the company to understand which system they use.
- Before approaching the software providers, one must ensure that all needed information has been obtained about the current FX trading functionalities used by successful organizations and which functionalities from one's old system must be also added.

- After checking the findings with the actual users, in our case the FX traders, and having their confirmation of what an ideal system should be, one can approach the companies under consideration.
- Ask the software providers for their proposals.

In most cases the possibility of online research is not used appropriately in order to avoid a tunnel view during the evaluation project. According to Stalk (2008), we need to use watch lists or alert signals in an environment which is changing in order to be able to compete. A change can affect a business, based on outsourcing, sub-contracting, partnering, offshoring, best-shoring, etc.

6.4.7 Social Networking

Being an entrepreneur for many years now and because of my passion for art, I was able to network with a diversified group of experts, compared to my time as an employee. For 3 years the company has offered art programs for bankers and collectors. The art programs were often in collaboration with companies who share the passion for art, such as Allianz, Merryl Lynch, Gassmann fashion, Porsche, wealth management companies, art galleries, and international auction houses. It was an interesting group with inspiring ideas as well as many volunteers and supporters who liked to be involved in making the art activities a success. These art programs enabled us many interesting encounters with senior bank managers, entrepreneurs, and excellent artists.

Many large organizations follow their own social media strategies to promote their corporate brand. I think the future social networking will be a balance of meeting in person and online.

References

Goleman D (2006) Social intelligence. The new science of human relationships. The Bantam Dell Publishing Group, New York

Hart T (2009) From information to transformation: education for the evolution of consciousness. Peter Lang International Academic Publishers, New York

Kaku M (2009) "The world in 2030: how science will affect computers, medicine, jobs, our lifestyles and the wealth of our nations" by Kaku on his speech at Queensborough Community College NY (on YouTube)

Kuchler H (2014) Technology groups take need for investment in security to heart. Financial Times

Snyder S (2009) The new world of wireless. How to compete in the 4G revolution. Wharton School Publishing, Upper Saddle River

Stalk G (2008) 5 Future strategies you need right now. Summarized by permission of Harvard Business Press, Boston

7 Brain, Creativity vs. Bank, Innovation

According to Stibel (2009), brainGate is currently being experienced by science and allows people to control electronics with their mind.

The internet has connections like our brain, although it doesn't have yet as many connections as the brain, but the internet's connections are growing every day. Computers are already able to process data much quicker than our brain. The activities around the solution of Web 2.0 are more similar to our brain.

I think that it is only a question of time to be able to understand our brain better through computer as science are continuously trying to rebuild what human is able to do. Is there any other objects than the exact copy of a human that might be more useful for our world to make a computer to copy?

© Springer International Publishing Switzerland 2015

S. Thuiner, *Banks of the Future*, DOI 10.1007/978-3-319-07554-9_7

3. A Busy City

7.1 Practical Approach

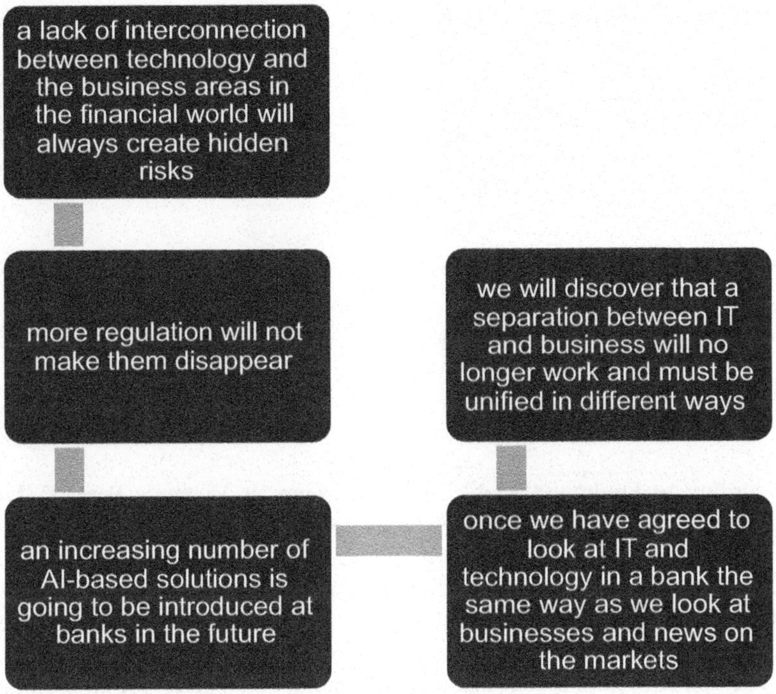

A lack of interconnection between technology and the business areas in the financial world will always create hidden risks; more regulation will not make them disappear. An increasing number of AI-based solutions are going to be introduced at banks in the future. Once we have agreed to look at IT and technology in a bank the same way as we look at businesses and news on the markets, we will discover that a separation between IT and business will no longer work and must be unified in different ways.

7.1.1 Viable System

Beer's (1967) model of a viable system explains that organizations act in an environment, with management regulating processes. Our problem is managing the complexity and therefore need to measure the complexity, which varies. In today's world of technology and huge amounts of information we have massively increased the variety of complexity. Therefore it is very difficult for managers to regulate this complexity by ignoring its variety. A large organization has many small environments, processes, and managements, with their processes being connected with each other to different environments.

7.1.2 De-centralized and Centralized Systems

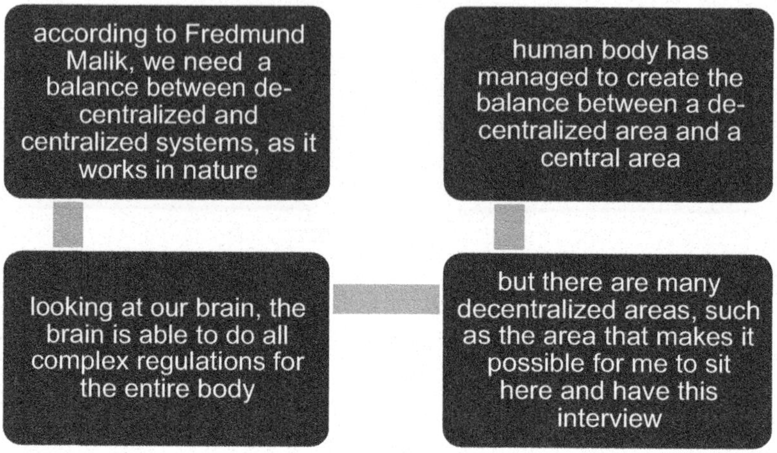

According to Fredmund Malik in an interview at Vienna's Peter F. Drucker Forum in 2009, we need a balance between de-centralized and centralized systems, as it works in nature. Looking at our brain, the brain is able to do all complex regulations for the entire body, but there are many de-centralized areas, such as the area that makes it possible for me to sit here and have this interview. The human body has managed to create the balance between a de-centralized area and a central area. The viable system model is a useful organizational setup for an organization, which confirms that the matrix organization is not good enough for today's world.

7.1.3 Creativity

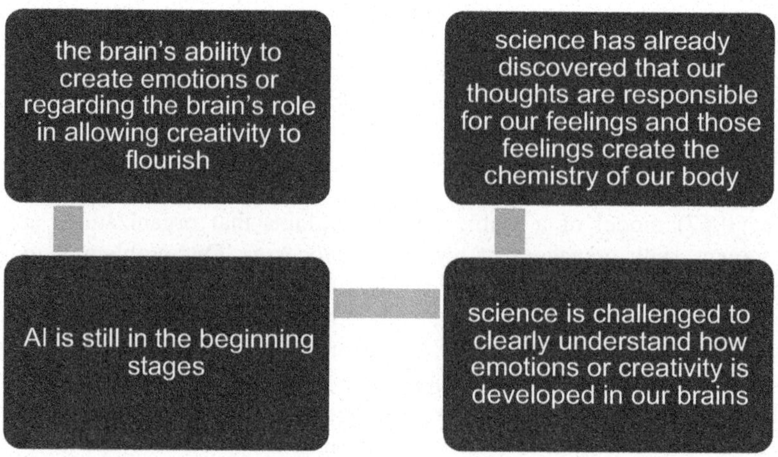

In the field of the brain's ability to create emotions or regarding the brain's role in allowing creativity to flourish, AI is still in the beginning stages. Science is challenged to clearly understand how emotions or creativity is developed in our brains. In medicine it is possible, with the help of modern technology, to see which area of the brain is activated when we, for instance, have a creative moment, but the mechanism that is at work to achieve it is unclear. Scientists Like Joe Dispenza have already discovered that our thoughts are responsible for our feelings and those feelings create the chemistry of our body.

7.1.4 AI

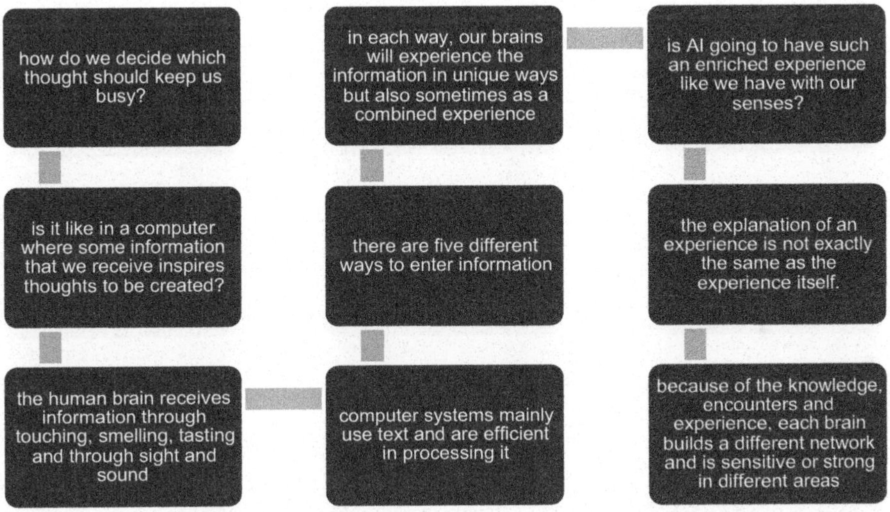

How do we decide which thought should keep us busy? Is it like in a computer where some information that we receive inspires thoughts to be created? The human brain receives information through touching, smelling, tasting, and through sight and sound. Computer systems mainly use text and are efficient in processing it. We have no way to enter text into a human's brain, but there are five different ways to enter information. In each way, our brains will experience the information in unique ways but also sometimes as a combined experience.

Is AI going to have such an enriched experience like we have with our senses? The explanation of an experience is not exactly the same as the experience itself. It is like giving our children advice from our life experience and hoping that they will use our experience to live an easier life, but they do not have the same beliefs and thoughts as we do after having the experience. It is clear that every person has different experience, and because of the knowledge, encounters, and experience, each brain builds a different network and is sensitive or strong in different areas.

7.1.5 Volume of Data

I think that a brain based on strong beliefs experience things and creates lasting impressions. The human brain is not like a laptop computer where, after it has been used for 5 years, we can see exactly what the volume of data is that we have collected over this period of time. I think that this is also true for organizations. Our brain is sometimes too busy with working all received information and in case it is too long too busy we feel that we need to have a break and maybe a holiday in order to let the volume of information structure itself.

7.1.6 Organization–Human Characteristics

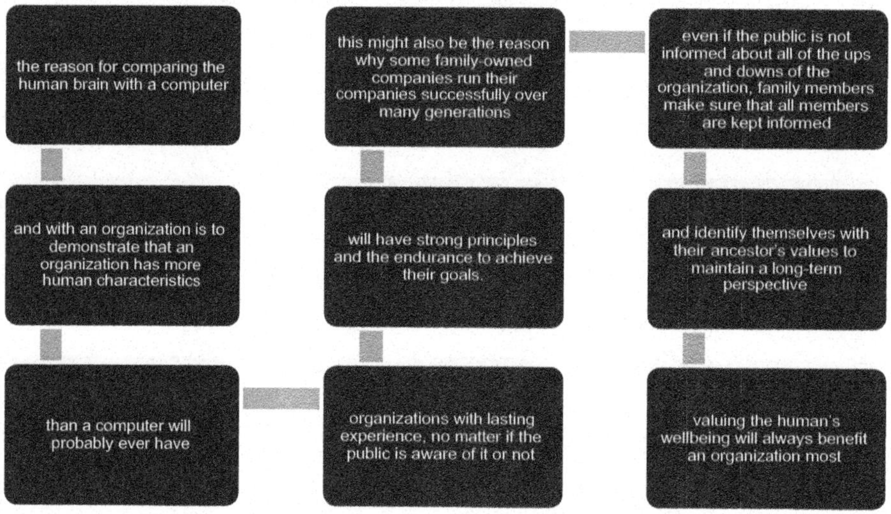

The reason for comparing the human brain with a computer and with an organization is to demonstrate that an organization has more human characteristics than a computer will probably ever have. Organizations with lasting experience, no matter if the public is aware of it or not, will have strong principles and the endurance to achieve their goals. This might also be the reason why some family-owned companies run their companies successfully over many generations. Even if the public is not informed about all of the ups and downs of the organization, family members make sure that all members are kept informed and identify themselves with their ancestor's values to maintain a long-term perspective.

An organization is made up of humans, with most humans acting similarly. An organization that values human resources will make their employees feel like family members. According to Iyer and Davenport (2008) in an article for the HBR called "Reverse Engineering Google's Innovation Machine," "Google's founders and executives have thought about many different aspects of the knowledge-work environment, including the design and occupancy of offices (jam-packed for better communication), the frequency of all-hands meetings (every Friday, with beer), and the approach to interviewing and hiring new employees (rigorous, with many interviews). None of these principles is rocket science, but in combination they suggest an unusually high level of recognition for the human dimensions of innovation. I think that recognizing and nuturing a human's well-being will always benefit an organization most.

7.1.6.1 Real Value to Organizations

The fact is that some of today's internal guidelines should be changed so that IT is applied in a more practical way. Only then will IT be able to provide high quality solutions and create real value to organizations. Organizations will also be able to monitor their core processes according to high standards and almost effortlessly. One way to build a natural bridge between business and IT is, as mentioned, to have experts with specific business and IT experience, like engineers in the automobile industry, who drive their own car and are crazy about it. We need few IT people who are also crazy about some activities in business such as having a passion for accounting or trading in their spare time.

Example

The best example is to look at the automobile industry and their engineers. Imagine the car industry employing engineers who have the theoretical knowledge of driving a car, but don't have actual experience of driving a car. In such a case they would need to have car drivers to tell them what they need to know, and, once understood, they would be able to build in a missing feature. This would slow down the development and production process and would be riskier and more expensive, because of potential misunderstandings. Apple, Facebook, or Google have for sure IT specialists with a passion for what the company is offering as a service or product and this is what banks of the future needs to build. A passion normally follows after experience and is hardly created after theoretical collection of information.

7.1.6.2 Valuable Assets

If financial institutions are supposed to become safer and more practical by using all available strengths effectively, they need to understand the way our brain works. The main valuable assets of an organization are the people and their brains. Even if an organization is technically advanced, there is even more need for intelligent control mechanisms. Although the computer has made much progress, the need to have humans to control it is still essential. I think that humans with their combined ability of logic, intuition, and five senses of collecting information are intellectually superior to machines, no matter how intelligent or advanced machines are.

7.1.7 Reduce Complexity

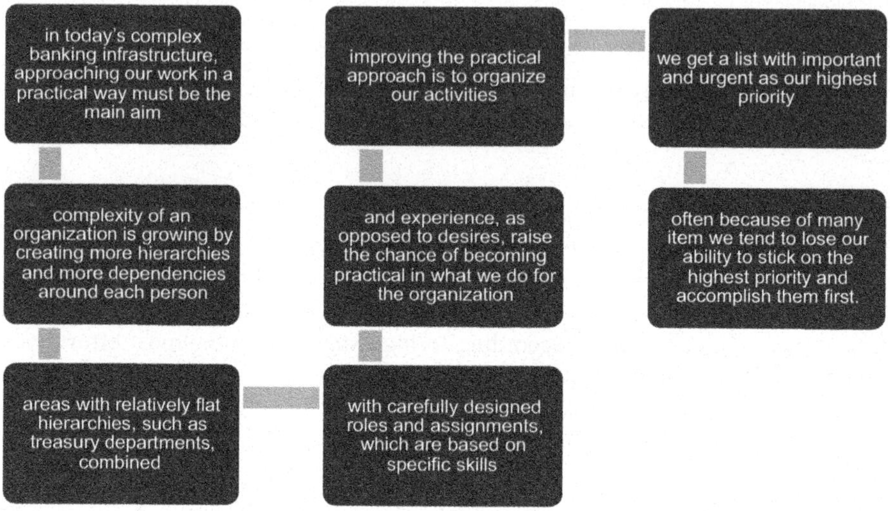

In today's complex banking infrastructure, approaching our work in a practical way must be the main aim. The complexity of an organization is growing by creating more hierarchies and more dependencies around each person in the hierarchy.

A practical approach is sometimes easier to implement than we think in practice.

Areas with relatively flat hierarchies, such as treasury departments, combined with carefully designed roles and assignments, which are based on specific skills and experience, as opposed to desires, raise the chance of becoming practical in what we do for the organization.

Another way of improving the practical approach is to organize our activities carefully. By putting together a list and starting with the most important subjects, we get a list with important and urgent as our highest priority and a list with important and not urgent as the second highest priority. In most cases we are carrying everything with us and think that we are able to do them all. Often because of many item we tend to lose our ability to stick on the highest priority and accomplish them first.

7.1.7.1 Complex Projects

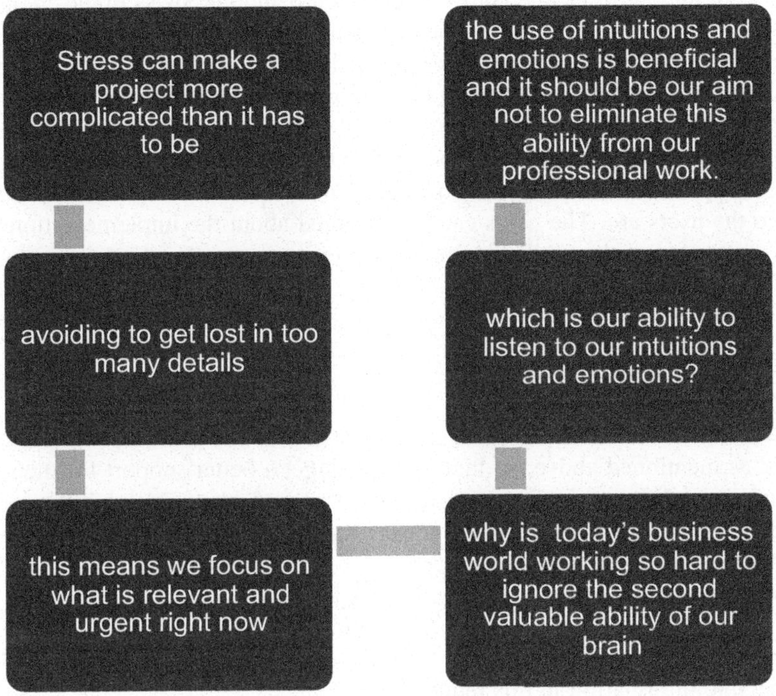

Stress can make a project more complicated than it has to be. A simple approach can be used to track a project's activities mindfully, while avoiding getting lost in too many details. This means we focus on what is relevant and urgent right now. There are consultants that are focused on offering mindful management, but they avoid the word mindful in their daily interaction with clients in order to avoid objections. Why is today's business world working so hard to ignore the second valuable ability of our brain, which is our ability to listen to our intuitions and emotions? The use of intuitions and emotions is beneficial and it should be our aim not to eliminate this ability from our professional work.

The prioritization of complex topics must be performed by humans, but their connections can be maintained and monitored through new AI-based solutions. I think that we are approaching a stage where such a list with prioritizations related to simple topics will be created and maintained by an AI-based solution. This will mark a significant progress in helping with today's changes via ongoing projects.

Example

For hedging purposes, the par rates of the Euro and the Swiss Franc are needed. A future AI solution will be able to identify which system provides the par curves; which reports need to be adjusted or newly created; who is currently using these currencies for trading purposes; and which overnight reports need to be adjusted or newly created in order to make it possible that an overnight decision about hedging an open position can be executed automatically. This list will support the IT specialists to understand what the necessary steps are and who the users are. The users can be informed about the implementation of the new curves and they will be able to use these curves for the running of their hedging reports.

7.1.7.2 Support IT

Furthermore, future AI solutions might also be able to add additional information to the list as mentioned above, so that IT experts get a better support for their work. Depending on the organization, AI might have a lot of other existing information so that the AI solution becomes more powerful and able to provide solutions and its dependencies to other areas and systems.

Future interactions between internal experts and AI could look like this:

- Enter your request in AI's global change management system and include all available information in this request.
- Describe the outcome that you expect from your request.
- Specify what you mean with your description.
- Confirm my understanding of your request.
- Enter the needed format for the report.
- Enter the names of the involved areas.
- Etc.

The AI solution as described above might look more complicated than it will be in reality in the future. In fact, today's process of doing what has just been described is time intensive and can be relatively easy covered by future AI solutions automatically.

Today's manual method of handling activities like explained above is not only cumbersome, but also allows hidden risks to emerge. Many analysts and experts must collaborate in order to set up a process to evaluate the impact of this change. Experts from business areas as well as from IT must be involved to discuss the findings and let people confirm what has been found.

After a long process of running the evaluation project and receiving the confirmation that the findings are correct and nothing is missing, the information can then be handed-over to a project team to make a proper project plan and set up a core team of all those people who must be involved in implementing the change. Sometimes the evaluation process is stopped or takes longer than the project itself, as people tend to be involved in several projects and get distracted when they are involved in additional tasks or projects. Business experts are needed only to provide explanations in order for decisions to be taken.

7.1.7.3 AI Solutions for Accuracy

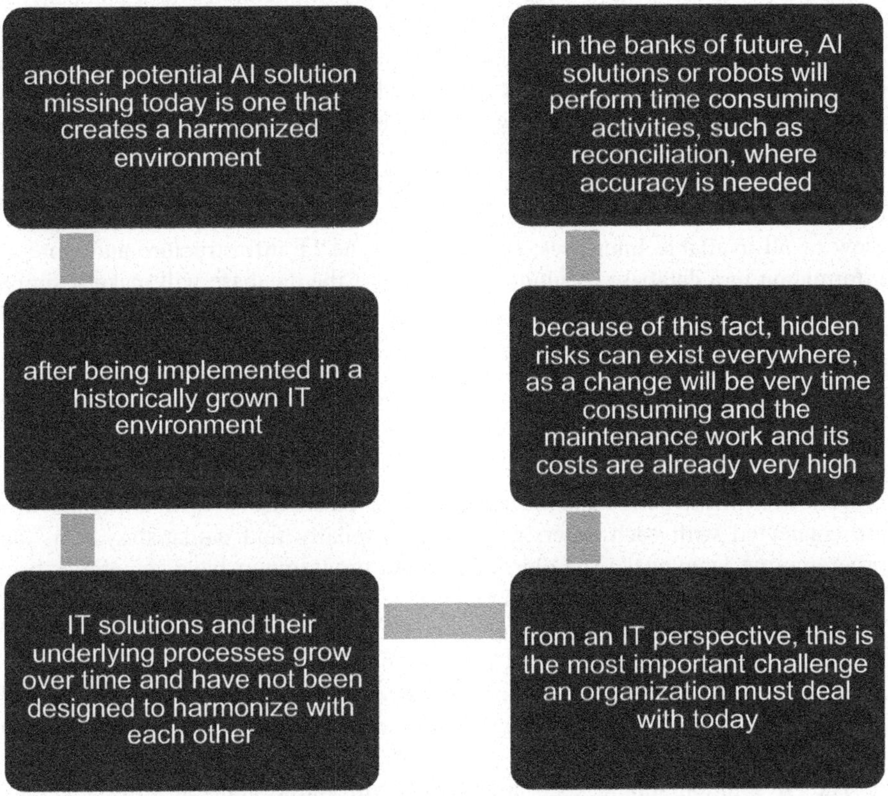

As mentioned before, another potential AI solution missing today is one that creates a harmonized environment after being implemented in a historically grown IT environment. IT solutions and their underlying processes grow over time and have not been designed to harmonize with each other. From an IT perspective, this is the most important challenge an organization must deal with today. Because of this fact, hidden risks can exist everywhere, as a change will be very time consuming and the maintenance work and its costs are already very high.

In the banks of future, AI solutions or robots will perform time consuming activities, such as reconciliation, where accuracy is needed. Robots are already available today for different tests and it is a question of time for having them involved in daily banking activities. Kuchler argue in an FT (2014) article titled "White-collar robots roll into schools, hospitals and offices" the following: "Shiny and white, the autonomous guard robot patrols an area, using data from optical and sound sensors along with licence plate recognition to feed information. . .."

7.1.7.4 AI Systems Develop AI Systems

Building potential future AI solutions as described before is simple for IT expert organizations and can have wide-spread, positive implications for a company. In the future there will be intelligent software in place which is able to develop AI solutions like described above. They can develop a new AI by simply collecting data from the intranet about one particular subject from all over the organization automatically. The more flexible the software is in collecting information, the more intelligent the created AI solution will be.

Future software will be able to create new AI solutions for organizations by collecting all the information around a particular department and create an overview of all available interfaces, can overview the IT infrastructure and store all information in a database. A unique definition of the database will make it simple for an organization to extend the data and to use the data when needed.

7.1.8 AI: Processes

Since the IT infrastructure and the underlying processes are set up in a way that they are connected with each other, we can occasionally find outdated systems and programming languages. The old systems and programmes have sometimes been used for decades and are maintenance intensive, with experts having experience and knowledge of old technologies and programming languages hard to find. Due to this fact, the future will see potential AI solutions that can harmonize the infrastructure. In order to build a solution like this, a company needs an attention to details; then it is simple to offer it to large financial institutions, which will be thankful to be able to use it.

The AI solution should keep interactions with old systems at a low level and provide access to the old system when needed so that the requested information can be collected automatically. The objective of the future banks will be to get rid of old systems which require high maintenance efforts and have high levels of risks embedded. Additionally, information about old systems can be maintained in the AI solution in order to make a replacement of those systems easier to accomplish.

Example

At one of my assignments the project's task was to look for information that one senior expert claimed to have access to in a system and can provide files which contained that information. The old reporting system had been already removed from the production environment, but he managed to keep access and used the old system as backup.

7.1.9 Human Intelligence

Research in the field of AI is attempting to find a way to incorporate higher logical skills into their solutions than humans have. Numerous available solutions on the market prove their success.

When it comes to incorporating human intuitions, science is stalled and does not progress. Any small achievement in this field looks insignificant. While the logic inherent in AI developments beats human skills, it cannot compete with human abilities with respect to soft skills, such as empathy, emotions, charisma, and creativity to solve problems.

According to Zweig (2007), our brain does not make financial decisions based on profit and loss, as there are additional factors involved, such as surprise, happiness, fear, risk, emotions, intuitions, and interpretations. We therefore act rationally or instinctive and we question our decisions afterwards. We test our assumptions and use common sense and so on.

7.1.9.1 Intuition

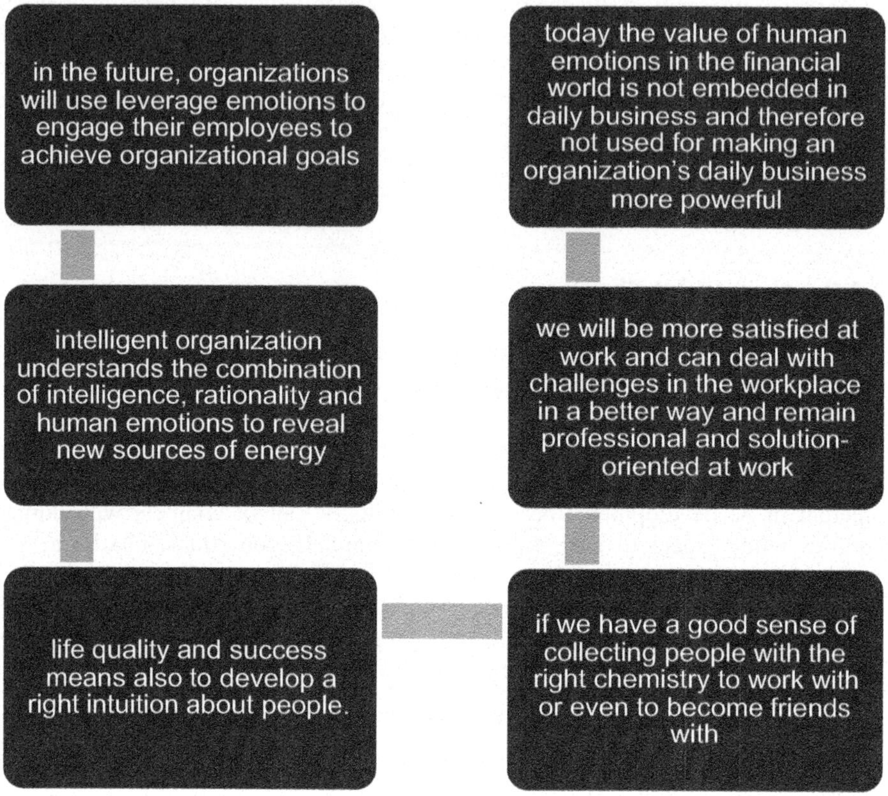

In the future, organizations will use leverage emotions to engage their employees to achieve organizational goals. An intelligent organization understands the combination of intelligence, rationality, and human emotions to reveal new sources of energy.

Life quality and success means also to develop a right intuition about people. We need to look at ourselves sometimes and ask who our close colleagues are, our close friends, and close family members. If we have a good sense of collecting people with the right chemistry to work with or even to become friends with, we will be more satisfied at work and can deal with challenges in the workplace in a better way and remain professional and solution-oriented at work.

Today the value of human emotions in the financial world is not embedded in daily business and therefore not used for making an organization's daily business more powerful.

There is no doubt that humans have a desire for social interaction, which, as Buettner (2012) described in his book about the world's "Blue Zones," has a strong impact on longevity. Working as an individual is as important as working in a team and therefore if we isolate ourselves and hide our emotions, the team cohesion will be weak and the quality of the result of a team collaboration will be below its potential and thus harm an organization.

7.1.9.2 ELIZA

Many decades ago, an AI system called Eliza tried to fake human soft skills and gain human's trust by giving them the impression that they are talking to a human. Since then, many AI solutions have tried to incorporate it, but with only little success.

The reason for science to replicate soft skills is that even humans have difficulties seeing through themselves and understanding the mechanism behind their creation. In addition to the fact that science does normally not want to interfere with emotions or creativities, it has difficulties with incorporating it in system solutions.

7.1.9.2.1 Soft Skills

Emotions are a door to develop many of our soft skills. We become excellent in soft skills by exposing our emotions at a time and in a level of intensity that needs to be expressed. If somebody loses a close friend or family member and does not allow himself to experience emotions of sadness for a while, then we suppress an important element of human nature.

After some time you also need to decide when to move on. It is our rationality that takes control after time has passed and tells us to move on. As human we will good to go through emotion when the time is suitable and feel stronger afterwards. Is the computer going to be able to do this? It would be difficult for a machine to be programmed that way and the more important question would be for which purpose?

Another important human ability is to listen to one's intuitions. How can technology create a new knowledge because of the "got feeling"? I think that an excellent technology will always need humans for their intuitions and feelings in order to be enriching and make the civilization to grow. A world without empathy and intuition is incomplete, and therefore in a better future we will see a combination of the intelligence of technology and human's emotional intelligence.

7.1.9.2.2 Empathy: Sympathy

If an organization does not allow human emotions, then the organization will be a colder place where colleagues are only connected because of work or benefits, with no human emotions involved, such as empathy or sympathy.

I think that an extraordinary collaboration is enabled when we become transparent with our emotions. This is when we gain sympathy, can afford to make mistakes, and are still respected as part of an extraordinary collaborative team.

Example

Another example to demonstrate why we benefit through emotions in our working life is the following: If we get a promotion and do not allow ourselves to express joy and celebrate with colleagues, family, and close friends, then we will not be able to recharge ourselves and get stronger in what we do.

We are also not going to experience that authentic people around us expressing their happiness to us, and we will end up feeling isolated and not integrated. If we hide a promotion because we are afraid of losing it, then we have no trust in people around us and it is a sign of poor life quality. This fact might not be true but will frustrate us.

7.2 Brain and Stress

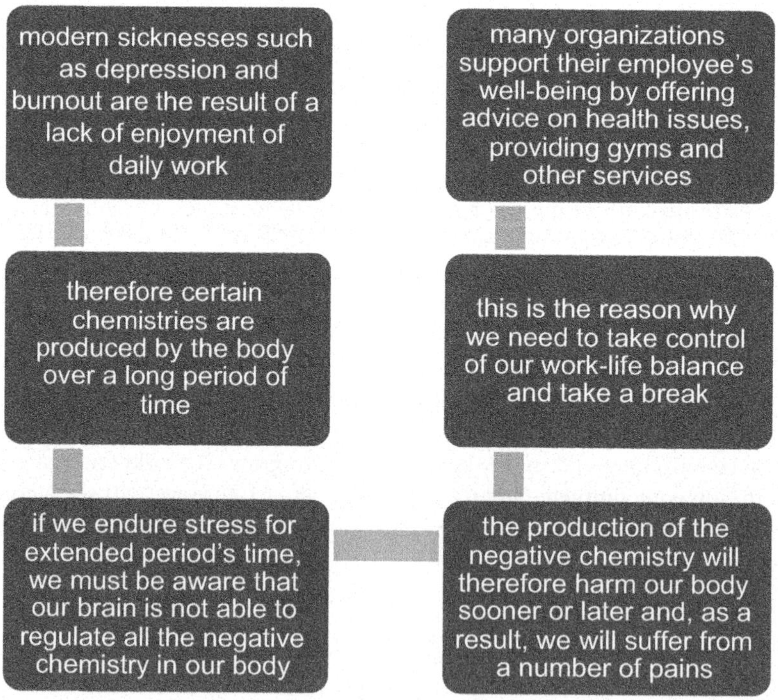

Modern sicknesses such as depression and burnout are the result of a lack of enjoyment of daily work, and therefore certain chemistries are produced by the body over a long period of time. Despite our brain's ability to control our body with all its complexity, we ask ourselves why it is the case that the brain is not able to regulate the volume of body-harming chemistry?

The brain regulates bodily functions from the beginning to end of life, but if there is long lasting stressful work, our brain releases stress to the body, as it is not able to handle it and lets the body create harmful chemistry, for instance, cortisone, for a longer period of time.

If we endure stress for extended period's time, we must be aware that our brain is not able to regulate all the negative chemistry in our body. The production of the negative chemistry will therefore harm our body sooner or later and, as a result, we will suffer from a number of pains.

This is the reason why we need to take control of our work-life balance and take a break. Many organizations support their employee's well-being by offering advice on health issues, providing gyms, and other services.

Example

I remember when we were implementing a system for a bank, it was necessary to work during weekends almost every weekend for 8 months. Luckily I was able to enjoy what I was doing so the stress did not harm my work-life balance. In 1999, during a major data migration process that I was responsible for and which took place over a weekend, I knew that the migration would take at least 15 h and therefore there was no time to repeat it if there was an issue. We were in a group of three people using a clock to ensure that we did not fall asleep during the migration in order to be able to deal with potential issues quickly and do not loose time. This was just one of many similar weekends. After this project, I also learned to appreciate free weekends much more than before.

The reason for mentioning this example is that I was happy to work in this project, with my manager being too busy to sit in my neck, and as I had the freedom, I felt more responsible to deliver the expected result and enjoyed the long working hours and even the stress. Since then I started to realize that I experience stress positively only when I have complete responsibility for what I do and I think many employees have similar experiences.

7.2.1 Systems, Processes, and Employees

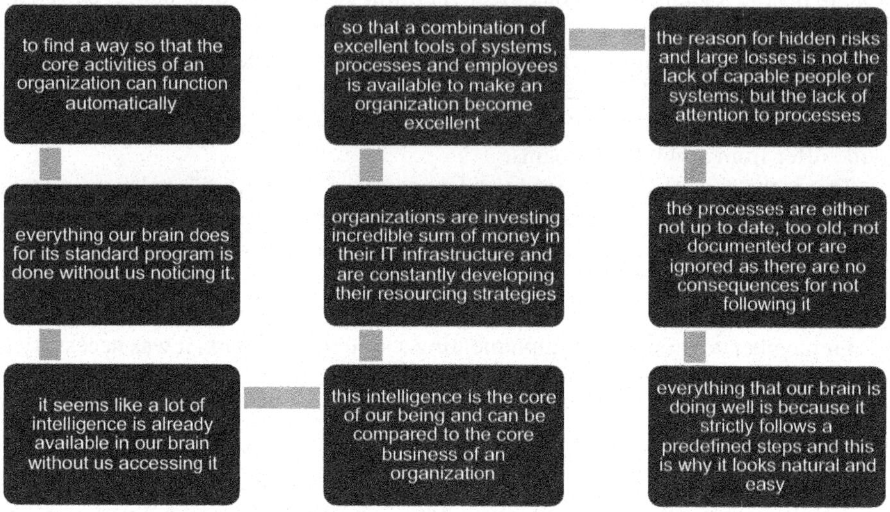

If an organization can be compared to the human brain, it is interesting to find a way so that the core activities of an organization can function automatically. Everything our brain does for its standard program is done without us noticing it. It seems like a lot of intelligence is already available in our brain without us accessing it. This intelligence is the core of our being and can be compared to the operating system of a computer or the core business of an organization.

An organization has an IT infrastructure and humans have defined processes to enable them to collaborate with each other in order to achieve an expected result. Today, all organizations are investing incredible sum of money in their IT infrastructure and are constantly developing their resourcing strategies so that a combination of excellent tools of systems, processes, and employees is available to make an organization become excellent. The reason for hidden risks and large losses is not the lack of capable people or systems, but the lack of attention to processes.

The processes are either not up to date, too old, not documented, or are ignored as there are no consequences for not following it. Everything that our brain is doing well is because it strictly follows a predefined steps and this is why it looks natural and easy.

I think that in the future, organizations will pay as much attention to their processes as they do to their IT infrastructure and resourcing. The best way to measure attention is to look at the amount of investment in each area and if an organization wants to function automatically and naturally strong, then they need to spend the same budget on setting up and controlling their daily processes as they use for IT infrastructure of resources.

This is definitely not the case and will be changed sooner or later. As mentined, in the future a new system will be built, which might be called the brain of the future bank (BOFB). This system will have many focus areas and is basically able to control the collaboration between humans, technology, and their underlying daily processes. This system will be also seen as the core intelligence of a bank, which is able to prevent risks which a bank is not able to take.

7.2.1.1 Core Intelligence

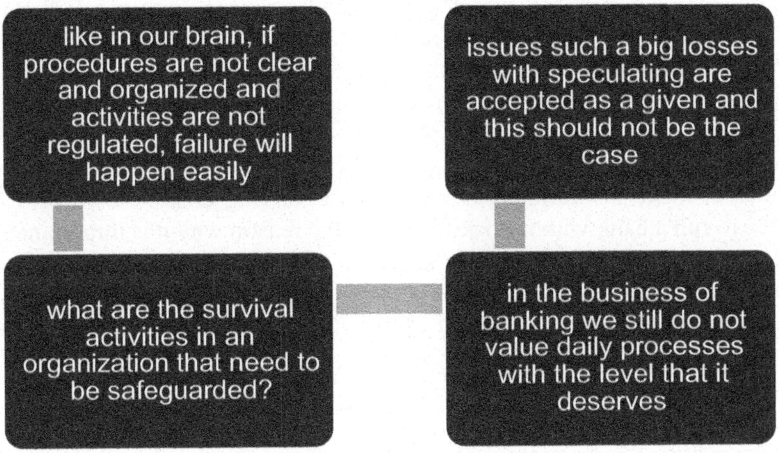

We agree that we wish that we could have a core part of banking such as a limit to risk that was untouchable or regulated by authorities and strongly monitored by control processes. Can we build such secure core intelligence for banking so that we know that survival activities are done already in a practical way with less effort and are safeguarded? Not every single employee or client may be able to understand this core intelligence of the banking business but they all will trust it as it is based on natural logical intelligence and it assures that the technology, humans, and their underlying processes are in harmony with each other.

Like in our brain, if procedures are not clear and organized and activities are not regulated, failure will happen easily. What are the survival activities in an organization that need to be safeguarded? As explained before, in the business of banking we still do not value daily processes with the level that it deserves. Issues such a big losses with speculating are accepted as a given and this should not be the case.

The introduction of a new product on the market or carrying the risk of this product must be seen as the core intelligence of banking and must be regulated with guidelines before it is implemented in the organization.

7.2.1.2 Core Activities

Banking has always been creative when it came to ideas about new financial products. In the past, regulators have had difficulties to cope with the range of product innovations. In the past creativity was more focused on increasing profits and less on controlling the risks behind creative financial products.

Core daily activities/processes are all processes taken so that a great risk for the organization can be avoided if these activities are not governed and monitored permanently. Lehman Brothers Bank was one of the largest investment banks as well as was one of the banks that created Wall Street. The bank went bankrupt in September 2008 because of large real estate-related losses. The risks the bank took were much bigger than the bank could withstand. The core business of banking, such as lending, must be managed with a strictly monitored limit system in place as well as a governance process which reflects regulatory requirements. Following the Lehmann case and the aftermath of the financial crisis, Basel III was introduced to reduce the risk of insolvency of banks.

Banking crises have always been a feature of economic activity. The lessons learned from such events tend to result in stronger regulation and higher risk awareness. It is essential to understand and control the risks involved in banking activities to make institutions safer and avoid banking crises. However, it is not possible to run a bank without risks, which is the reason why it is important to have good control procedures in place so that risks are monitored and reported to senior management in the organization as well as to regulators. The meaning of accepted risk is how much a bank is allowed to lose. This can be easily defined in a daily processes and controlled.

7.3 Logic or Intuition

I think that the source of creativity, creation of emotions or the existence of "gut feeling," is a part of our brain's core intelligence, which we have no access to today and there is no science that could build a copy of it and there is no sign that a copy can be built, which suggests that this is unique to humans.

7.3.1 ELIZA: HER

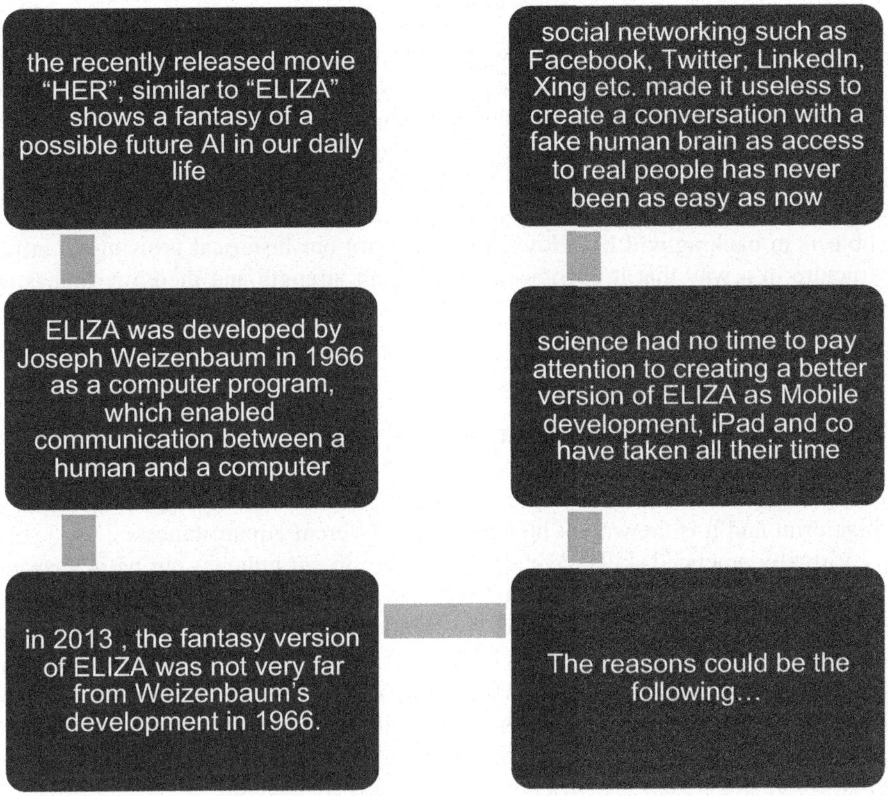

The recently released movie "HER," similar to "ELIZA" shows a fantasy of a possible future AI in our daily life. ELIZA was developed by Joseph Weizenbaum in 1966 as a computer program, which enabled communication between a human and a computer. The program was able to generate different speaking partners based on different descriptions. Weizenbaum wrote this program in MAD-SLIP for an IBM 7094. In 2013 the new version of ELIZA was called "HER" and although it was a fantasy and there no system has been developed, the fantasy version of ELIZA was not very far from Weizenbaum's development in 1966.

The reasons could be the following:

- Science had no time to pay attention to creating a better version of ELIZA as Mobile development, iPad and co have taken all their time.
- Social networking such as Facebook, Twitter, LinkedIn, Xing etc. made it useless to create a conversation with a fake human brain as access to real people has never been as easy as now.

- The creation of robots and their use in the nursery business is not really necessary as many real people are available to do this job.
- The creation of real feelings has not been proven to be possible at all.

Besides all these obstacles to create the soft skills for a machine, I think that it would be only a little benefit for the banking business. Being competitive does not mean implementing everything that is available in the market quickly. Everybody is talking about mobile banking and it has become a culture of banking during the past decade that a bank without the latest technology is not competitive.

I think that this culture will change. In the future one of the most important subjects in banking will be "How can we control our historical growing IT infrastructure in a way that it becomes a sign of our strength and therefore makes us more competitive on the market."

7.3.2 Left Part and Right Part of the Brain

According to Davidson and Begley (2012), our emotional style is unique like a fingerprint and it is the way of how we act in different circumstances.

Virtually practiced skills have a similar effect in our brain, as our brain answers to the external or internal world. Our negative emotions will increase the activities of the right part of the brain and positive emotions will increase the activities in the left part of our brain. Our emotions have many dimensions, such as resilience (if it takes time to recover from past emotions), outlook (sunny personality), social intuition (reading non-verbal messages), self-awareness (being aware of your feelings), sensitivity to context (different behaviors are appropriate in different situations), and attention (don't allow to be easily distracted).

7.3.3 The Fingerprint of Our Brain

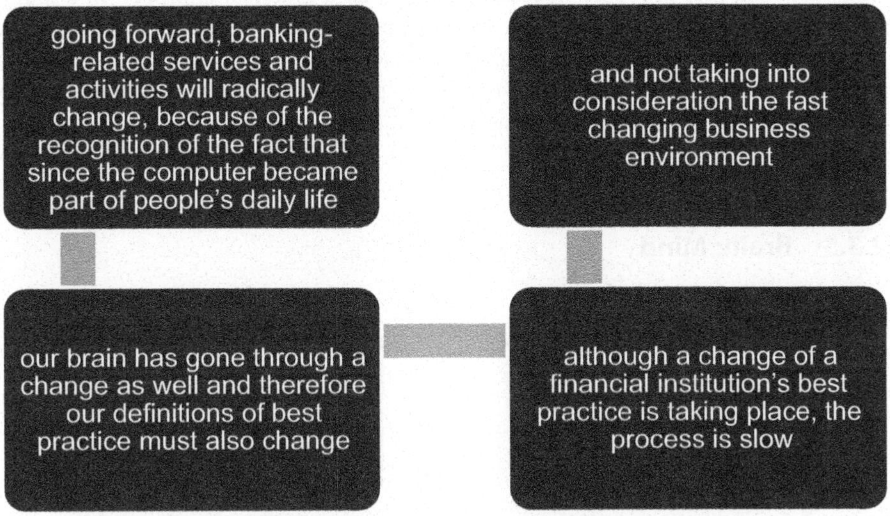

According to Sharot (2011), we have no control about the way we think and feel. An automatic optimism is an illusion and our brain has an optimism bias. Although we know that we die one day, we see our future sunny and plan for it as it would never end.

This ability makes us to consider our past and wonder about our future, which is supportive to see a better life and remain positive in hard times. Highly emotional situations will affect our brain strongly and will be remembered for a long period of time.

Brain according to Watson (2010), scientists know that our brain is changing all the time and the computer has an influence on this change, for instance, it changes the way we read. The book calls today's teenagers "screenagers," who like to spend their spare time online or using digital media. There are already many intelligent solutions available in the market, which are making decisions for us like our brain does.

7.3.3.1 Change of Best Practice

Going forward, banking-related services and activities will radically change, because of the recognition of the fact that since the computer became part of people's daily life, our brain has gone through a change as well and therefore our definitions of best practice must also change. Although a change of a financial institution's best practice is taking place, the process is slow and not taking into consideration the fast changing business environment.

7.3.4 Practicality and AI

In conclusion, it is probably necessary to say that a practical approach in a multi-dimensional IT environment with interaction with peoples, processes, systems, networks, and the outside world can only be achieved by introducing AI solutions to control existing solutions. This will make it possible for experts to act practically and leave today's way of implementing a solution by using more time.

7.3.5 Brain: Mind

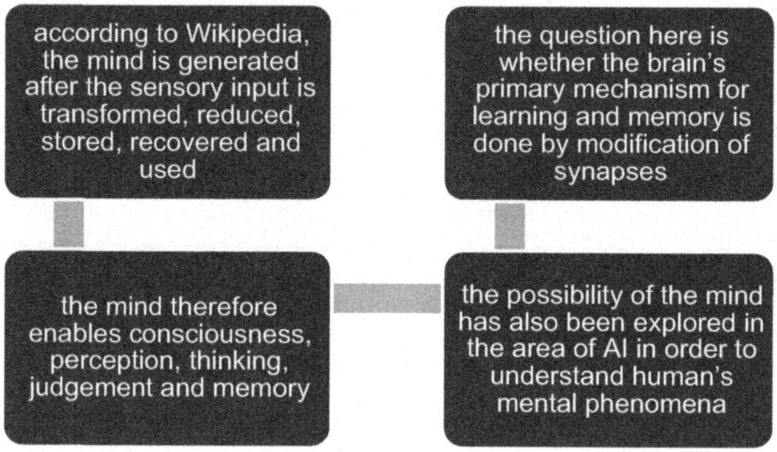

According to Hawkins (2005), a lot of progress has been made over the last few years to understand how our brain functions. Each region of the brain is related to a particular functionality for which there is a reason behind it. For example, the vision region is physically connected to the brain. Our brain is located at the center of the nervous system and is the most complex organ in our body. It evaluates information from the primary sensory organs such as sound, smell, vision, taste, and balance.

According to Wikipedia, the mind is generated after the sensory input is transformed, reduced, stored, recovered, and used. The mind therefore enables consciousness, perception, thinking, judgment, and memory. The possibility of the mind has also been explored in the area of AI in order to understand human's mental phenomena. Information is transformed via synapses. A synapse is a structure that permits a neuron or nerve cell to pass an electrical or chemical signal to another cell. The question here is whether the brain's primary mechanism for learning and memory is done by modification of synapses.

7.3.6 Sixth Sense Technology

Pranav Mistry is exposing the idea of sixth sense technology and has developed a number of ideas of how our current desire to interact with machines could give back to our physical environment and how this world would be like. He exposes the human imagination by using all the technology that we use in our physical world without any technical devices, such as chaptering a picture by only using our hands and downloading it to our computer. The future computer might allow us to enter all information related to the senses into the information, such as respect, etc. What about the virtual picture by using our hands on a wall? Will this be a future development to happen? Using the paper ticket and see already the adjustment after the ticket has been changed online on our paper ticket. Imagine to use everything in our computer we can play with on paper, like we read newspapers, but it acts like a TV and shows the change of the weather. These ideas have been developed to avoid a world of spending time with devices and not having actual interactions with our physical environment.

7.3.7 The Brain's Frustrations and Narrow-Mindedness

According to a documentation called "There is God in Neurons," which says that, depending on which neurons get simulated, certain connections become stronger and more efficient, while others may become weaker. Rationality and emotional resilience work the same way. These are neural connections that can be strengthened. Whatever you are doing at any time, you are physically modifying your brain to become better at it. Since this is a dangerous situation such a foundation at mechanism of the brain, being self-aware can greatly enrich our life experience. Specific neurons and neurotransmitters, such as norepinephrine, trigger a defensive state when we feel that our thoughts have to be protected from the influence of others.

If we are then confronted with differences in opinion, the chemicals that are released in the brain are the same ones that try to ensure our survival in dangerous situations. In this defensive state, the more primitive part of the brain interferes with natural thinking and the limbic system can knock out most of our working memory, physically causing narrow-mindedness. We see this in the politics of fear, in the strategy of poker players or simply when someone is stubborn in a discussion.

No matter how valuable an idea is, the brain has trouble processing it when it is in such a state. But, when we express ourselves and our views are appreciated, these defence chemicals decrease in the brain and dopamine neurotransmission activates reward neurons, making us feel empowered and increases our self-esteem. Our beliefs have a profound impact on our body chemistry, which is why placebos can be so effective. Self-esteem or self-belief is closely linked to the neurotransmitter serotonin.

When we grow up, our moral and ethical compass is almost entirely forged by our environment, so our actions are often a result of the validation we get from society.

New developments in neuroscience are giving us a better understanding of culture and identity. Recent neurological research has confirmed the existence of empathetic mirror neurons. When we experience an emotion or perform an action, specific neurons fire, but when we observe someone else performing this action or when we imagine it, many of the same neurons will fire again, as if we were performing the action ourselves.

These empathy neurons connect us to other people, allowing us to feel what others feel. Since these neurons respond to our imagination, we can experience emotional feedback from it as if it came from someone else.

7.4 Magic Moment

In a letter to shareholders some years ago, Warren Buffett was telling the story about Berkshire's entrance into the insurance business when buying National Indemnity. The owner of the insurance company was late for the closure of the deal, explaining that he was driving around looking for a parking meter with some unexpired time, which Buffett described as a magic moment to him, knowing that this was the kind of manager he was looking for. Buffett values managers with a certain sense of frugality which is also needed in the banking business. The answer to cost pressures is not always to outsource to other countries where labor costs are low. The answer could also be which other actions need to be taken so that costs are reduced. The actions could be the following:

- What do we have and do not really need?
- What should we change to make a particular solution more efficient?
- Who should be responsible for providing the answers for the questions above?

7.5 Ongoing Projects and the Brain's Nature

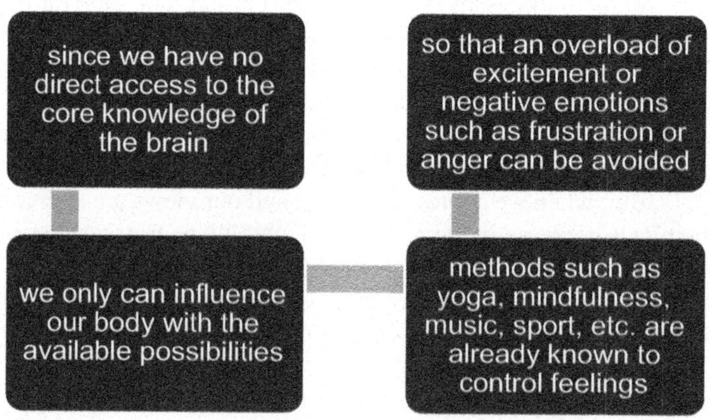

Today more attention and budget goes to the two factors of technology and humans. In order for an organization become more practical, as explained, it is necessary to pay more attention to daily processes. Everybody with decades of experience in banking will confirm that almost all projects must be done as quickly as possible. We receive the order from our managers and pass it to our working colleges. In fact, all projects are urgent.

In projects we also sometimes tend to make our work even more stressful by informing stakeholders either too frequently or too little or by including the wrong group of people and ask too many managers for their opinions. The creation of confusion will produce negative stress for all involved people.

This is why we need to keep an eye on the level of stress we are creating or listen to our imitation when it comes to informing or involving experts. This also means that we need to become more practical so that only good stress is generated and negative stress is not created at all.

In order to understand practicality better, we should look at our brain once again. Since we have no direct access to the core knowledge of the brain, we only can influence our body with the available possibilities. Methods such as yoga, mindfulness, music, sport, etc. are already known to control feelings so that an overload of excitement or negative emotions such as frustration or anger can be avoided. This will help not only our body to recover and avoid becoming sick, but it also means that we can remain productive for our project.

7.5.1 Frustration in a Project

Schäfer (2014) wrote the following in an article for FT called "Banks fear effects of stress on workforce": Banks are worried about a rise in mental health issues and stress-related illnesses ... bankers struggle to cope with more work and less job security. Frustration in a project is a hidden risk and can be controlled by the project manager. This can easily be achieved by assigning the project team members clear responsibilities and by managing authentic. As a project manager in a great organization, they will give you the power to introduce a change to the organization, and as far as you follow their processes of running a project, you can achieve the goal by applying the right soft skills. In a short period of time, a small group of people can change the working culture because of your project.

7.5.2 Escape Rooms

4. Beautiful Lake

As humans have different understanding of enjoyment, they also have different ways of releasing stress. During a conversation with the CEO of a private bank in Zurich in the summer of 2013, I was surprised that he liked the idea of a painting room in a bank's office. He found that it was a good idea to offer his employees the option of painting to relieve stress. In most of my assignments for banks, I have to use instrumental music to avoid the creation of frustrations and negative stress. I was told that I am more happy than sad and most of the time I am more optimistic than pessimistic and I think that it is a decision that we have to make and stick to it. I know a saying that goes; who does not enjoy will become unenjoyable.

I think that in the future, organizations will offer "stress releasing room" in each of their buildings so that employees can go there to relieve stress. The room could be described like an escape place, where talking is forbidden. It is empty with an expert who demonstrates small relaxing movements and lets you do it. On the other corner, there is a canvas to paint on an unfinished painting that many colleagues have already worked on, and instrumental music, such as the four sessions from Bach, is playing. I think that in the future large organizations will provide entertaining and stress relieving practices, in a simple room like this, but there will also be more sophisticated ones, potentially with a virtual teacher who instructs how to practice yoga, move or breath.

7.5.3 Modern Ways of Reducing Stress

The best way of reducing stress that I have discovered is Monika Anneliese Koch's yoga dance class in Salzburg. Monika's work was introduced to me in 2002 in London. Since then I have visited her seminars regularly. She teaches to breathe correctly, while copying her slow movements. She also introduces her students to Pina's dance technique to experience their emotions in a positive and intense way.

She helped many of her students to escape their busy days and to find themselves in an environment where they have more strongly experienced the calmness and silence around them than the cruddy noisiness. She is continuously studying new philosophies and techniques so that she can share them with her students.

I could imagine that the future banks might offer similar classes to their employees where they can relax and take a break to return refreshed. With the help of modern technology, artists like Monika could offer virtual, 30-min classes for employees in many different places.

According to Amy Cuddy, a professor at Harvard University, we can reduce the level of stress by only changing poses. The "stress-relieving room" could also represent Amy Cuddy's poses virtually to help you to do the same and relive stress. According to Cuddy (2012), you can change the chemistry in your body and reduce stress with how you sit or stand. She says that if we stand, talk, and sit like a person with high confidence; we will already reduce the level of cortisone even if it is fake and we actually do not feel confident. By changing our pose to a power pose, we will already feel powerful.

7.6 Avoid Hidden Risks

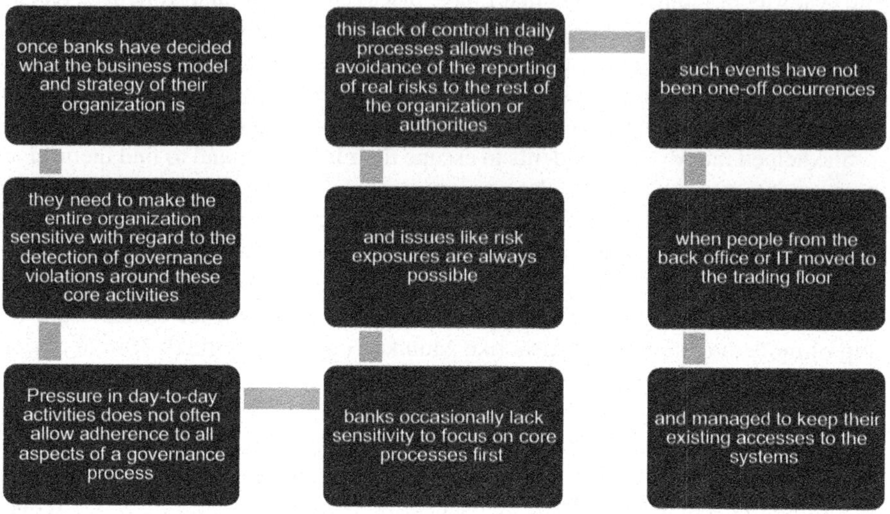

Management of client data is a crucial activity and is of central importance in the day-to-day running of a bank. All procedures around client data need to be strongly monitored and controlled.

It is a fact that more and more big data will be used in the future in a higher quality and predefined way so that only data from chosen sources will be allowed. This can help a bank to better understand and therefore to better support their clients and their employees.

The point is that once banks have decided what the business model and strategy of their organization is, they need to make the entire organization sensitive with regard to the detection of governance violations around these core activities.

Pressure in day-to-day activities does not often allow adherence to all aspects of a governance process. Therefore banks occasionally lack sensitivity to focus on core processes first, and issues like risk exposures which are in breach of limits related to risks are always possible. This lack of control in daily processes allows the avoidance of the reporting of real risks to the rest of the organization or authorities. Such events have not been one-off occurrences when people from the back office or IT moved to the trading floor and managed to keep their existing accesses to the systems.

7.6.1 Investment Banking

An employee from the back office is interested in trading and can finally move to the trading floor. A lack of control in daily processes allows him to keep his old permission and is therefore able to become his own back office. The separation of duties, which can avoid risks because of the embedded control, is no longer the case with this person. He can allow himself to speculate far beyond his limit.

Do we really think that mistakes like these have only happened seldomly, with the loss at Société Générale also being an exception? In most cases it is only one person who can manage to ensure his fictitious hedging trades are not only undetected by the middle and back office, but that they can also be shown as a real trade on the daily PnL statements and value at risk (VaR) reports. If the daily processes are not clear and strictly controlled, issues like a huge loss are possible. This is the case when nobody in the organization recognizes the open, unhedged position for a long time. Following large losses there will be internal and external experts working diligently on uncovering the real reasons for a massive loss on the trading floor and most of the people involved in investment banking probably know right from the beginning what the final reports will say. Their report will say that there was a weakness in the internal control processes about, for instance, forward ETF transactions (Case UBS/London 2011).

The daily processes in this area allowed these kinds of transactions to be accepted. Internal system weaknesses allowed the fictitious hedges as a real trade through many interfaces into other areas, such as risk management, etc. Once we draw conclusions from such instances, the expectation is that it will not happen again, but, unfortunately, these issues have always been part of the trading culture of investment banks and will happen again, unless there is a fundamental change in today's way of controlling.

In the future, at least the key people in IT will have gained work experience on the trading floor before they start to work in, for instance, IT, unlike in the past. The experts from a trading floor in the area of IT are able to understand all the trading-related creativity to find solutions and make sure that the IT infrastructure is able to create a control mechanism that is not harming the entire organization.

7.6.2 The Benefit

This is why experts with a combined IT and business expertise will become essential for controlling risks. Their involvement from the beginning in system implementation and innovation activities will ensure a higher quality in controlling and avoiding risks.

The most capable experts in risk management are those people who have worked as experts in both areas and do not only understand the business, but also bring along an understanding of the cultural differences between IT and business areas. They are able to establish better collaborations between these areas and can easily gain trust and collect the requested information about a particular subject.

7.6.2.1 Cultural Differences

There are fundamental cultural differences between the various business areas in a bank and IT. If there is no willingness to account for and to understand these differences, management will create frustrations and complicate collaboration between the various areas and the desired best solution can hardly be realized.

In the future there will be experts with a combined professional IT and business experience in all areas of the bank. These experts are going to be involved whenever it comes to controlling risks. By professional experience I mean that the person was, for instance, an accountant, controller, or programmer and is not working in accounting as an IT specialist or in IT as a business specialist. The most effective combination is a diversified working experience.

Every project can be seen as an innovation, and people with a combined experience are much more needed in projects than in the various areas of a bank. During a project, a change will come up and creativity in searching for new solutions is more needed than ever.

7.6.2.2 Innovator's Brain

In an article in the Harvard Business Review about "The Innovator's DNA," the authors find that one of the strongest skills that most successful CEOs of our time have is associating. Associating, or the ability to successfully connect seemingly unrelated questions, problems, or ideas from different fields, is central to the innovator's DNA.

Entrepreneur Frans Johansson described this phenomenon as the "Medici effect," referring to the creative explosion in Florence when the Medici family brought together people from a wide range of disciplines: sculptors, scientists, poets, philosophers, painters, and architects. As these individuals connected, new ideas blossomed at the intersections of their respective fields, thereby spawning the Renaissance, one of the most inventive eras in history. In order to grasp how associating works, it is important to understand how the brain operates.

The brain does not store information like a dictionary where you can find the word "theater" under the letter "T." Instead, it associates the word "theater" with any number of experiences from our lives. Some of these are logical, while others may be less obvious. The more diverse our experience and knowledge, the more connections the brain can make. Fresh inputs trigger new associations; for some, these lead to novel ideas.

As Steve Jobs has frequently observed, "Creativity is connecting things." It became essential, and a lack of interconnection between technology and the business areas in the financial world will only create hidden risks; more regulation will not make them disappear. Once we have agreed to look at IT and technology in a bank the same way as we look at businesses and markets, we will discover that a separation between IT and business will no longer work and must be unified in different ways. One way is, as mentioned, to have experts with work experience like engineers in the automobile industry who drive their own car and are crazy about it. The fact is that today's setup should be changed so that IT is applied in a more practical way. Only then will IT be able to provide high quality solutions and create real value to organizations. Organizations are also able to monitor their core processes according to high standards and almost effortlessly.

The most valuable resources of an organization are the people and their brains. Even if an organization is technically advanced, there is even more need for intelligent control mechanisms. Although the computer has made much progress, the need to have humans to control it is still great. I think that humans are intellectually superior to machines, no matter how intelligent or advanced machines are.

7.6.2.3 Conclusion

A practical approach is sometimes easier to follow than we think in practice, such as driving a car. In case we drove a car we were able to use all our senses to collect information and are therefore able to access a richer knowledge from our brain.

References

Beer S (1967) Cybernetics and management. S. Fischer; Wiley, New York

Buettner D (2012) The blue zones: lessons for living longer from the people who've lived the longest. National Geographic, Washington

Buffett W (2006) Berkshire Hathaway Inc. Shareholder Letter

Cuddy A (2012) Your body language shapes who you are. TED Global, June 2012

Davidson RJ, Begley S (2012) The emotional life of your brain: how its unique patterns affect the way you think, feel, and live – and how you can change them. Plume

Hawkins J, Blakeslee S (2005) On Intelligence. St. Martin's Griffin, New York

Iyer B, Davenport TH (2008) Reverse engineering Google's innovation machine. Harv Bus Rev 86 (4):58–69

Kuchler H (2014) White-collar robots roll into schools, hospitals and offices. Financial Times

Malik F (2009) Interview at P.F. Drucker forum, Vienna

Mistry P (2009) The thrilling potential of SixthSense technology. TED India, November 2009

Schäfer D (2014) Banks fear effects of stress on workforce. Financial Times

Sharot T (2011) The optimism bias: a tour of the irrationally positive brain. Pantheon Books, New York

Stibel JM (2009) Wired for thought: how the brain is shaping the future of the Internet. Harvard Business Review Press, Boston

Watson R (2010) Future minds: how the digital age is changing our minds, why this matters and what we can do about it. Nicholas Brealey Publishing, London

Zweig J (2007) Your money and your brain: how the new science of neuroeconomics can help make you rich. Simon & Schuster, New York

Banks of the Future

8

My professional experience in the banking sector led me to believe that there must be better ways of controlling and running a bank to avoid crises than we have seen in the past. History has shown that crises are a feature of the banking business, which entail regulatory changes in order to make banks safer. I think that crisis could be now largely avoided, as we now have the right systems and tools available. We now have the advantage to use intelligent systems that the old banking system could only dream about. I think that we are missing only one point today, and this is the creation of a natural bridge between business solutions and IT solutions.

When I researched new ideas and information around technology and banking, I came across a number of interesting authors and thinkers, like Michio Kaku, as well as concepts and approaches which helped me to better understand the subject of innovation. In this chapter I have taken the input of some of these experts and applied it to the banking world of the future. The future of banking will have new characteristics which will be introduced in this chapter.

8.1 Workplace

The meaning of smart workplace is when an employee can work at any place and has all needed facilities available, like a computer and telephone, so that there is no need for a permanent office desk or location. There is no doubt that the banks of the future will replace their currently used laptops with something smarter and easier to carry for their employees, like in the past when terminals were replaced with laptop computers.

In the future there will be smarter work places than today that are designed in different styles, such as in a living room style, home office style, coffee shop style, seminar room at hotel-style etc., so that employees can choose the environment where they feel most comfortable. The infrastructure in these environments enables employees to log-on to their work environment via mobile phone instead of a heavy laptop.

© Springer International Publishing Switzerland 2015

S. Thuiner, *Banks of the Future*, DOI 10.1007/978-3-319-07554-9_8

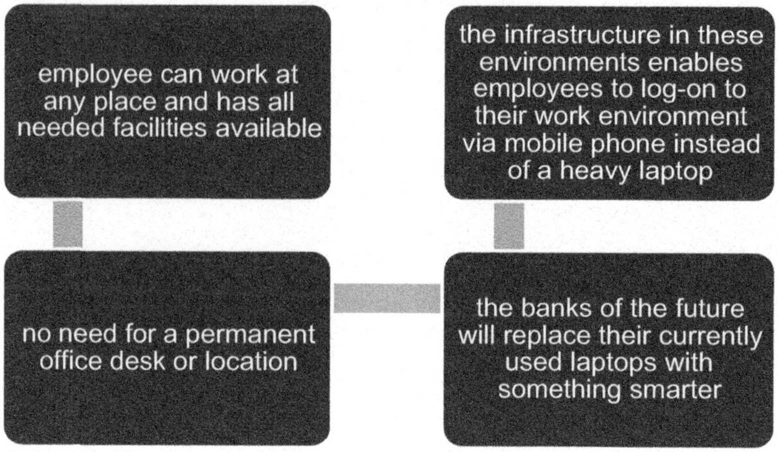

8.1.1 Mobile Phone as Future Laptop

As we carry our smart phones with us all the time, our mobile phone will have two operating systems, which are completely separate from each other. The same device will provide employees with one operating system access to their work environment, while the other operating system is for private purposes only. The phone will be able to separate the two activities from each other. The possibility of running more than one operating system in phones is only a question of time. According to Hannah Kuchler in the FT article "Facebook reaches out to developers with mantra of stability," Mr Zuckerberg is planning to provide a "cross-platform platform" so that different mobile software, like Google's Android and Apple's iOS can run next to each other. I think it is only the start of having fewer devices in a more intelligent way (Kuchler 2014).

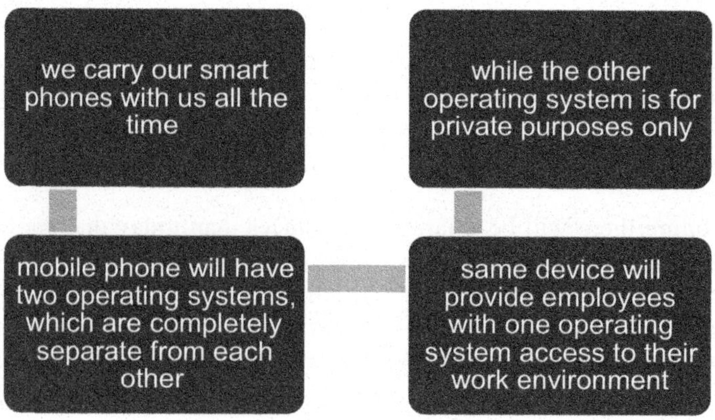

8.1.2 Modem, Cable, TV, Radio,...

Using the internet has become part of our lives, but future usage will become more straight-forward, with no cables or additional devices being required. A future blue chip company will offer an intelligent solution, which does not require cables or other devices, like modems to access the internet, movies, music, etc. will slowly disappear, and everything will be accessed comfortably via internet based on cloud data.

This development will not only change our homes, but also today's office environment, with cables largely disappearing. The main devices in the future are going to be smart phones and large screens. Future screens will be touch screens only. The usage of head-sets will become more wide-spread in work environments, with traditional key boards slowly disappearing.

Additionally, our phone is going to connect us to a future intelligent software so that most of our writing will be voice dictations to a software, with the software being able to ask questions in order to specify and clarify. Our future work environment will provide excellent software that creates our documents in a default format, which can be personalized by ourselves. Emails will be read to the recipients and the answers will be recorded and sent as a voice mail or text. Employees of future banks will not carry a heavy device from or to the office, as all what they need will be their smart phone and headset.

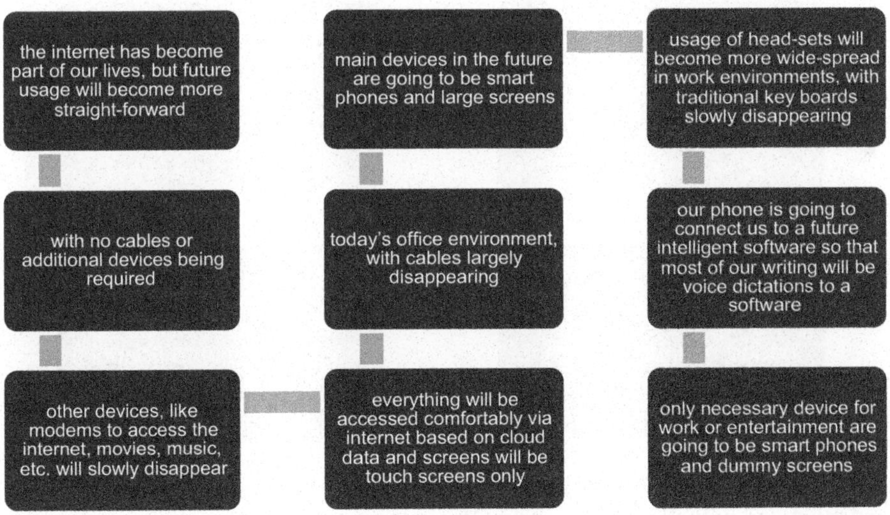

The development of these solutions will also change today's office environment, increasing the comfort. Even at home, shops, hotels, and restaurants, the only necessary device for work or entertainment are going to be smart phones and dummy screens. Technology will further transform businesses through new possibilities, like infinite bandwidth or a more secure access to the web.

8.2 Complexity in the Future

After the latest crisis we have learned that a change is needed, but the change is not only about implementing better regulation and making the daily business more transparent, but also about moving forward with the progress around technology and proving that comfortable solutions based on innovation are essential. I think that simplifying the complexity of the banking infrastructure will be the best response to financial institutions' current situation.

Considering the changes in our society and the new abilities that we have created with the improvements in technology, financial instruments will need to reflect this in their fundamentals so that this will make business less complicated than it is today. However, we are currently far away from implementing radical change so that an improvement in one area will trigger improvements in all relevant areas.

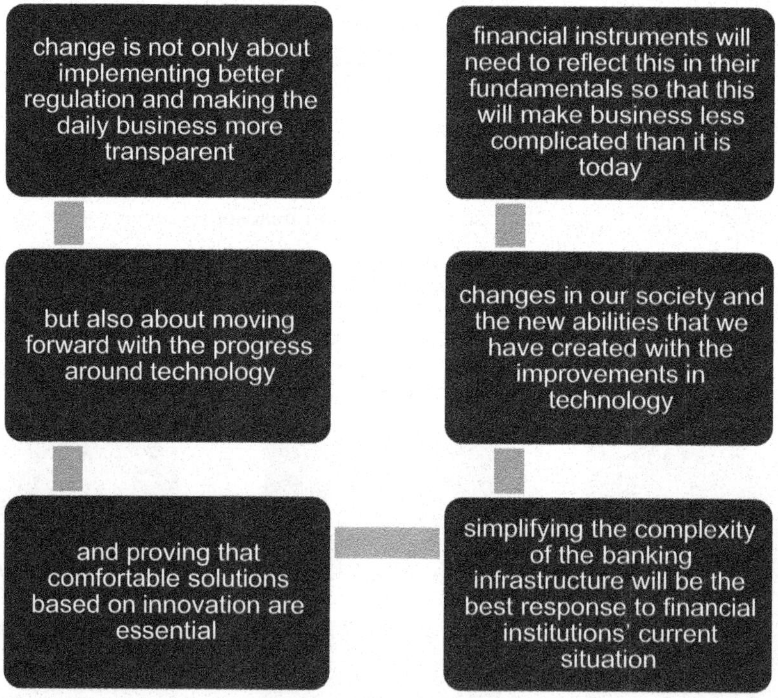

According to Burstein (2013), the millennial generation was born between 1980 and 1994 and will change our world. This generation is more optimistic, visionary, and fully committed to social responsibility and willing to accept change.

Could it happen that today's banking culture and the millennial generation will generate more complexity, as they are not matching perfectly? I think the implementation of holistic IT solutions will not only reduce the creation of island solutions and the rise in maintenance costs, but will also enhance security to fundamentally change the operations of a bank.

8.2.1 Modern Banking Solutions

I think that the future bank will have many AI solutions in place in order to control risks. As explained I call the future intelligent solution "BOFB" (Brain Of the Future Bank). Depending on the subject, these solutions apply a holistic view and will eliminate the island approach in the future, based on highly sophisticated software solutions of the future.

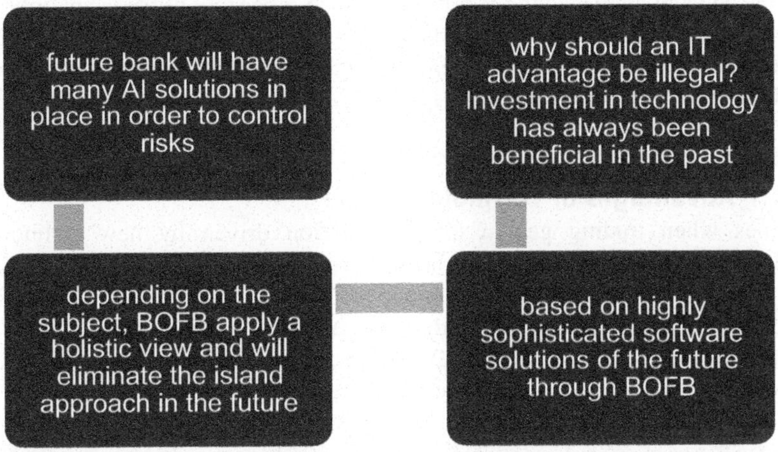

Scannell and Massoudi (2014) argue the following in an FT article titled "NY attorney-general subpoenas high-frequency traders": "New York's attorney-general has sent subpoenas to six high-frequency trading firms, as its investigation into whether certain traders have an unfair advantage over others widens beyond the stock exchanges." According to this article, trading firms such as Tower Research, Chopper Trading, and Jump Trading have received subpoenas. A request for information was also sent to other trading platforms such as NYSE Euronext and Nasdaq OMX in order to understand what kind of services are provided to the high-frequency trading firms. They also focused on the arrangement of giving traders a better bandwidth to improve their speed for the flow of information.

Why should an IT advantage be illegal? Investment in technology has always been beneficial to banks in the past. Here I use trading as an example to explain the advantages of technology and clarify its relation to ethics.

Example

During a project where a trading system for derivatives was supposed to be implemented throughout the organization after two of the largest banks in Austria merged, we had to set up many services and servers from scratch. The decision was made by senior managers that the bank needed a different speed in the front office than in the back office or in controlling. Although this decision was made 15 years ago when we discussed the bandwidth in the organization, the same concept applies to the World Wide Web. The front office is not only acting for the bank, it also provides a crucial service to the bank's clients. This is why we need to separate improvements in technology from other point of views, which deal with ethics and legal issues.

8.2.1.1 Advantages of Technology

In times when trading gets a lot of attention driven by new technological developments, we need to differentiate between unwanted risks, which will harm organizations and their clients, and an uneven playing fields created by technology. Should we consider intelligent trading systems that advise banks how to trade smarter in the market as illegal? What about intelligent systems that support financial institutions in creating structured products?

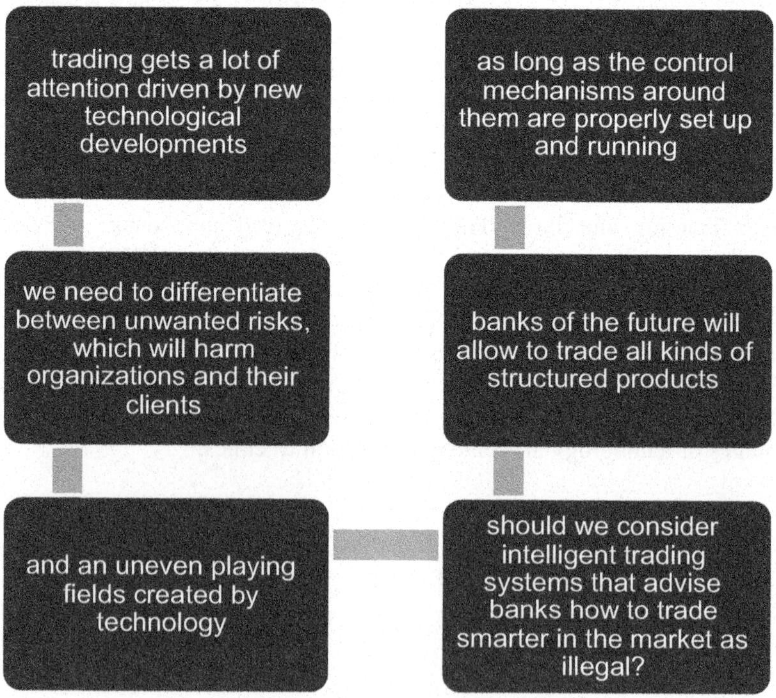

I think that the banks of the future will allow to trade all kinds of structured products, as long as the control mechanisms around them are properly set up and running before the product has even been introduced to the market.

8.2.1.2 Controlling Processes in the Future

Control mechanisms ensure that, for instance, a trade can be priced in the front office systems. It can be settled via back office and controlled by the controlling department. Furthermore, risk management is able to evaluate the risks correctly and accounting is able to book the trade accordingly.

Banks of the future will order internal auditors to confirm formally to their shareholders that the process behind a new trade has been tested. Only when all involved departments have confirmed it and a written confirmation from the auditor has been received by the board of directors and the shareholders, then will the banks of the future will be able to introduce a newly developed trade or product to its portfolio.

The process above might sound complicated, but it is simple and can be set up and monitored by an intelligent application as a part of BOFB, and therefore issues like the following cannot happen in the future. Alloway (2014) argues in an FT article titled "Finance parts ways with economic reality" the following: "In March, Virtu Financial, the high-frequency trading firm, revealed as part of a regulatory filing for its now postponed initial public offering, that it had found a "material weakness" related to its "inability to prepare accurate financial statements"." According to this article, they did not have adequate resources to cover the complexity of such transactions. The article also reports that in late April 2014, after a stress test, Bank of America (BofA) discovered an accounting error based on structured notes that made BofA to postpone their plan in returning $4 billion to shareholders....

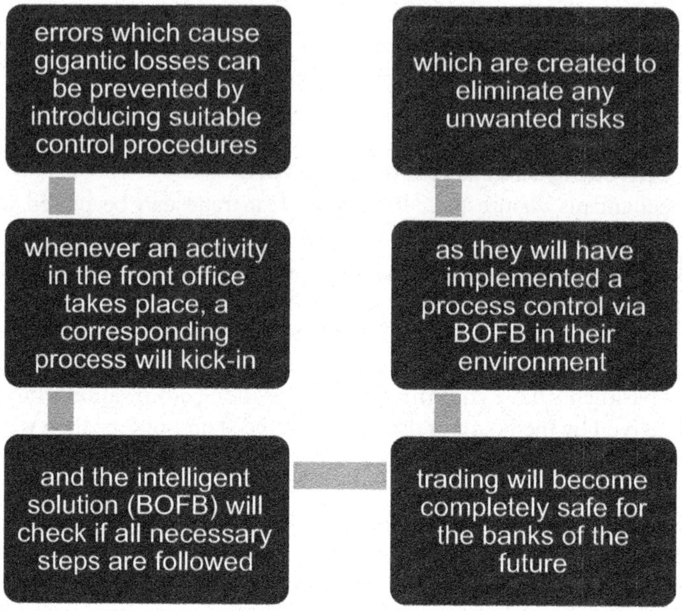

Errors which cause gigantic losses can be prevented by introducing suitable control procedures, and processes which can be run automatically in the background. This means that whenever an activity in the front office takes place, a corresponding process will kick-in and the intelligent solution (BOFB) will check if all necessary steps are followed.

Therefore, trading will become completely safe for the banks of the future, as they will have implemented a process control via BOFB in their environment, which are created to eliminate any unwanted risks.

8.2.1.3 Standardized Solutions

In the future, there will be many standardized IT solutions, such as IT solutions for OTC derivative contracts, which will be used in case a safer derivative market is requested. It is only possible to trade risky, complex derivatives if BOFB allows taking the risk. A standardized IT solution will allow traders to have fun again and be able to play freely in the financial markets, but only with a calculated risk.

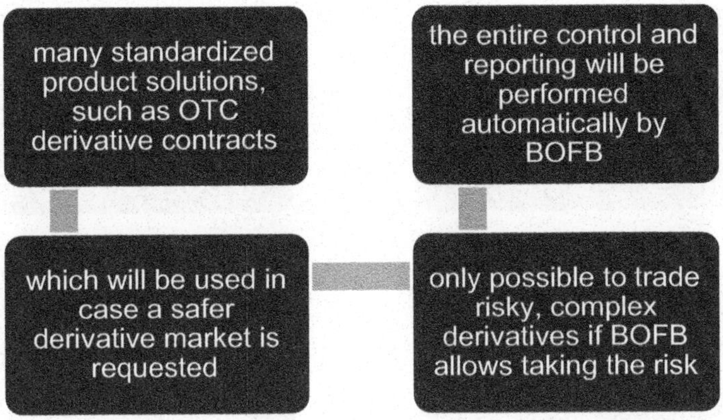

The limits related to derivative trading will no longer be only monitored by risk management or individuals from the IT departments, as we could see in the past that mistakes will happen. The entire control and reporting will be performed automatically by the future brain of the organization (BOFB) which will be part of a standardized solution. In case the BOFB would have been implemented at Lehman Brothers, due to the direct communication of BOFB with senior executives, shareholders and clients as well as authorities outside of the bank, in the run-up to the bankruptcy, the situation would have been evaluated as risky, and because of the high risk, all stakeholders would have been informed. The reporting line would have depended on the subject and been determined by the involved experts.

8.2.1.4 Monitoring Risks

A future intelligent AI solution will be developed so that risks can be monitored automatically and will send reports to senior executives, shareholders, and clients as well as regulatory authorities. In case there is no risk, none of these people will be directly contacted. This is why the implementation of the BOFB can prevent a crisis and, in a case of Lehman Brothers, the process of de-risking and removing all related obstacles would have been started months before and 28,600 employees around the world would not have lost their jobs overnight.

8.2.1.5 Clearing Houses

Clearing houses will continue to rise in importance in the future. All special financial instruments such as derivatives or structured products will go through clearing houses and must be supported with more capital to secure a trade. There will be new collaterals, which will provide a secure ground for trading derivatives.

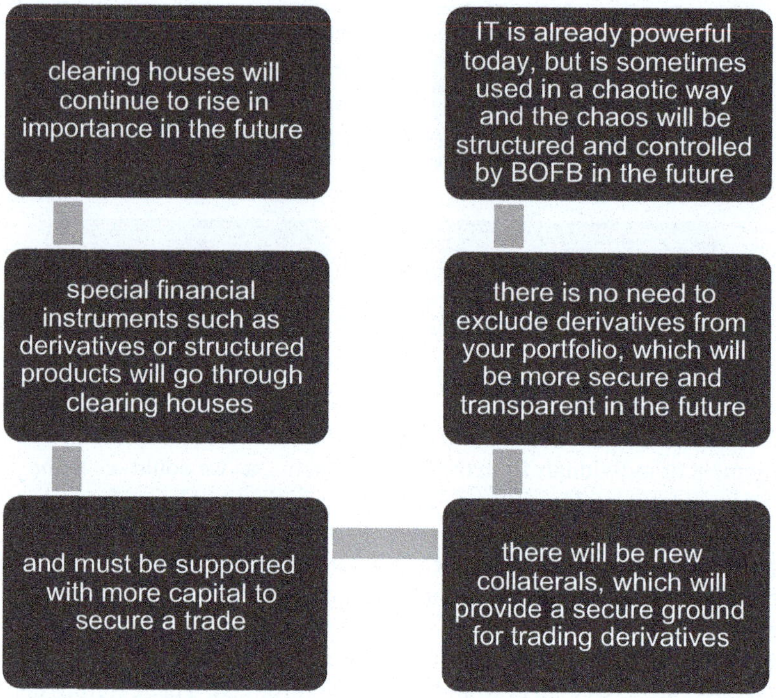

Therefore there is no need to exclude derivatives from your portfolio, which will be more secure and transparent in the future. The understanding of derivatives and knowing how to use it in a secure environment will be a big advantage on the market and should not be given away just because we do not have our IT and underlying processes under control. IT is already powerful today, but is sometimes used in a chaotic way. The chaos will be structured and controlled by BOFB in the future by simply implementing control and monitoring mechanisms around systems and activities in the organization.

8.2.2 Banking's Core Activities

Going forward, there will be a clear definition and understanding of the core activities of a bank. Implementation in the organization will be accomplished by setting up transparent processes and governance structures. Clear and consistent communication will ensure the information transfer between all involved areas in order to maintain the functionality of the daily processes and structures. These transparent processes will naturally give all people in core functions or with access to sensitive information such as client data a better radar to discover weaknesses.

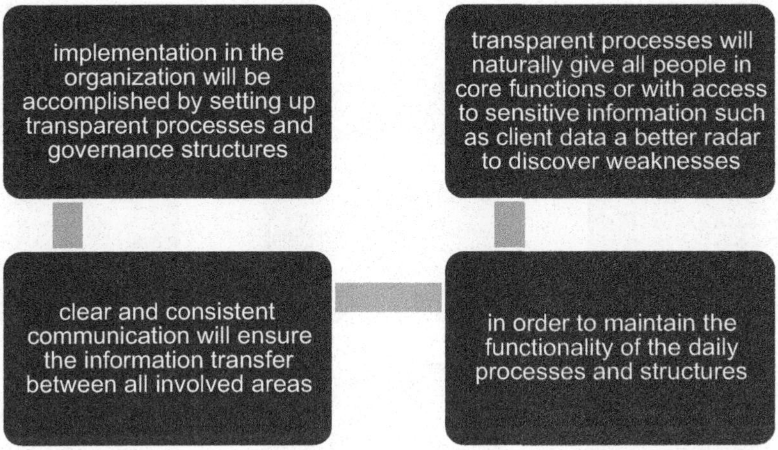

The daily activities of people in an organization and their permissions in existing systems must be set up properly and controlled by another daily monitoring mechanism. Most of the monitoring activities can be performed overnight, with so-called overnight jobs such as a "cronjob." These overnight jobs could be implemented as part of the daily monitoring that control the core activities in a bank, such as monitoring risks, limits, or monitoring of permissions.

8.2.2.1 Automatic Monitoring of Daily Processes

I think that in the future, BOFB will help with the secure monitoring of daily processes automatically and will create reports to the board or any other defined stakeholder or manager to inform them about any deviation from core processes as soon as it happens. In the future IT will hire more experts from business areas in order to be able to create intelligent solutions for monitoring critical areas via BFOB and will set up controlling mechanisms and automate them without involving the business areas to a large extent. All what the business areas will need to do is to confirm the setup and to test it jointly with the IT department.

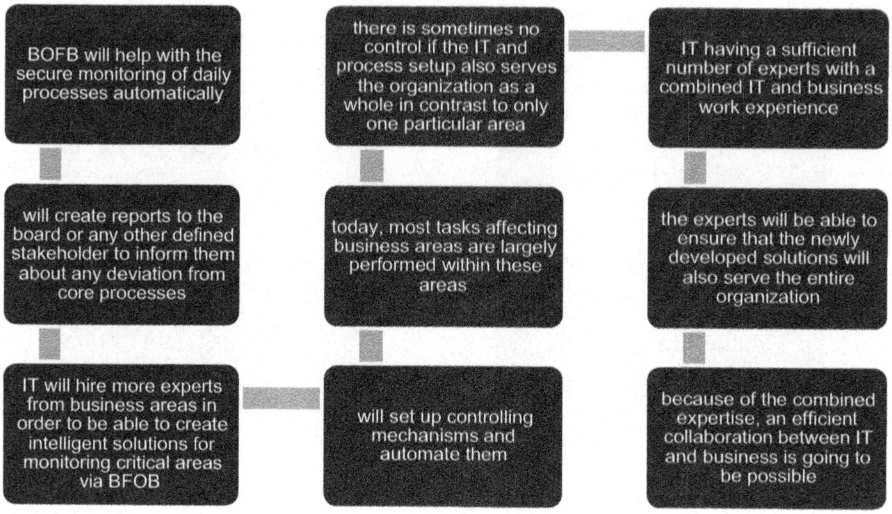

Today, most tasks affecting business areas are largely performed within these areas. There is sometimes no control if the IT and process setup also serves the organization as a whole in contrast to only one particular area. In the future, with IT having a sufficient number of experts with a combined IT and business work experience, the experts will be able to ensure that the newly developed solutions will also serve the entire organization, as it will be harmonized with the rest of the solutions in the organization and will also serve the business. Because of the combined expertise, an efficient collaboration between IT and business is going to be possible, with the business people in the IT area acting as IT's guidance so that a natural understanding of a business activity is available in IT. New solutions for controlling core activities will be implemented almost effortlessly.

8.2.2.2 Automobile Industry vs. Banking Industry

Implementing an IT-solution for a business is a complex subject, with many aspects involved. In most cases there is a strict separation between IT and business, which increases the potential for hidden risks, meaning, that a new implementation can bring along issues that will only be discovered later.

As already explained, I think that in the future, IT areas in well-managed organizations will have at least one expert with experience in a particular business area as a member of their team. This is not the case today, as we hardly find people in IT with work experience in a business area. In the past decade the involvement of IT people in business areas was considered necessary and as a result, many IT people were hired to sit in business areas to provide support for improving existing IT solutions whenever it was needed. Although important, these IT experts sit on-site and do IT work. In fact, the communication between IT and business became more practical. The missing part is that not only the communication must be improved, but also the understanding of business within IT needs to be improved.

Currently, the practical knowledge about day-to-day business activities is missing in IT. It is comparable to having the most innovative solutions in a car or to improving the weakness in current models of a car, with many engineers being involved who have never driven a car.

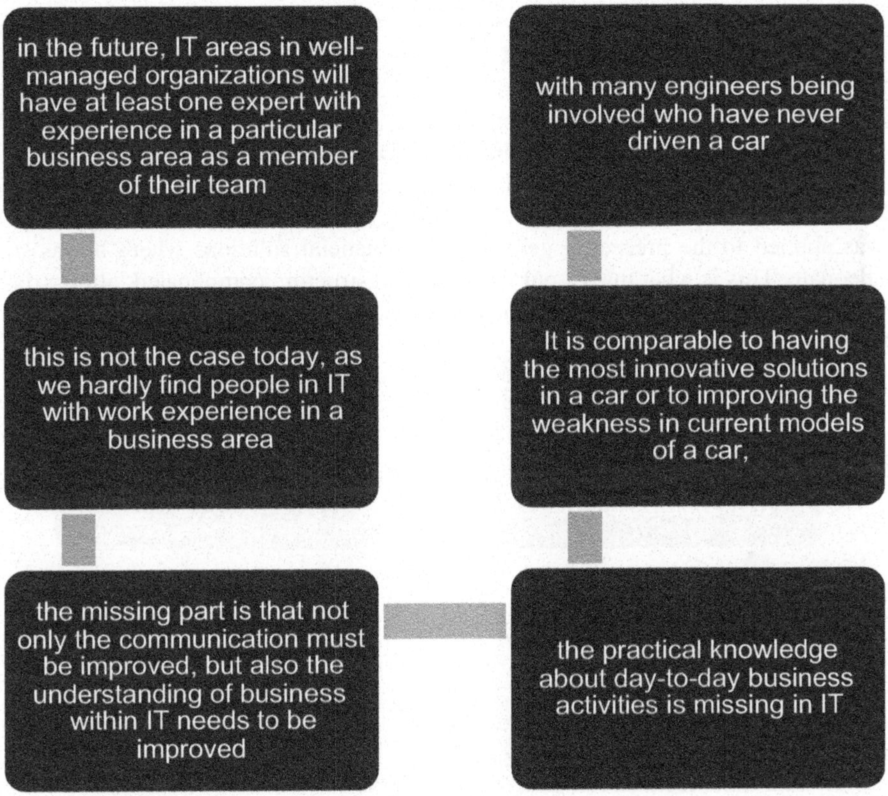

In case the engineers of automobile manufacturers lack the experience and understanding of driving a car, they need to ask the driver a lot of questions. Having efficient communication helps to define priorities and to monitor daily activities efficiently, but it would be even more helpful to automobile manufacturers to employ engineers who know the technological possibilities and have user experience with the end result, in this case the car. This is exactly what the banking industry must copy and not the matrix organisation as a structure.

8.2.2.3 Apple vs. Banking Industry

Would Steve Jobs have been that successful if he had created Apple's innovative products only for other people and not for himself to use? Carrying thousands of songs on an iPod or using an iPad to experience new ways of enjoying entertainment would have been difficult to come up with if he had never used the product himself. He not only knew about the possibilities in IT, but also experienced and recognized what was missing from the user point of view. IT is no longer a back office or support function, like an archiving department, a controlling department, or human resources.

8.3 Project Management

According to Christensen and Raynor (2003), the difference between sustainable and disruptive innovations is fundamental. Disruptive innovations are all of the sudden available in the market and change the market by affecting other available solutions. Innovative financial solutions often run on outdated technology, which was applied to the preceding generation of financial solutions where it was still adequate. This is what makes our banking infrastructure complicated, allows risks to emerge, and causes high maintenance costs.

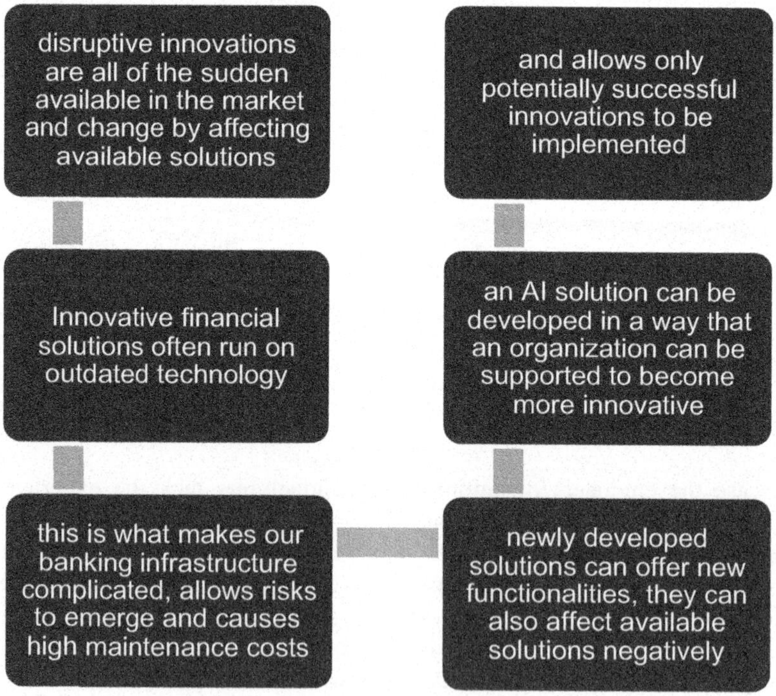

Although newly developed solutions can offer new functionalities, they can also affect available solutions negatively by creating additional risks. I think that a BOFB can also be developed in a way that measures the available data and allows only potentially successful innovations to be implemented.

I think that an AI solution can be developed in a way that an organization can be supported to become more innovative. According to Dyer et al. (2011), we are able to improve our innovation techniques. The main skills that all successful innovators have had are the following: they practiced associative thinking, asked questions, observed, liked to network with people with a diversified background, and experiment around what they did. The authors define these five skills as the innovator's DNA.

This is what Steve Jobs did when he drove the invention of a range of new products at Apple. He made sure the entire company applied associative thinking by involving different areas of the organization to work on new solutions early on. How often do we experience this in a financial institution? I think that a BOFB will be surely set up to do so.

Example

- A derivative trader has a preference for Monte Carlo simulations when pricing derivatives.
- He programmed the pricing methodology in C++ and implemented it in the test environment.
- Once the result is satisfying for the trading floor as well as a number of other areas that treasury has involved in the testing process, the IT department was asked to add this solution to production.

Steve Jobs probably would have set up a project where all critical areas, including internal audit, are involved at every level of the creation process of the project deliveries and asked all to combine their expertise before implementing the solution.

8.3.1 Internal Collaboration

In banking, the issue is that internal audit is acting more like a policeman and therefore a collaboration would have been more complicated. Another point is that the business cultures today do not appreciate IT at a level that it deserves. In most cases IT is seen as a back-office area. In the past as well as in the present, managers spent huge sums of money to ensure that the IT-risk is delegated to a suitable person, department, or company. This is an approach that cannot be afforded anymore, as banking infrastructures become ever more complicated and generate consequences that are expensive to deal with.

In order to simplify the existing infrastructure, we need to involve all areas that are affected by a new solution right from the beginning in order to foster an associated thinking approach, which includes having open discussions with questions and answer sessions, observations, networking with people with a diversified background, and experiments around a particular innovation.

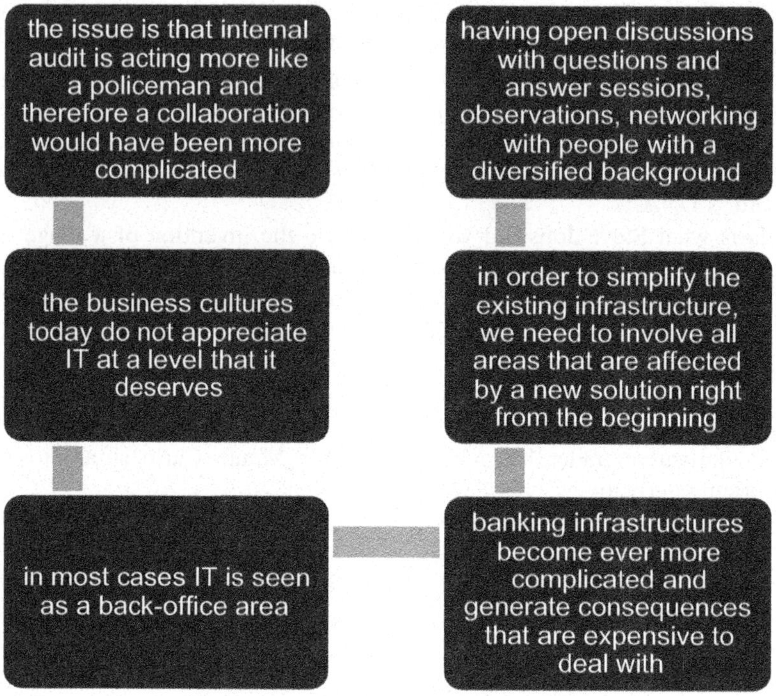

Today every financial institution is following the latest technology trends, but I think that their approach will change in the future. They will have a clearer understanding about which development will never be part of the organization, as it would conflict with their current IT and business solutions or cultures and strategies.

8.3.2 Complex Projects

According to Cooke-Davies (2011), complex projects must have project managers who can handle the complexity with knowledge and intuition, based on many years of experience. The expectation is that today's complexity will increase even more.

A complex project includes uncertainty, lack of clarity, dynamic interfaces, and significant political or external changes. Additional factors in a complex project are scope and technical complexity. There are many other factors, such as multiple teams which will also increase the risk of issues in a project. The project manager's behavior can also increase complexity and confusion in a project. This is some of the best practice for managing a project: active and passive empathy, positively influencing stakeholders, development of a lexicon to simplify project complexity, avoidance of optimism-bias in forecasting and cost estimations, use of small steps, and adaptation of project management methods. According to the author, at least 15 years of solid experience can help a project manager to manage a USD

100 million contract and at least 25 years of experience will make it possible for a project manager to manage a USD 1 billion contract.

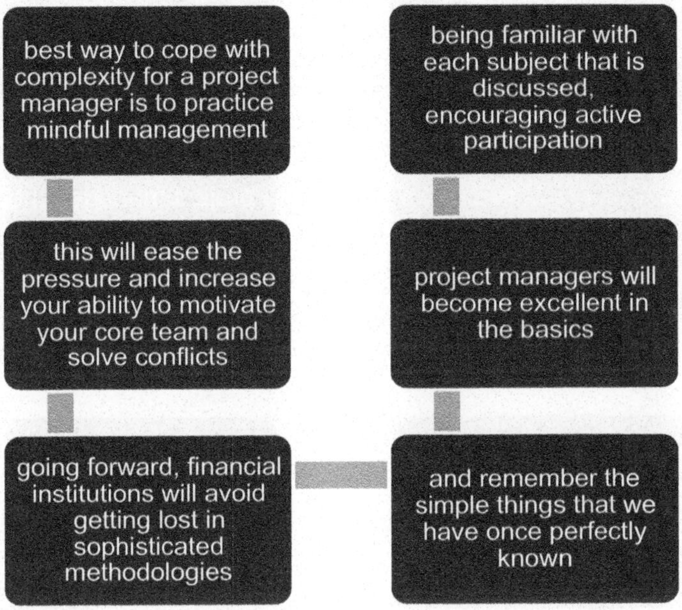

I think the best way to cope with complexity for a project manager is to practice mindful management. This will ease the pressure and increase your ability to motivate your core team and solve conflicts. Going forward, financial institutions will avoid getting lost in sophisticated methodologies and remember the simple things that we have once perfectly known. They will ensure that their project managers will become excellent in the basics, such as being familiar with each subject that is discussed, encouraging active participation by all team members, and cultivating open discussions.

8.3.2.1 Challenging Soft Skills

A project manager who lacks empathy and always acts strictly rational, focused on achieving the goal, will likely expect his team to work long hours and over weekends on a repeated basis. The likelihood that his team will accomplish less optimal results than otherwise possible is high, without the project manager noticing the sub-optimal outcome.

A project manager should be skilled in striking the right balance between showing empathy for the sensitivities of the team members while at the same time challenging them to get their maximum contribution.

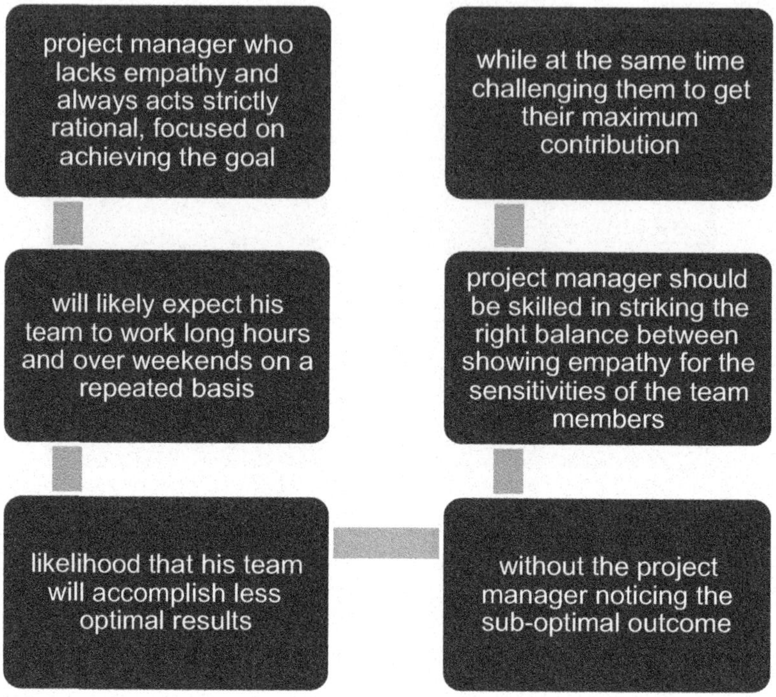

I think that project managers who are not afraid to express emotions and are open with their concerns will receive more loyalty and support than project managers with no sense of authenticity and empathy towards their teams. A project manager who does appear too controlled will never achieve above-average results for his project. The reason is that most of us will do everything for our managers if we experience their human side.

8.3.2.2 Presentations in Projects

During one of my projects, I have made a number of presentations to the core team members and sometimes to the managers. I used pictures and questions, and when the questions were asked, the pictures were supporting my explanations. The presentations were always done quickly and the information flow was easy to follow. As we have recorded all the project steps, we have generated a huge project documentation in order that the project members and their managers could find the details of each presentation in the comprehensive document if needed. This project was successfully finished with an excellent result, which was the provision of a solution costing much less than originally suggested. At the end of the project the project team was asked to present the project and its results to the top executives of the bank. The generation of the Power Point presentation for this meeting was frustrating. It was a level of frustration that you normally only experience when your project is not moving in the right direction.

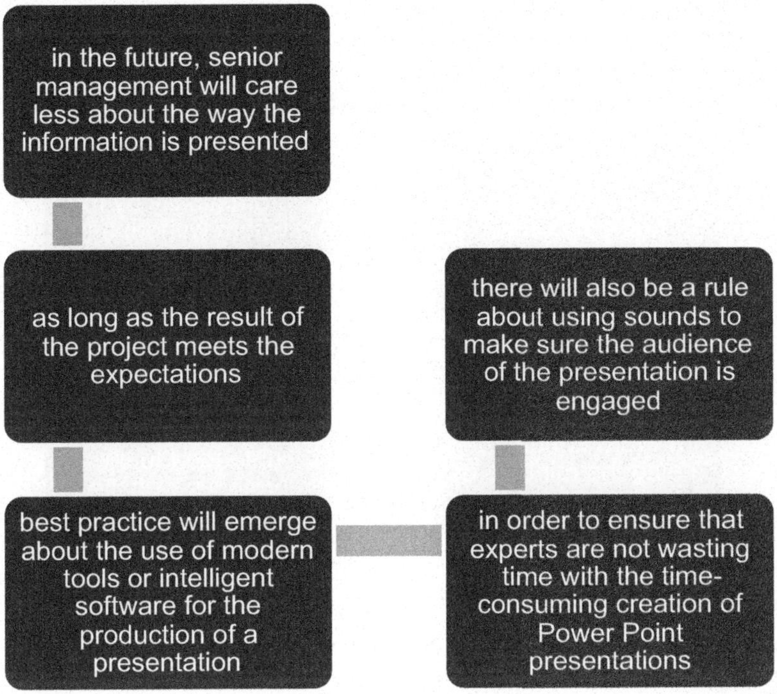

We did not understand why, after a successful project, we could not use our previous style of presenting the content, as mentioned before. We were not allowed to use pictures and questions and to refer to the final project documentation to look up details in case it was needed. A team was put together to produce the project presentation. A number of senior managers were involved to provide us with feedback to our suggestions, which required a number of adjustments in the presentation. I was convinced they decided to take control of the presentation to make sure we did not embarrass ourselves in front of senior management with a poor style.

I think that in the future, senior management will care less about the way the information is presented, as long as the result of the project meets the expectations. A best practice will emerge about the use of modern tools or intelligent software for the production of a presentation in order to ensure that experts are not wasting time with the time-consuming creation of Power Point presentations. There will also be a rule about using sounds and maybe cartoons to make sure the audience of the presentation is engaged and can deliver all the needed information if requested.

8.3.2.3 Core Team

At project meetings, experts will be photographed by their online video conference facility. This picture will be added to the recorded conversation through an AI solution, which will be a Word document being the minutes of the meeting. Going forward every project will have a project website. All relevant data for the project will be uploaded to the project's website. By making photos of participants during each project meeting, the project website looks more alive and gets more attention from all involved busy areas. Note that in the future this will be done automatically by the system without any effort by the project members.

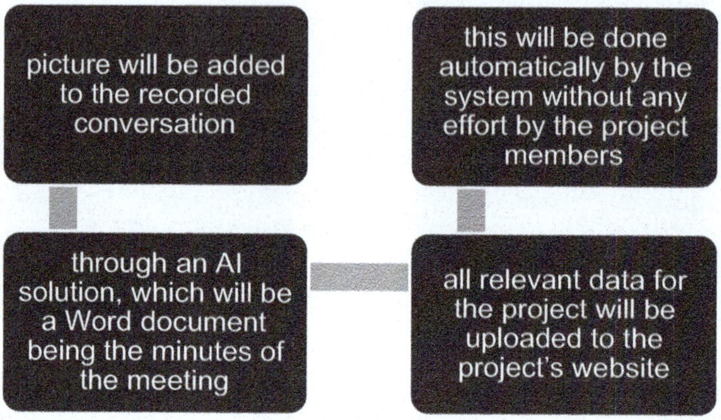

8.3.2.4 Collaboration

According to Dawson (2011), our issues are either about money or about people, and one of the main questions that one should ask is: Do I really have an issue or is it only a misunderstanding, and do I need to make a decision? If there are no consequences, one does not need to waste time on it and should forget the issue, and if you were wrong, just say it and move on. This wisdom can be useful for all kinds of complex projects and can be followed by the project manager.

There are numerous methodologies around decision making and problem solving in organizations. These are sometimes patented and practised by consulting firms. Here is an example: in order to speed-up decision-making processes, a new methodology was patented by Capgemini Consultants called Accelerated Solutions Environment (ASE). This methodology was seen as an alternative solution to the bottom–up or top–down methodology of making decisions. Whenever the traditional methodology was not able to come up with a decision, the ASE methodology was introduced by Capgemini. The methodology is about reducing time in the search for a solution, generating a number of ideas and valuing it, involving all relevant areas of an organization. The result is a number of options, even if the collaboration took place in a virtual environment. There are many cartoon videos, etc. that are used in such an environment to ease the collaboration from the beginning to the delivery session. The philosophy behind ASE is that people matter and results count.

Although the concept of ASE is great, a competent project manager must be able to take the exact action for his project every time. In collaboration with the core team, most of the ideas behind the concept will be generated automatically. The project manager applies his approach to engage the project team and make them decide by jointly applying their knowledge to make a suggestion of what the options are. All senior managers or stakeholders will understand the reason behind a decision and will support it.

It is sometimes the case that people with a particular knowledge can come up with a recommendation, however, they meet first with senior managers and ask them for recommendations. This is a disaster for many projects, as there is a failure in thinking if experts think that managers can show them a way that they did not yet consider. The role of senior managers is to have objections in case there is a piece of information missing and the team does not have it, but the recommendation for a decision must be made by experts.

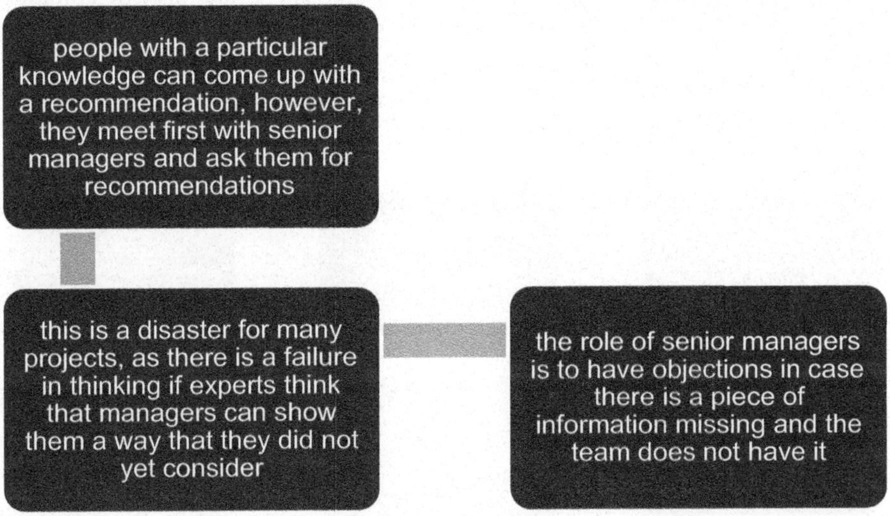

Today we are dealing with many methods and guidelines in daily banking business. The need for methodologies or guidelines is essential, but we always need to ask ourselves "How many of these methodologies are needed in what way so that an organization remains productive?" Will each organization define only one methodology to cover all areas in order to keep tools around organizational excellence simple?

8.3.2.5 Success Formula

According to Hansen (2009), the iPod combined existing solutions from many areas in the organization and created something new. Through this work they also have redefined a new culture of enjoyment through collaboration.

I think that if a manager or project manager can create enjoyment for collaboration in the team, an extraordinary solution can be achieved. The future bank will value the enjoyment of teamwork, not only because they want to prevent burnouts in their projects, but also because that will be where extraordinary solutions can happen if the team is structured clearly and experts are having fun by being responsible for a particular subject and being respected with their expertise in what they cover in the project. This is not the case today and will therefore continue to generate hidden risks for all those projects that cause frustration for their project team.

Again, the understanding of different cultures in different areas will improve collaboration within a project, and this understanding comes with professional experience. It is comparable to understanding the cultures of countries. In case you have lived there, you will have a better understanding than from reading books about it.

If the future banks are not able to find people with combined expertise in the market, they will have to start developing them internally via the promotion of a change to other areas within the organization. There are always ambitious employees who would be thankful to get the opportunity to change their job to a completely new task without getting penalized. The future bank will change their usual thinking patterns and make it possible for their employees to bring different values to new areas in the organization which will lead the way to outside-of-the-box solutions.

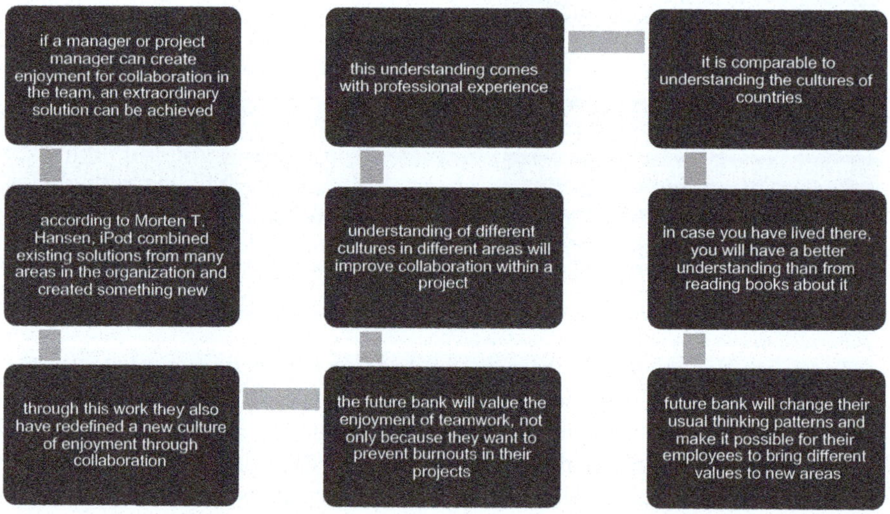

According to a Harvard Business Review article, the two major reasons for Google's success are the following: they are not afraid of failure in their innovations and they make it easy for their employees to change within their organization. These employees are not only more motivated, they also develop a combined expertise which will generate more knowledge and competence in an increasingly complex world.

8.3.2.6 Agile of the Future

In the future, Agile will be the most preferred project methodology used. I have already explained in the previous chapters what the meaning behind Agile is. In case of Agile, the project manager is asked to plan all iterations temporarily and to take one iteration at a time to focus and take the next one after completing the preceding one.

The goal will be to keep the project as simple as possible in order that it will be easy to finish on time and budget and with appropriate resources. If we focus to keep the project as simple as possible, it would be easier to estimate relevantly. By being focused on only one iteration at time, we are able to keep the project reasonably sized and easy to analyze, design, implement, test, and document.

In the future, the stand-up meetings will be changed to a new way of daily video-based meetings for durations of around 20 min each time, and all employees will remain at their workplace. All discussions and agreements will be recorded via AI and stored on the website of the project. The recordings of discussions in each meeting and taking of pictures of participants during a conference call can be uploaded to the project website automatically which serves a high transparency along each step in the project. All involved experts and stakeholders will have access to the website automatically. Because everything around the project is done automatically, the efforts around administration in the project will be low.

The project website will offer the possibility to add text files with pre-defined information in a pre-defined format. By updating these text files, the website is able to generate a Power Point presentation with audio, video, pictures, and data. Picture and sound are instrumental to engage the visitor to remain focused. The pictures are generated based on the information of the text file and is able to be explained without any further support.

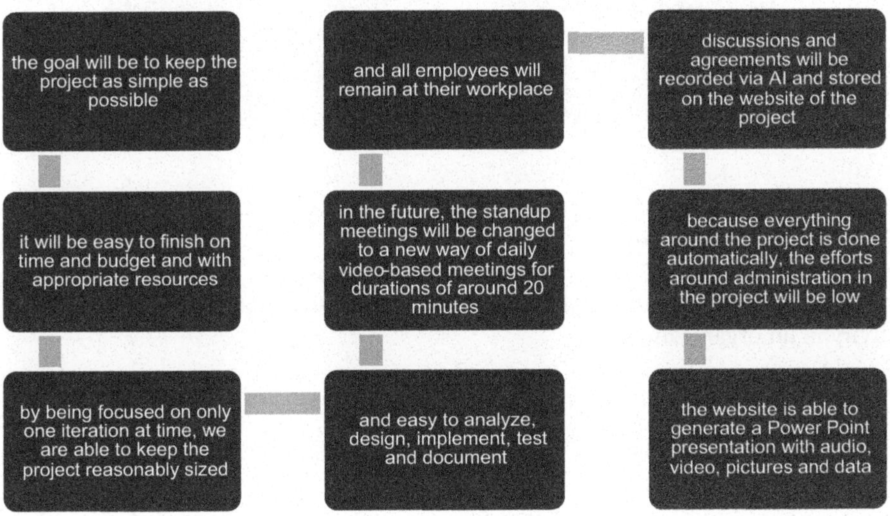

8.3.2.7 Matrix Organization

The matrix organization replaced the traditionally vertically structured organizations. According to Malik (2006) at the Peter Drucker Forum in Vienna in 2009, a matrix organization should not be the first choice, because it inhibits the efficiency of the staff. My experience was that project managers did not care if they are in a matrix or not, as they were measured by the result of their project. Apart from project managers, almost all experts that I worked with and who worked in a matrix organization did not really like the idea of having two bosses and at the same time felt less important. It is well known that negative emotions affect the result of our work, as more mistakes happen. I think that matrix organizations will disappear from the banking industry in the future.

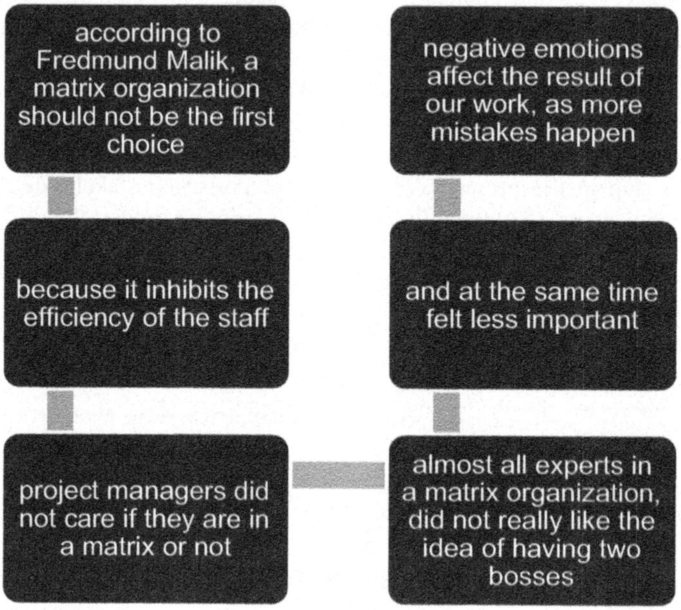

8.3.2.7.1 Deficiencies

We work better and are more collaborative when we are not bothered by deficiencies. Frustrated employees do certainly not contribute to improved productivity in an organization.

Example

In one of my projects the project plan was set up very ambitiously in order to keep senior managers satisfied. The initial cost calculation for the project was therefore much lower than the actual costs in the end. As a business analyst I needed to analyze a subject in-depth in order that an update could be given to the developer by the end of the day. After every couple of days we discovered that something was missing and needed to be changed or adjusted the status of the analysis to pass it on to the developer in order that the program could be changed, with the eventual solution passed on to the business users to test it again and confirm. Because we were under constant pressure, we lacked the time to find out whether the project is running as planned, but when the project was finished, we agreed that the project plan was insufficient from the start and that a more thorough evaluation of who needs to be involved in order to cover all aspects would have been necessary. An agreement between two people is quicker than in a large group which is dispersed around the world.

8.3.2.8 CMMI: Six Sigma

According to Snee and Hoerl (2002), Six Sigma can help to improve the result in daily business, with the focus being on the business process. It is important that the processes are consistent and reliable. Any variability in the process will reduce the quality in daily business and must therefore be avoided. They think that black belt project managers can be helpful for the success of a project.

The question here is if it would be better for the future to request a black belt in Six Sigma, CMMI, or another similar guideline. I think that in the future the value behind Six Sigma and CMMI will still be appreciated, but there will be more practical ways that can jointly lead to success in a project. The first step would be to review CMMI or Six Sigma's current documentation to make it shorter and to create the documentation for a group which already brings along a diversified expertise in the organization and therefore has a good common sense.

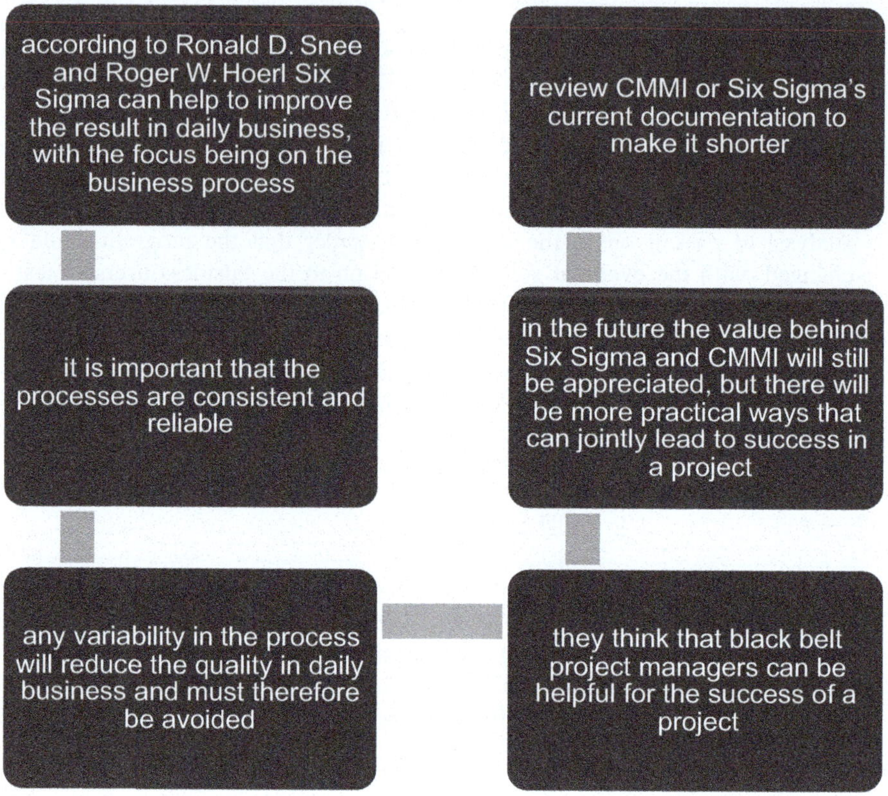

The fact that project managers will bring along a range of expertise is the reason why documentation of Six Sigma and CMMI will be much shorter in the future, which will ease the education process around CMMI Six Sigma or any other guidelines and thus will save time and effort.

I think that another important point is that the entire documentation of a project must be kept as practical as possible. Time consuming, well-formatted documentation or presentations for a project are not necessary, as you can be sure that these activities take your resources' time away from more important activities in your project.

We should keep in mind that the documentation of entire projects is only relevant during the project and will not remain valuable after a project has been successfully finished. Therefore, only results count, not the beauty of your presentation or document, as in the future nobody will bear the costs for this kind of time-consuming activities.

8.3.2.9 Becoming Practical

According to Tobis and Tobis (2002), activities in all projects should be run as routines regularly. The efforts of the project should be estimated, based on all single tasks, and important experts should be scheduled first for the entire project cycle, such as definition, design, construction, implementation, and testing.

I think that the best projects are those where a project manager is 100 % involved in a project and when managing parallel projects can be avoided. A less intense project should be combined with routine jobs and certainly not with another project in order to achieve the best possible outcome. According to Levine (2002), a project manager should have a good plan of how to measure risk and also a contingency plan in case of issues. I think that the creation of a contingency plan needs creativity and the ability to think outside-of-the-box.

According to Marchewka (2009), IT projects always involve complex IT solutions and the project team includes IT experts, but also users from business areas. The two groups of people bring along different knowledge, values, and cultures. While the author provides useful guidance on how a project manager should act in this kind of project, I would like to add one aspect that I think is missing here, which is the provision of a combined expertise.

In terms of projects which are IT-related, all project managers of the future will bring along a combined business-related and IT-related work experience. This will replace today's way of running a project with two project managers, where one manager is from IT and the other one from business. It will not only reduce the costs of the project, but also improve the efficiency, as it is often the case that the culture differences between ITPL and BPL create conflicts, which will cause distractions for the project team members.

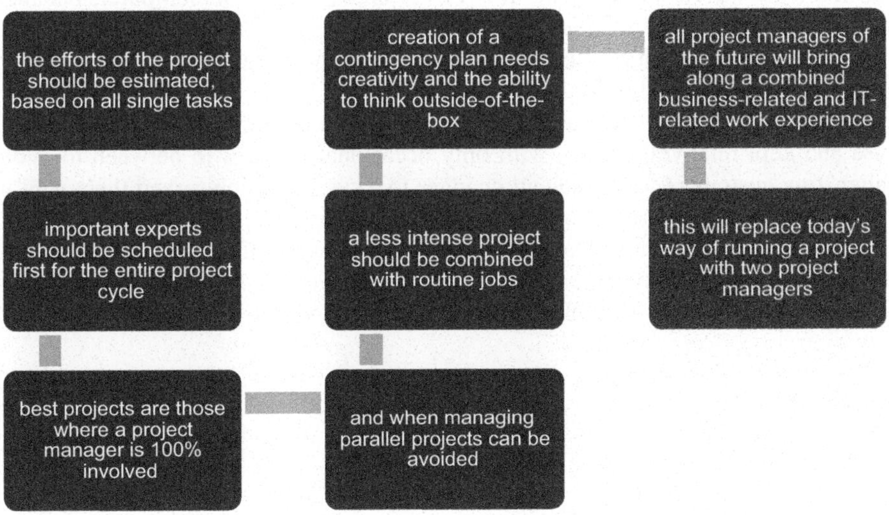

8.4 Security

Palin (2014) argues the following in an FT article titled "Payments via mobile to open to 30 m bank customers": "The launch of a new mobile payment service will allow 30 m bank customers to make payments using a mobile phone number alone." Financial institutions are working on innovations to provide their clients new services, like mobile phone banking and Web 2.0. Behind each innovation there will also be the aspect of security to consider.

Daniel Thomas (2014) argues the following in an FT article titled "Mobile devices open new front in battle": "Smartphones are now being used as much for mobile computing as they are for making phone calls. And, like any device linked to the internet, they are open to hacking." The high and still growing number of smart phone users makes the market for mobile banking solutions an attractive prospect. This is also the reason why financial institutions cannot ignore the fact that interaction with clients as well as the security around it must be redefined.

8.4.1 Client Services

Today, many clients can be reached via their social networking accounts and smart phones. The traditional way of attracting clients is no longer a promising source of business. However, some clients feel to be forced to use the computer, but they might have less trust in IT security or would rather like to have interaction with people. A continuation of this trend might lead some clients to ponder remaining with a more traditionally focused bank.

I think that banks of the future will provide IT-based services which are easy to use and kept relatively stable, with only occasional changes in between to avoid alienating customers with frequent changes to a system which served them well in the past. Going forward we will likely see a co-existence of mobile banking and internet solutions next to traditional offerings. Despite the growing number of technology-minded customers, it is unlikely that we will see a disappearance of the old-fashioned way of banking over the next 10 years.

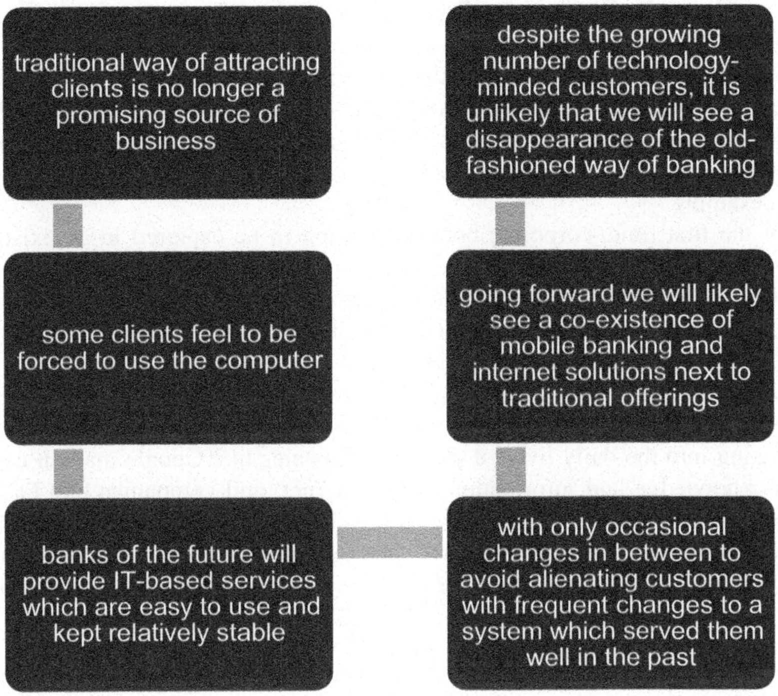

Research has shown that every person is unique in its personality, which is why I think that the assumption that all clients would like to use the latest technology is wrong.

Some of the existing security weaknesses, such as around wireless networks, might be solved eventually so that we do not mind to combine our finances with the latest technology. In fact, we might even enjoy the comfort, but until then it would be difficult to make a final, unambiguous decision on whether one way or the other way of banking is right.

8.5 Technology

According to Kaku (2011), societies of the future will benefit from future new developments, like special contact lenses, AI, and nanotechnology.

How would sunglasses, which provide information about the person you meet in your project or organization, benefit the organization or yourself? In a large core team, sunglasses which give us background information about all our project members are useful, as the project manager can collect the information in a way that makes leading a subject much easier than it is today. It could also be the case that the internal information related to the project will be reported and stored in the database through the recording functionality of the sunglasses, while participants are discussing and confirming it.

8.5.1 Historically Grown IT

There is no doubt that technology will continue to drive change in the world. Today, we need to deal with historically grown IT landscapes, with the implemented solutions not being harmonized. This fact causes high maintenance costs and hidden risks.

An Example

For the first time, corporate bonds are going to be captured in an existing IT system. This not only means to adapt the system accordingly, but also to adjust all existing interfaces and all related reports generated by various systems. Other aspects to consider are a change in potential overnight processing jobs, provision of user training, IT support training, etc.

Companies like IBM, Microsoft, and Apple introduced the benefits of personal computing into the daily lives of people; companies like Google made it easier to access knowledge and information in the internet, and companies like Facebook connected people. In the future, companies which offer solutions for harmonizing IT infrastructures will rapidly gain in importance, based on wide-spread demand for such solutions in the banking sector. There are already solutions available on the market, but for some reasons financial institutions could not be convinced about them yet, which probably means that more efforts are needed to make these solutions excellent so that financial institutions realize that they can't afford not having these solutions implemented in their organizations.

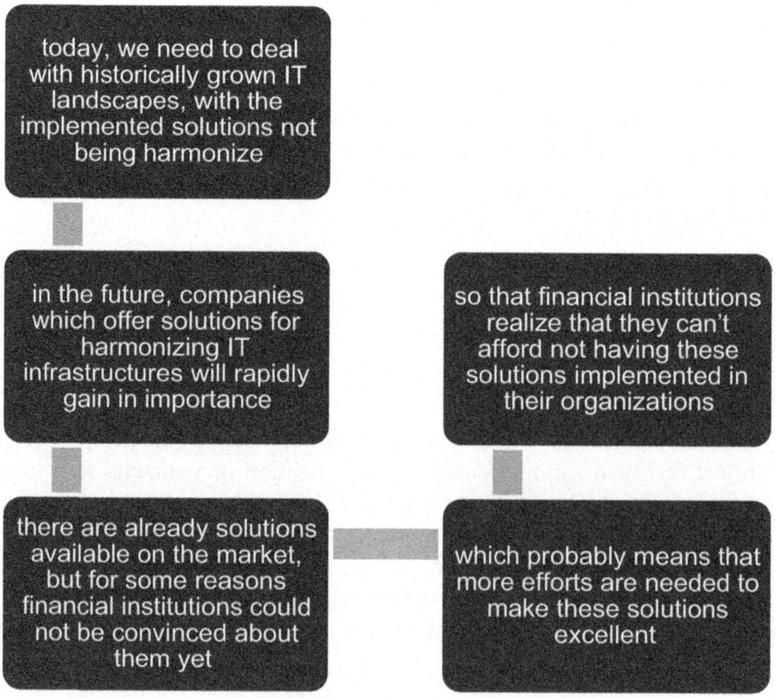

8.5.2 The Need

There will soon be a new blue chip company offering a solution to financial institutions that will eliminate the need for interface maintenance, which will remove many of the activities in our example above regarding corporate bonds. This will not only dramatically affect the costs of implementing a solution or running the bank, but will also eliminate the risk of changes to interfaces and increase data quality.

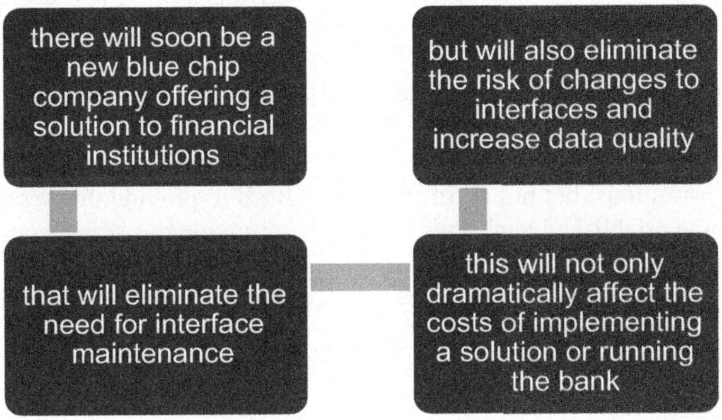

This future solution will support banks in addressing the problem regarding legacy systems with high maintenance requirements and to avoid that the old solutions rise in importance, but disappear naturally over time. In the future, banks will prefer system solutions which simplify processes. For instance, in data warehousing, it recently became possible to define the source of your data in the data warehouse, with the data warehouse collecting the data itself. This approach, however, is still in the early stages, but will get more attention in the future in case it's a better version of existing solutions.

8.5.3 Some Ideas

According to Shaikh (2012) at a TED talk, we see developments such as app-ification, game-ification, crowdsourcing, consumerization, and big data. We live in a time where consumerization and services are at the heart of numerous efforts. Banks offer services, such as risk management, FX transactions, payment services, etc. where a positive and lasting customer experience is the key to retain customers. In this context, Germany-based Fidor Bank came up with an innovative solution where it offers clients an account which can be used for 140 different currencies and for investments in a range of financial instruments. Nadeem Shaikh also talks about a new view of buying and selling ideas, such as the fact that Fidor Bank paid 10 EUR-cents for each new idea entered into their online system.

Here are some of other Nadeem Shaikh's observations: Simple (BankSimple) in New York is based on a very simple concept and focused on consumer experience of how people interact with the bank. "MoBank" is keeping people connected with their money. They provide a mobile infrastructure to their clients. The most interesting topic in this talk was the comparison between a real currency and a virtual currency and the fact that the population of the Eurozone is 332 million people (2011), and there are around 800 million users (2011) on Facebook, which are using Facebook credits on Facebook. Nadeem Shaikh's question is what our world would become if we bring the virtual currency into our real life?

8.5.4 Mobile Banking and Established Banks

Due to the popularity of mobile phones, mobile banking is attractive for almost all financial institutions, but not all of them can afford to provide this service to their clients. Some established banks might be able to provide this service only at a later stage.

Going forward, mobile banking is only going to be successfully introduced in established or newly setup banks if it's secure and if the security is insured (cyber insurance). This means that any failure or lack of security is insured in order that a customer can use the smart phone for all kinds of communication and interaction with banks. This subject of security will become more and more transparent for financial institutions' employees as well as their clients than it is today.

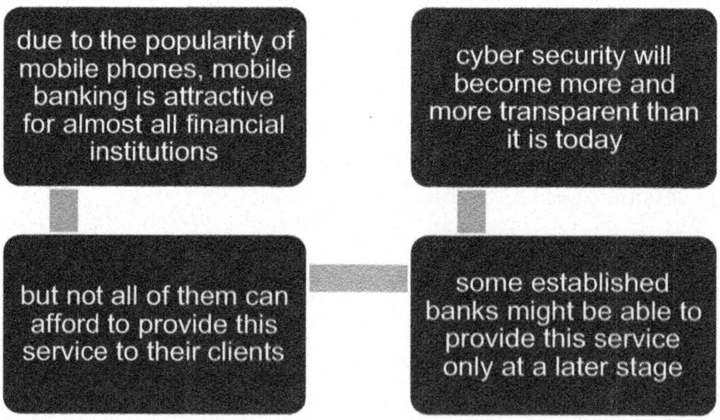

If mobile banking is possible in countries like Ethiopia or countries in Asia or Europe, it does not mean that established financial institutions with their entire complex IT infrastructure and IT solutions from every generation of IT development must compete as soon as possible.

I think that in the future financial institutions will want to stand more for identity, values, and principles, which might become more valuable in future markets than to compete with IT-related commutability. What is more important than the latest technology is implementation or new ways of controlling an organization. In order to be able to do it, we need to identify the risks inside of an organization. This subject will be more explained for different views later in this chapter.

8.5.5 BOFB and Innovative Solutions

I think, in the future we will use our mobile phones connected to big screens in order to do our work and avoid using laptops or other heavy devices. Additionally, head-sets will become more important for daily business. It will be used to communicate with software, to document a subject, or write emails. For instance, there will be more software in place to interact and communicate by voice instead of keyboard. This solution is also a part of BOFB and will certainly transform banking in the future in terms of controlling and productivity.

This explains why the hardware costs for financial institutions will be lower, as there will be no need to have a laptop for each employee, and employees will not bring along heavy devices to the office, but just their smartphone and a headset.

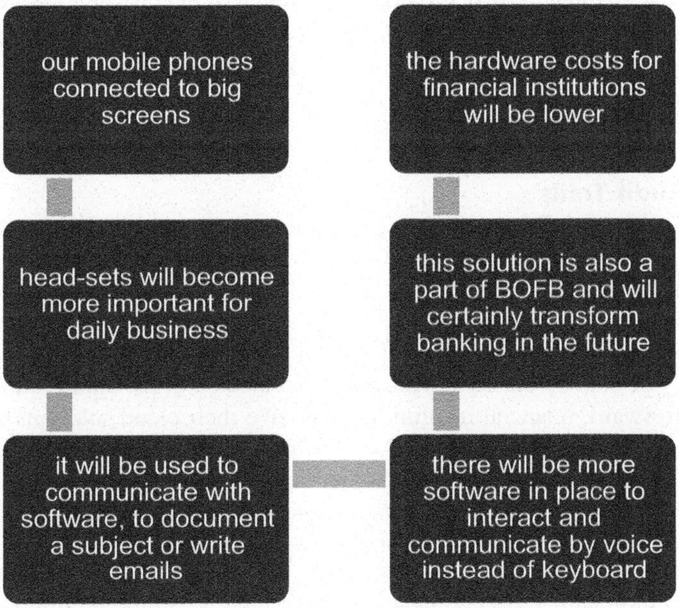

8.5.6 Cloud of the Future

Experience with cloud computing so far has proven the benefits of permanent data availability. It will make more and more banks to consider this as a solution for their daily business. Data will be increasingly stored in the cloud, based on file hosting.

These data will be accessible from everywhere and will allow the exchange of data between different areas of an organization, independent from time and place.

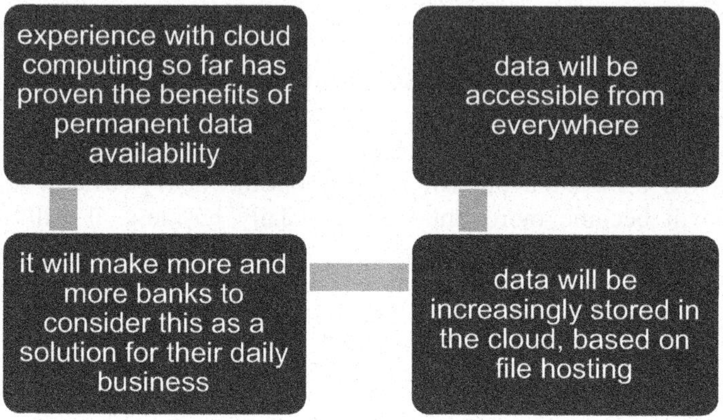

Andrzej Kawalec, chief technology officer at HP Enterprise Services, says in an article by the Financial Times (2014): "If a cloud provider has no processes in place for monitoring access, or does not track data consumption at device level, it is a sign they cannot offer a complete view of threats, and valuable assets may be vulnerable."

8.5.6.1 Audit Trails

In the future the cloud from the banking industry will provide the possibility of an audit trails process, which will be developed as a part of the monitoring via BOFB and is based on users, data, or other criteria. All critical information, such as who read or changed which data or report, will be stored to support the audit trail process and can be used if needed. Financial institutions have the possibility to define the availability of data by clusters, which are also located in the cloud (cloud cluster).

Going forward, financial institutions will have their cloud solutions as a part of BOFB incorporated in the intranet of the organization, which might be called "cloudy." All applications, data bases, operating systems, archiving solutions, etc. will be run on the cloudy of the organization, which is the more secure version of the cloud and belongs to the organization. Therefore, authorized employees as well as pre-selected clients will be given a secure access to a part of the infrastructure of the organization with a pre-defined role so that their activities are limited, based on their permission.

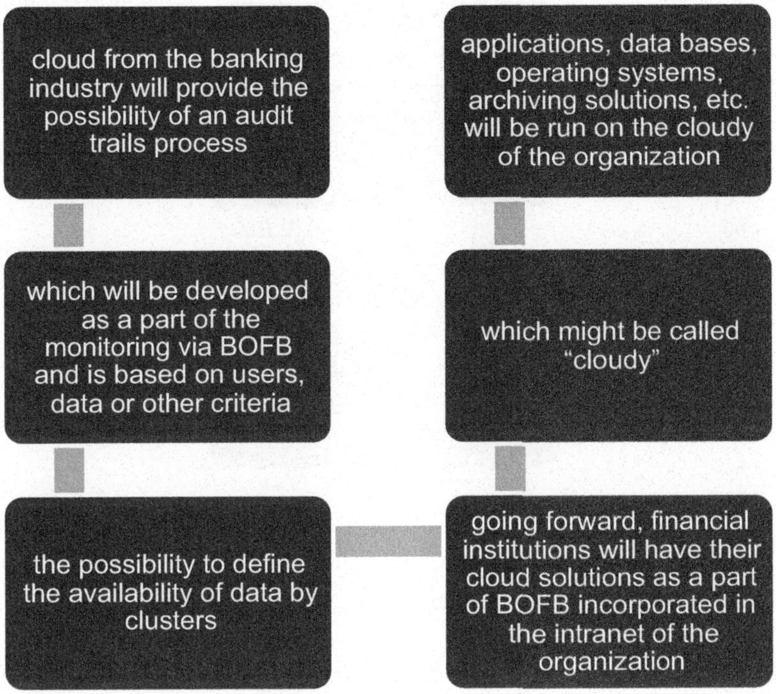

Through cloudy, a new log-on system will be provided as a super secure access so that clients' or employees' IT access in the future banks will no longer be a pain. All activities based on cloudy will be recorded. A client is able to review all the processes behind his portfolio and understand it. There will also be a hotline for clients only so that they can contact their advisor at any time and ask questions. This solution provides a new level of transparency to clients, as they will be allowed to generate reports or to change existing agreements, with notification to the bank.

8.5.7 Productivity

Creating a powerful intranet will increase the productivity of employees in an organization. Using a powerful intranet can support employees to access the knowledge of experts from all areas of the organization. In one financial institution I made the experience that I was not able to work as effectively as I could have when the intranet was down for a whole day, because of maintenance, while in another financial institution the intranet was not a big advantage and therefore was not used at all.

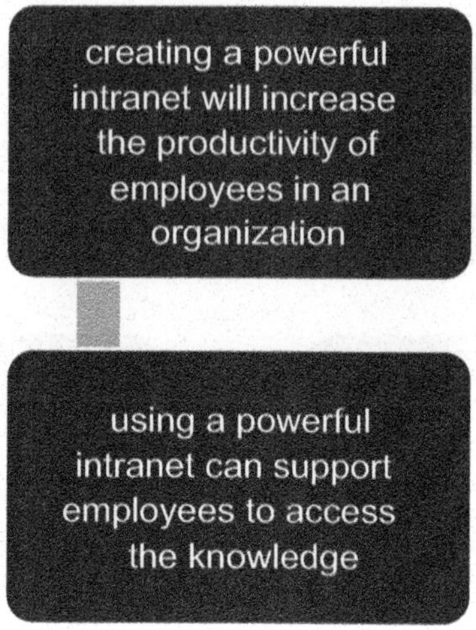

8.5.8 Benefits

Thus some of the benefits of cloudy are going to be the following:

The power of corporate intranets will increase, based on more information and data being available, in addition to more IT-related solutions. User administration will be simplified and this will be done centrally in cloudy. Software administration and availability will be easier to manage, as it will be done centrally. Therefore a new level of transparency can be offered to employees as well as to clients.

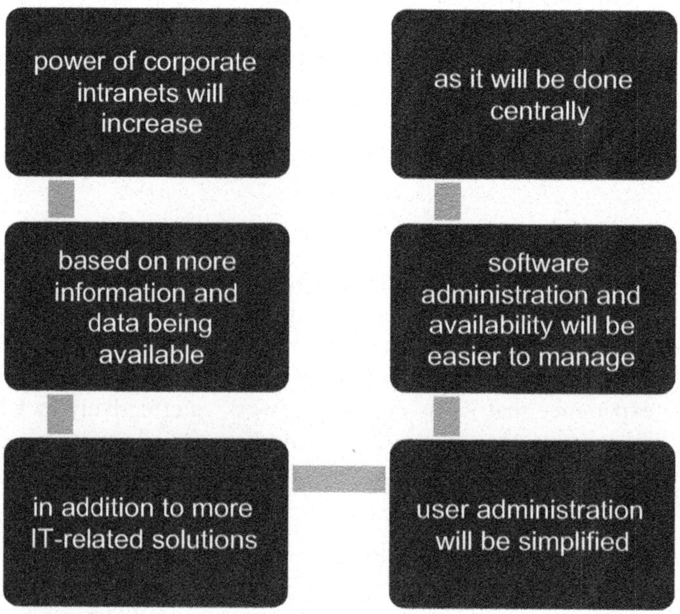

Access to the system environment of the workplace, no matter if at the office or outside of the home country or while travelling, will only be done by smart phone and therefore very efficiently. Future phones will be smaller and more intelligent than we can imagine today, supported by intelligent new software.

The smart phone uses dummy screens, and cloud computing to access the work-related data. Cloud computing will become the center of data management, and even archiving and data sharing within teams, project members, or departments will be performed by cloud computing in the future, as today's island way of data storage and the creation of several copies will disappear. This will be a benefit, especially for the management of security around sensitive data, such as client data.

8.6 External Service Providers

Based on studying the most successful service providers, Frei (2010) presents the principals of success for HBR in an article called "The Four Things a Service Business Must Get Right": "As the world's major economies have matured, they have become dominated by service-focused businesses. But many of the management tools and techniques that service managers use were designed to tackle the challenges of product companies. Are these sufficient, or do we need new ones? When a business takes a product to market, whether it's a basic commodity like corn or a highly engineered offering like a digital camera, the company must make the product itself compelling and also field a workforce capable of producing it at an attractive price, because customers' involvement as producers can wreak havoc on costs, service companies must also develop creative ways to fund their distinctive advantages... When we look at service businesses that have grown and prospered, companies like Walmart in retail, Commerce Bank in banking, and the Cleveland Clinic in health care, it is their effective integration of the elements that stands out more than the cleverness of any element in isolation. ... The challenge of service-business management begins with design... customers may attribute convenience or friendly interaction to your service brand.

They may compare your offering favorably with competitors', because of extended hours, closer proximity, greater scope or lower prices. Your management team must be absolutely clear about which attributes of service the business will compete on. Strategy is often defined as what a business chooses not to do. ...In order to create a successful service offering, managers need to determine which attributes to target for excellence and which to target for inferior performance. These choices should be heavily informed by the needs of customers. Managers should discover the relative importance customers place on attributes, and then match the investment in excellence with those priorities. At Walmart, for example, ambience and sales help are least valued by its customers, low prices and wide selection are most valued, and several other attributes rank at points in between. . ..”

According to this article, once an attractive customer segment has been found, the objective of the company should be to offer services to attract customers in that segment. The offer can be a special service, such as extended opening hours (leaving the lower price to your competitors), combined with friendly customer interaction.

Example

Commerzbank: It provides the possibility for payment transactions to be made in a more flexible way, such as offering late opening hours as well opening hours over the weekend. The creation of a win–win situation in terms of operating service and value-added services in order to extend the customer experience is often offered around car insurance.

Innovative ideas which will not cost the customer much, but will provide a higher customer satisfaction, can be copied quickly and will soon lose its competitive advantage. If a service was defined as free and suddenly has fees associated with it, customers tend to react with displeasure.

According to Scholtissek (2011) quality, purity, and value will become less relevant for consumers, and having IT services from other countries is appreciated. The innovations are either product innovations, service innovations, business model innovations, or organizational innovations. The process behind innovation can be based on the idea of what is missing, planning, prototyping, testing, exploiting in real markets, and on market penetration.

8.6.1 Outsourcing

The outsourcing trend is continuing so that not only IT-related expertise is outsourced, but also other expertise, like marketing, HR, etc. Maybe the future makes it even necessary to outsource activities like trading or risk management or activities related to the monitoring process of innovations. The question is how beneficial the outsourced solution is over a period of, say, 5 years and what is the best way to measure it.

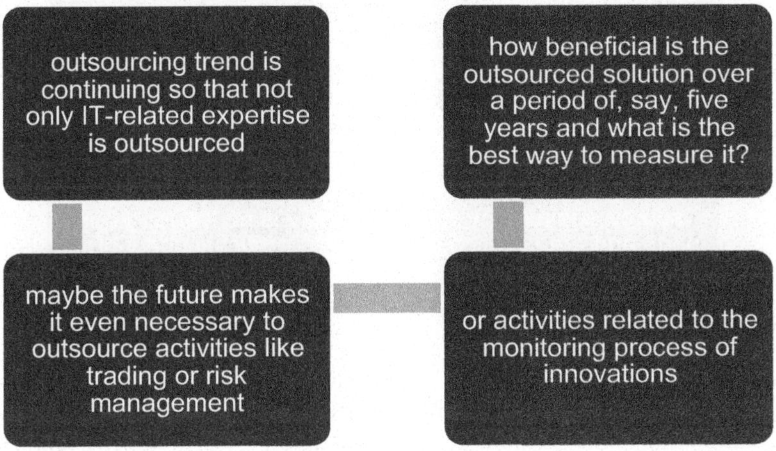

8.6.1.1 Local Economy

A country with strong immigration laws might even support outsourcing, as organizations might decide to rather outsource than have a local, expensive solution in place. The main question will be how far can we outsource without severely affecting a local economy.

8.6.1.2 Short-Term Benefits of Solutions

In today's banking world, the short-term benefit is the main driver of almost every decision implemented. There is no real measurement methodology used to re-assess an outsourcing decision. I think that the future banks will only outsource the non-critical areas of the organization's activities and will start to in-source again many parts and areas which are currently outsourced. We need to recognize that IT is no longer a non-critical aspect of banking as before. This recognition will lead banks to review and change some of their existing procedures and guidelines, such as in relation to critical knowledge that has to be available in the organization as well as in the country.

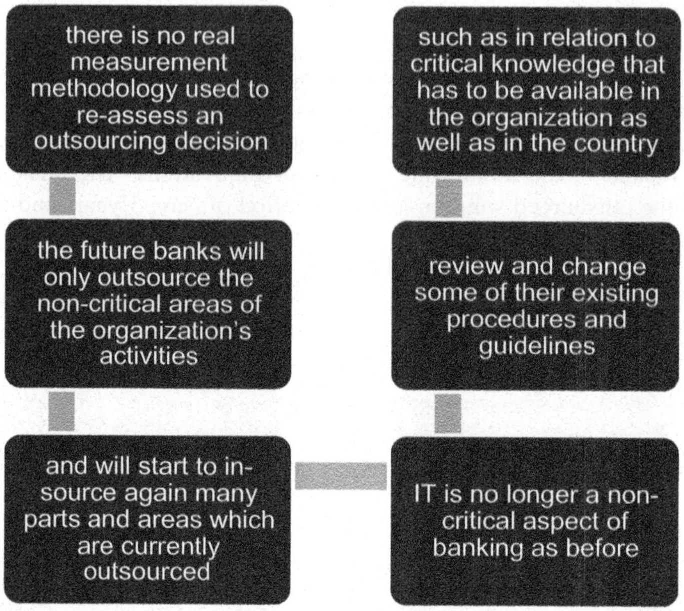

Below are a number of different ways of looking at outsourcing topics which I found interesting to share: FT published an article on growth that said it will depend on inventions and imagination. It was written by Cienski (2013): Global tech companies such as Google and Samsung have built up substantial research facilities in Poland. Skype, the Microsoft-owned internet phone service developed in Estonia, has a significant research presence in the Czech Republic.

According to Vitasek et al. (2010), organizations have outsourced departments such as HR, IT, call centers, etc. and provide ways to achieve better results with outsourcing with a new model called "Outsourcing 2.0." They provide new ways to keep both clients and providers satisfied.

According to Lacity and Rottman (2008), in today's world with all the progress being made in technology, it is easy to outsource IT and manage cost reductions in your IT department. Although it is not easy to optimize outsourced activities, there are other benefits which should be considered, such as additional employees who are either on-site at your office or off-shore or routine tasks with low priority that can be forwarded to the off-shore supplier, running of a project management office or development teams or business processes that can be performed off-shore. I think that future banks will avoid outsourcing their core business processes, as they are the critical for controlling purposes and must remain in the organization.

8.7 External Employees

There are several types of external employees, such as consultants, contractors, or freelancers. In fact, their tasks are to support internal employees and their managers to accomplish a task. After the crisis financial institutions became more bureaucratic in terms of the selection of external employees. There are guidelines on how to select external employees.

Everybody involved in the selection process is keen on sticking to the guidelines and does not question the appropriateness of the hiring approach. This means that people only select from a given internal list of people, with qualified external alternatives (consultants, contractors, or freelancers) not even being considered, as potential candidates have to be selected from the list. This approach does not make use of the available potential in the marketplace in order to find the best people. Today it seems to be move important to rather choose the right company than the right people.

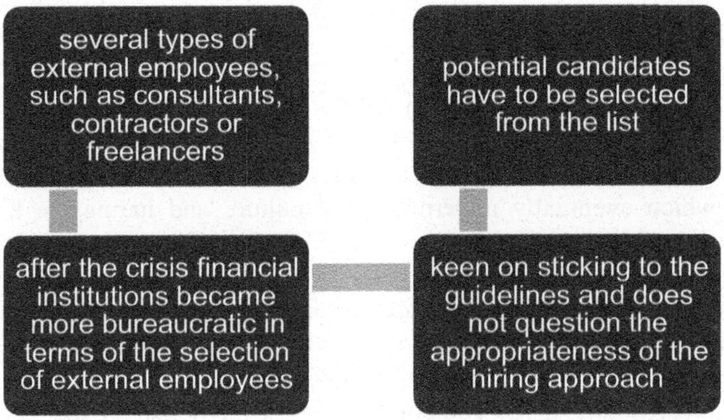

8.8 Employees

The banking business is based on the service quality provided to its clients by its employees. This is the reason why the selection and training of employees is important for their organizations, as these people will also determine the service reputation of the bank. The main aim of a bank should be to provide excellent specific service to specific clients. What makes people in an organization able to achieve excellence? What motivates these employees to achieve excellence?

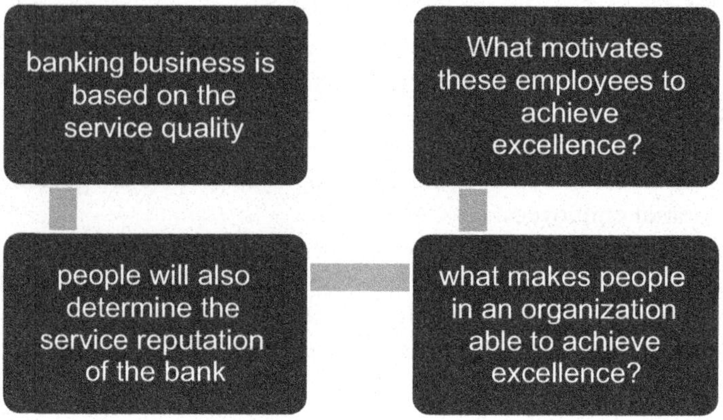

8.8.1 Lasting Values

After the crisis, bank employees have been frequently told that there are many experts on the market who are looking for work, which can be annoying to employees who think that, even if it's true, there is no need to put them under pressure, which eventually undermines the culture and harms the business, as people with positive emotions will not only perform better in their job but also satisfy clients.

I think that a bank with a high understanding for essential values of the organization will be sensitive to all the little things and continuously educate their employees so that they not only grow professionally, but also personally. It is part of human nature to be sometimes positive or negative, but changing our moods and emotions to positive can become a habit and will benefit us as well as our organization continuously.

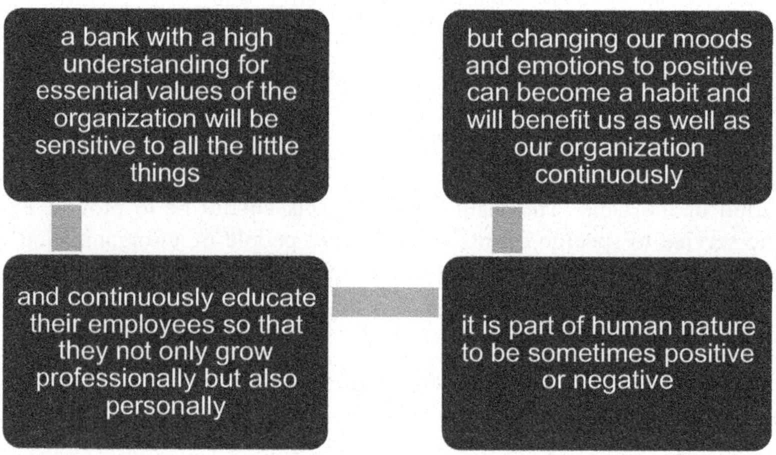

8.8.2 Performing Employees

An organization which has reached a high level of acceptance in the market applies a balanced way of assessing its employees. The performance assessment is split between results and the employee's behavior. The valuation of yearly profit must be seen as a part of amortizing valuation within 5 years. This means that an annual profit will be split over the ensuing 5 years. With this simple idea, employees are encouraged to hold on to their jobs.

In this case employees are discouraged from making huge profits today and not caring about the next years, as they probably won't take the bonus and move into a different job. The longer an employee remains in the same area of an organization, the bigger the bonus will become.

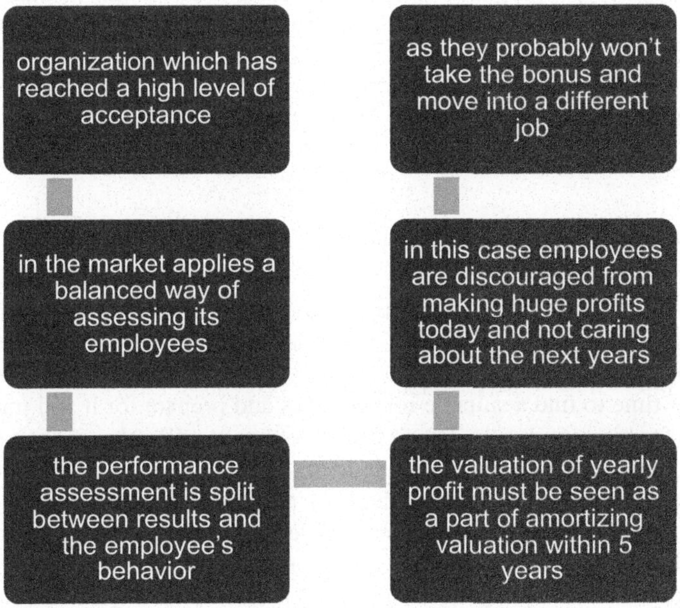

8.8.3 Rewarding of Employees

Nelson (2012) thinks that the most important asset of a manager is the ability to keep satisfied and motivated employees and that there are many ways to keep them satisfied and motivated. A manager can provide flexibility, regular communication, compliments even for small achievements, support, and autonomy, but also the culture of an organization can provide new ways of creating a satisfactory working environment. I think the most important way of satisfying employees is to assign clear responsibilities, show respect, and be authentic.

Even managers are forced sometimes to get involved into internal politics, but they should try to separate politics from the way they manage their team. Large organizations need internal politics, but this should be avoided in teams, departments, or small organizations.

Authentic mangers are able to earn the trust of their employees, and even if they make a mistake, they tend to be forgiven easily. An authentic manager is focused to maintain a productive environment, as they are not bothered with signs or actions that they do not understand. Authentic managers who never complain about or criticize their people in their team are those managers who will have a loyal team which supports him beyond what's expected from them. I think that being able to act authentic is the most important skill for a manager, a trait which strongly influences cultures.

Schäfer (2014b) argues the following in an FT article titled "Banks' skills gap forces up pay for talented minority": "...banking has moved away from being a profession... away from professional exams in favour of narrow quantitative and sales training...created a cultural inability... to recognise and address risk in a holistic manner."

8.8.4 Employees of the Future

The employees of future banks will stick to their core expertise and extend their role in the next related role after each 2 or 4 years, and this change will be a process which will start 16 months before the 2 or 4 year ends and will be booked 10 % of employees time to find a suitable related tasks and prepare for it and train the new employee for his current role. Future culture of banks will only see their employees as heroes if they combine excellence in their work but also support their colleagues to become excellent. The entire process during these 16 months will be supported and monitored by another department, which has the responsibility to ensure a smooth change. By this possibility an organization will promote the change to another areas within the organization so that the diversified expertise can be built, which will benefit the organization.

Employees of future banks know that they will be rewarded if they add a new expertise to their current knowledge from the professional point of view, but they also need to develop their personality.

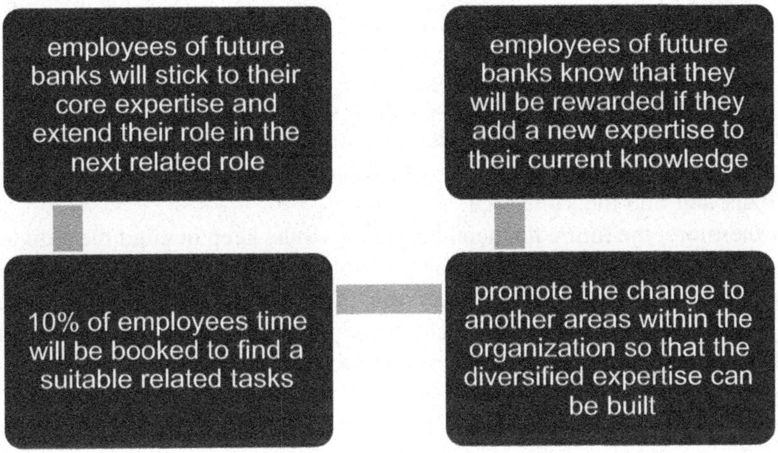

8.8.5 Future Senior Managers

Instead of presenting themselves as distanced and aloof, the future senior managers need to learn to become more natural and close suitable to the situation in order to ease the collaboration. Natural and authentic senior managers have the power to gain trust and respect combined with sympathy which will release a lot of energy for achieving their organizations' goal.

In the future managers will not look controlled or grumpy in their day-to-day business meetings or interactions with their employees, as they will be asked instead to become more transparent with their emotions and remain comfortable and trustworthy all of the time.

Furthermore, the matrix organization for the future banks will completely disappear as the future bank must become completely transparent in what they do internally as well as toward clients and regulators. Their experts around the organization are taken away from the matrix and are able to extend their expert knowledge.

They will be allowed to become more valuable for their company with understanding the dependencies around their subject in the entire organization. The culture of the future banks will value the uniqueness of their employees trust them and let them grow in their responsibility and leave their own finger print on the organization. This will create an incredible power to support the ongoing projects within the different areas, which will therefore benefit the organization as a whole.

8.9 Clients

Going forward, system interfaces are going to look identical, no matter from which environment the clients have had access more often. The more clients will use it, the more they will like it, discovering the benefits of interacting with technology, no matter if at home over the weekend or traveling or at work; they can always access their bank and find the same GUI.

Furthermore, the future financial institutions must keep in mind the individuality of each client in terms of personal preferences as well as social and cultural backgrounds when offering client solutions. Adding the possibility of customized online services would take into account the uniqueness of each client, a feature which is still largely missing in today's service offerings.

8.9.1 Possible Solutions for Attracting Clients

I think that banks around the world are facing a change in their cultures today, and since some of the banking laws have lost their validity, the need to improve services is stronger than ever. Clients are looking for transparency and simplicity, but also for a combination of comfort and benefits.

For instance, innovative banking in today's time, suited to a small independent country, which is respected for its achievements around the world, might be a combination of benefits, such as the beauty of the country, its culture of respecting other cultures, its transparency in running banks, an enriching integrations program when joining the bank and a unique, but simple financial instrument suited to different types of clients, such as retirees or entrepreneurs.

Future bank clients will have the possibility to select their advisor's personality and values by looking at their professional and personal development. They will also look at their bank as their closest friend where friendship counts more than money. They will have proof of this by being able to network with other clients that can report that they have the same quality of respect and support from their bank when they had a high income, but also when it was low. Future clients want to be entertained by their bank as well and will appreciate openness and authentic behavior of their banks.

There is no need to become a super bank by offering every possible benefit one can imagine, but in order to retain existing clients and attract new clients, a change in today's way of thinking is needed. In the future, an adviser must do more for its clients than just being polite and funny, although this will still be appreciated. Today's highly rated banks will have additional strengths, such as a bank's culture with all the right soft skills available in order to attract new clients. The value of the culture of a bank will only come from the human's involved, based on their well-being and the satisfaction of clients, authorities, and shareholders. The future bank will have a good overall intuition which will serve all involved people.

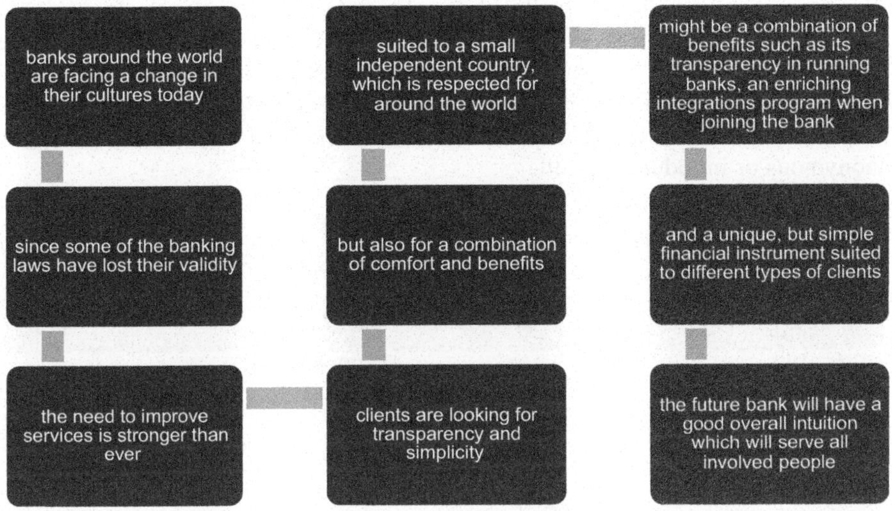

8.9.2 Interaction with Clients

Innovative banks already provide the possibility of virtual interactions amongst clients. Such services are soon going to be offered by more banks as one step toward more transparency. The technological capability is available today and its benefits are high. This new way of interaction between banks and their clients makes banking activities more sympathetic, as we find other clients sharing their ideas with us which might also be useful for our financial ambitions.

Additionally, in the future banks will also attract those technology shy clients by providing a location for these clients' banking activities based on their own mobile devices, but with all other facilities from the bank, like internet access and printing facilities on a fee basis.

These clients will also have the possibility to interact with each other in the location offered by their banks. The future banks will provide their marketing information as an enriching knowledge but also an entertainment to their clients and will provide a digital experience room in these locations for all their newly introduced financial solutions or offering a training for customization of the customer's access to online banking and more. In these locations clients can benefit from education about new developments in banking in an entertaining way at any time making new contacts to other clients if they like.

In a cutting-edge IT-environment with a mixture of latest solutions and a good cup of coffee or tea, clients can educate themselves and enjoy good company by meeting with other clients of the bank. Each location is designed to attract a special customer group, with similar interest and these locations are offering online documentary about bank's internal news or products, online games, some offer a

Bloomberg screen with the possibility for clients to search for particular information. This kind of locations could be also called the private bank's internal club to serve clients. This can be compared to a library, as all are sitting next to each other being busy. Clients can communicate with other clients online or still meet face to face with the bank's relationship managers or other clients and decide to remain anonymous or introduce himself.

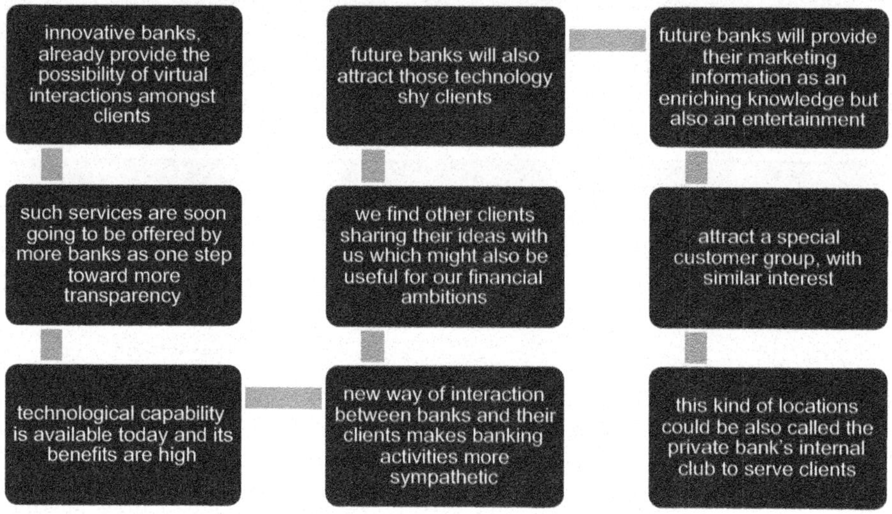

8.9.2.1 Understand Your Clients

According to Callaway and Callaway (2012) the client should always have priority over everything and the relationship to them should be based on competence, caring, and honesty. This will make your client to feel more satisfied while doing business with you. There are even more keys such as respect and communication that are needed for a great relationship with your clients.

Future banks will redefine the relationship with their clients and follow a pre-defined communication guidelines and put their client's interest first and then theirs as they appreciate the loyalty of their clients more than short-term benefits.

Not all banks are able to compete with technology as soon as their competitors, especially if they have a lot of old systems in place that cannot be easily replaced. Therefore there will be more types of banks that will attract many different types of clients. This process has already started but is currently insufficiently used.

There will be many banks that see the need to develop other higher qualities of services in terms of their clients so that they feel bounded with their bank and will create a closer relationship.

According to Beckwith (2003), if you want to have a good relationship with your clients, you need to start asking better questions. These questions can be first addressed to yourself such as what would my client love? Better questions will also help you draw new blueprints for your organization. The author also suggest avoiding perfection and becoming impatient while search for big answers and more.

Because of my interest in art, I came across a number of banks' clients, relationship managers, or private bankers and was surprised to learn that most of the clients liked to be asked questions and if one paid attention to what they said and used their word in the questions, they never wanted you to stop the conversation. It is a funny experience, like doing small talk, but the client has the freedom to decide what he or she wants to share and is not upset that you are asking about subjects that he/she is not interested in discussing at that time.

Asking questions builds a relationship with your clients and does not necessarily mean that your aim is to sell at the end of the conversation. Sometimes a sale takes much longer but it definitely only comes if you first build a relationship with your client.

According to Krause (2013) (Win More Clients with Fewer Cold Calls), the clients have more interest in spending time with you if you talk about their issues and how you could help. They are also interested in listening more if you know when a problem could be solved and you always need to find the right contact, which is able to buy your service and ensure that this person has the budget for your offer.

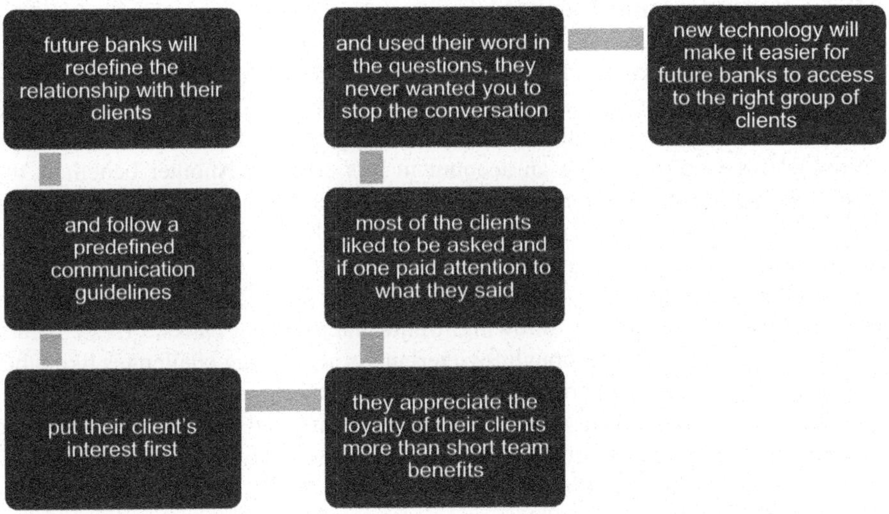

I think that new technology will make it easier for future banks to access to the right group of clients and offer the exact service that they are looking for. For instance, Fidor bank has already implemented a modern way of communicating with clients and also allows clients to exchange their knowledge of investment strategies with each other. I think this will also relieve clients' advisors as the bank will remain the same for their investments even if they talk to other clients.

According to Bleeke (2013), clients do not want to be approached for sale purposes but they like it if you focus on their goals and have a conversation with them about it. Thanks to social networks such as Facebook, LinkedIn or others, clients are already sharing so much information and if you belong to their network, you can follow it.

8.9.2.2 Reporting

In the future traditional banks will also use pictures and colors as well as videos in their documentation for clients or even the authorities are interested in a better service to clients and will avoid pure black and white documentation or text.

> future traditional banks will also use pictures and colors as well as videos in their documentation for clients

8.9.3 Banking and Pleasure

According to Barber (2008), due to the strong Swiss Franc as well as lower taxes, it would make sense to open an account in a Swiss bank. The author also describes the beauty of Switzerland and the benefits of being in the heart of Europe as an additional reason for opening an account in this country. Another benefit is the Swiss national character which is avid to be independent. The uniqueness of the country by having four different languages and cultures makes the people more cosmopolitan. The country has a reputation for quality and agile international tourism and is neutral since the Congress of Vienna in 1815. Switzerland has four kinds of banks which are the following: Major international banks, Private banks, Cantonal banks, Savings. Although Switzerland is also facing challenges like other counties since the financial crisis, they have largely mastered the challenges so far. Banking will remain a major factor in the economy and the country has made changes to laws and regulations in terms of confidentiality and privacy since the crisis in order to better control the banking industry.

8.9.3.1 Human's Brain

Studies have shown that over the course of people's lives, brains undergo individual development which makes them unique like our finger prints. Considering this will cause us to respect each client's individuality while providing a unique solution. By giving each client the ability to customize their solution, the bank will signal once again to the client that the uniqueness of their personality is respected. As a human we want to be treated like in first class no matter if within our friends, company, or as a client. We will be pleased to offer the same respect. This fact can also help the future bank to provide all those services where their clients but also their employees feel being treated like in first class.

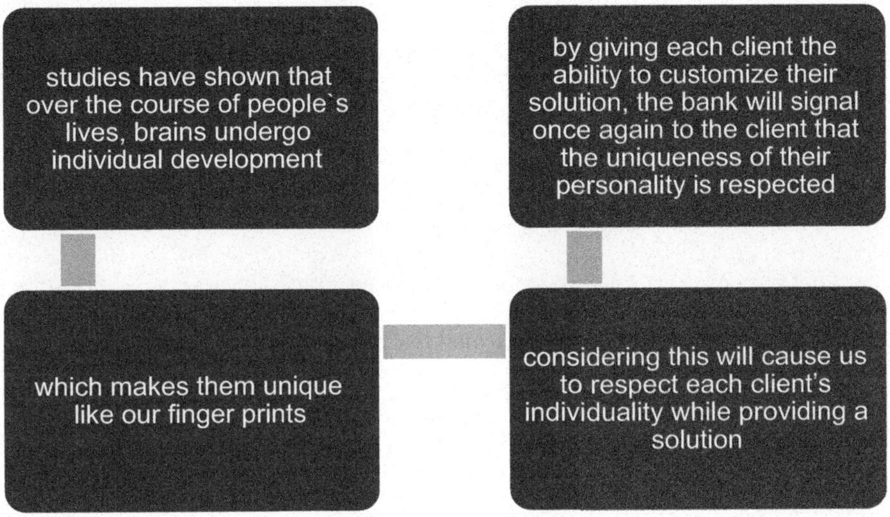

8.10 Added Value

The smart phone of a client or an employee that can enter a banking environment via internet will become the most powerful device in the future and can perform all the activities that the person is allowed to do, with the access being secure, no matter from where a person logs into the banking system.

In the future an organization can use a secure access via this company like an umbrella for employees' and clients' access to the organization's environment. There will be no technical possibility in the future to hack a client's or employees' access via mobile to the banking environments as the access is using bank's future internet solutions. In the future it will be possible to access a highly secure internet via the service provided by a new blue chip company.

There won't be many high quality service providers on the market for private purposes. Therefore the services of the new blue chip company will only be affordable for powerful organizations. The secure access can be added by the financial institutions to the basket of benefits for clients and employees. Therefore as an additional service, the bank will allow their employees and clients to use the same secure umbrella to access a secure internet service for their collaboration with the bank but also for personal lives if needed.

As our day-to-day lives will be strongly influenced by the use of technology, the security behind the usage will soon cause us headaches. Accessing this kind of secure internet environment will not be affordable for individuals.

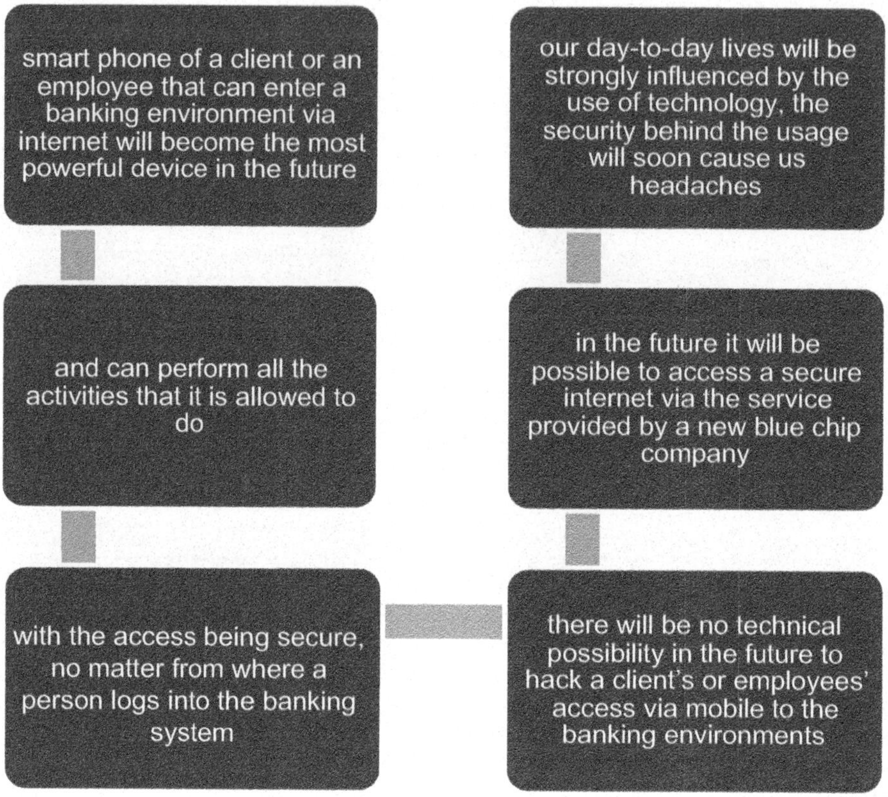

The first banks providing this service to their clients and employees will be more attractive to potential clients and employees.

8.10.1 Direct Benefit

It is a big advantage for a bank to provide support to their clients and employees in all those areas which are not related to a direct benefit for the bank, and this can also be seen as a good service to serve others. By providing the support in areas that are beneficial to clients and employees, banks will become more sympathetic act as a friend and enable the building of a stronger trust. This also requires adaptations in cultures, which allow people to explore potential solutions in those areas that a directly beneficial for a bank, without large costs involved.

This is like a new way of marketing a bank as a whole, which can be a mindful gesture and therefore a powerful approach. The meaning of mindful here is to develop an emotional intelligent that can help a bank to better understand their client's need and develop a closer relationship with the same available time.

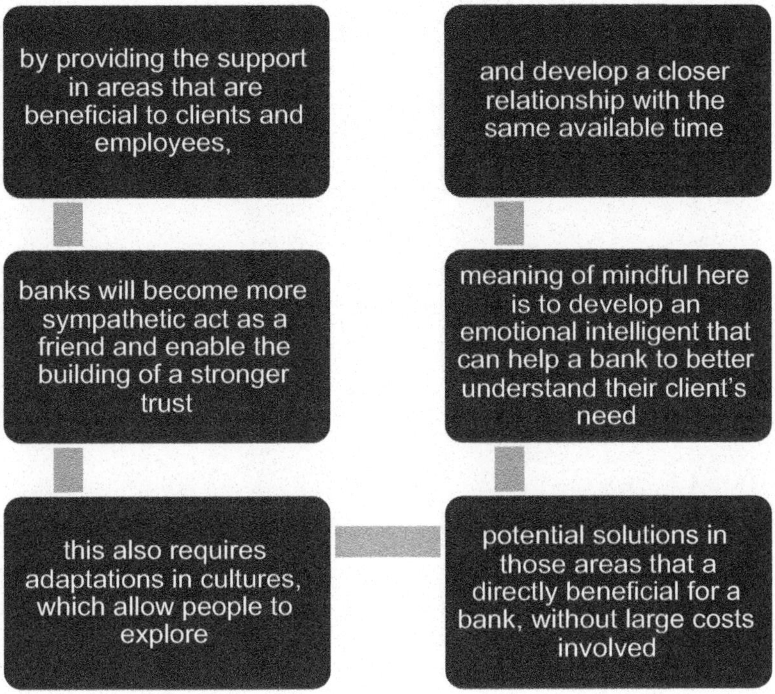

8.10.2 Benefits of Art

There are other ways of organizations that expose the experience around art/emotional intelligent and gain sympathy from their employees as well as their clients.

A good example in that respect, I think, is IBM. The company's commercials and advertisements seem to generate sympathy with its viewers and thus make them potential clients or future employees of the company. The company uses art to provide a beautiful picture, it uses stories to make us admire their achievements after many difficulties, and it uses knowledge to gain our respect. In the end, the perception remains that the message created a combination of positive emotions and professional knowledge.

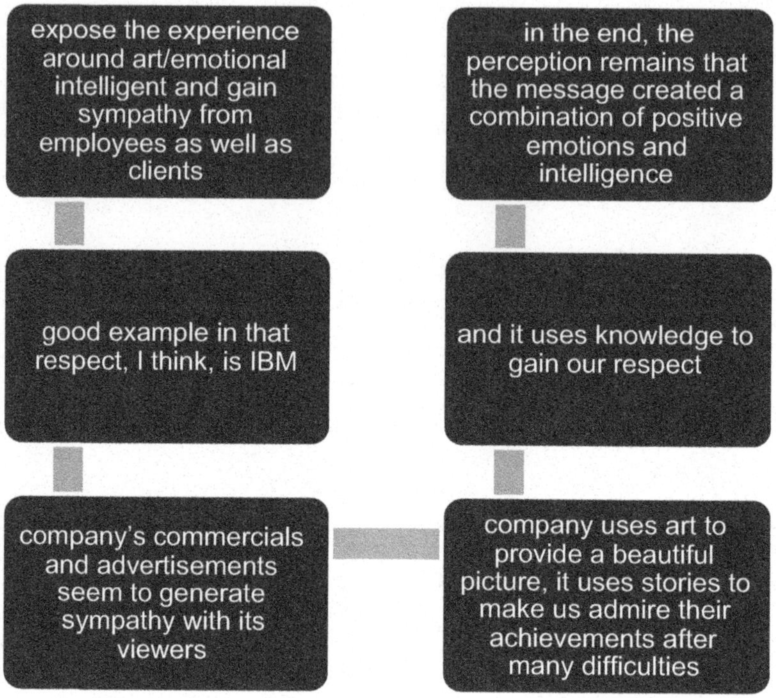

8.10.2.1 Rational Thinking to Rebuild Reputations

I think that being transparent with emotions is a strength and can help to get back the sympathy after mistakes. After the crisis financial institutions are applying more rational thinking to rebuild their reputations, as they had in the past. However, form an observer's point of view, they have worked hard since 2008, but don't quite achieve what they aim for.

Financial institutions today present themselves too distanced and aloof and are alienated from their clients. In the future financial institutions will not be afraid to admit weaknesses and will ask their clients as well as their employees to come up with ideas to deal with a particular weakness.

8.10.2.2 Ask Clients for Ideas

The internal project group, which is being set up to solve a particular weakness related to client's services, creates a window through the internet to the rest of the world in order to ask clients, employees, external consultants, etc. to enter their ideas. The project team will take into the account what they have collected. The project team will solve the weakness and communicate through the website what their achievements are via videos or art. This kind of approach will slowly remove the distance between financial institutions and their clients. The same approach will be required in order to remove the distance between senior managers and their employees.

8.10.3 Emotional Intelligence

According to Neale et al. (2011), we need to understand the value of emotions in an organization and develop an emotional intelligence, as emotions are important and influence our decisions. The authors are advising to pay attention to emotions and use them as a tool to achieve better results. We need to control reflexes such as breathing or sleeping. The authors also compare emotions to a lion and rational thinking to a tamer and explain that emotions are able to overpower rational thinking if we dont pay attention to control it.

The main components of emotional intelligence are to understand your reactions and the awareness of other people. Your emotional intelligence can be developed or changed and improved by exercising behaviors, such as relationships with others, self-regard, self-awareness, and self-management. There is a direct correlation between emotional intelligence and improving performance and is based on supporting others and understanding the feelings about a situation.

Using art and emotion is also true for Steve Jobs when he introduced his innovative technologies to the world. He has provided a product for everybody that combines intelligent technology and positive emotions.

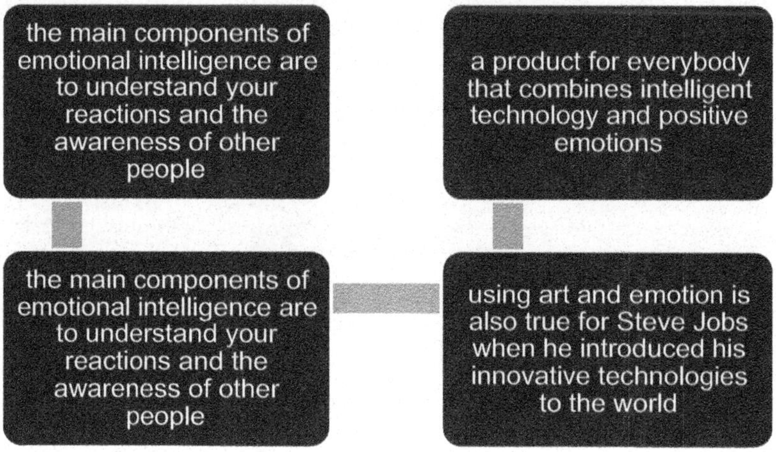

8.10.3.1 Values

The value of emotions is severely underestimated in the banking business, which is why it has received almost no sympathy for its challenges that arose since the last crisis. Many areas in the banking business are characterized by severe competitive pressures, difficult working relationships and burnouts, with little-to-no room for empathy and emotions. Instead we work hard to be seen as rational and define this as the highest level of intelligence.

I think that senior managers should encourage them as well as their employees to be more transparent about what they really think and can accomplish their tasks without having any frustrations.

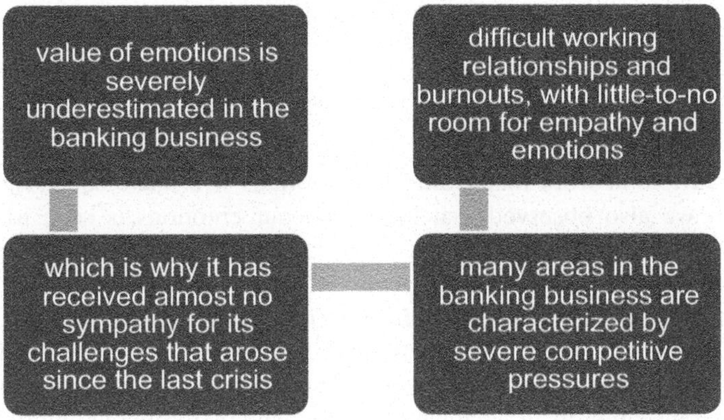

8.10.3.2 Influence and Presentation

Picard (2011) used an interesting device to measure the emotions of an audience while at a presentation via TED Talk. The device always changed color when the audience was excited. That is what is missing at regular company meetings when the audience is not engaged and potentially falls asleep. The "net generation" can probably better explain why there is a need for entertainment if we would like to engage our audience and have their complete attention over a longer period of time. This generation will be responsible for many fundamental changes in the future banking.

Rosalind Picard discovered that sounds keep listeners' or observer's attention high. This is the reason that the future software companies will have implemented the possibility of sound in the automatically generated power point presentations about project status. Imagine what it means for the project manager's time if the annoying power point presentations with time templates, risk status updates, and action plans with all the findings are generated not only automatically, but also arty in order to catch the attention, as they include colors, pictures, and music. In the future, a new intelligent project related software is programmed in a way that humor will be introduced with funny cartoons to keep the project team in a good productive mood during the presentation. The presentation itself will never be longer than 2 min and maybe via video with the rest of the meeting time being an online video discussion which will be recorded for communication or audit purposes.

The presentation will always be shown and available online and can be accessed during the entire project period either by the project team members, stakeholders, senior managers, or other involved internal departments.

In the future there will be no time wasting for the creation of a Power Point presentation. Power Point presentations will be done automatically in a practical way with colors, pictures and sounds. Can you imagine what this means for the productivity of the organization to avoid their experts working for hours on Power Point presentations, which make the audience falling asleep, due to most of today's presentations being overloaded with information, facts, and numbers and are kept like a difficult to read documentation.

8.10.3.3 Professional

We were all told at work that hiding our emotions will make us act more professional, but we also observed that hiding all our emotions is seen as not being authentic. Additionally we made the experience that controlling emotions is better than hiding them.

As a project manager understanding emotions in the project will always help us to better understand project team members, stakeholders, other involved people; it will support us more and better evaluate current status of ongoing projects. We need to become transparent in all what we do at work and therefore our emotions become transparent too but also should still be controlled instate of being hidden. Today's culture of hiding emotions will be replaced in the culture of our project with controlling emotions, as it will support our collaboration with each other.

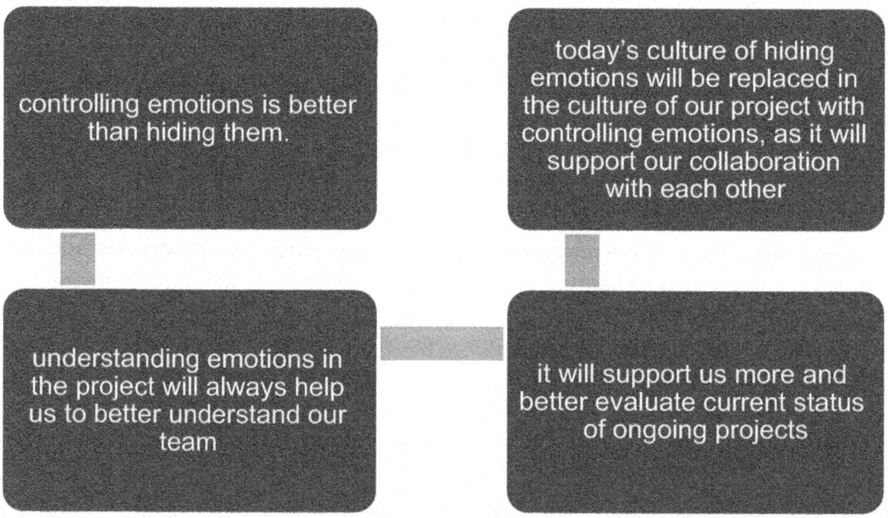

I think that in the future banks will have their managers and experts trained to become honest with sharing their emotions. This culture offers collaboration and will become the motor of the organization, as we are able to avoid conflicts and are therefore able to remain motivated and to go an extra mile for an important project if it is needed. This would also solve many issues that we have today towards teamwork and collaboration. The same rule about the benefit of emotions of employees also applies to clients of a bank. Imagine what this would mean for the relationships that a bank could build with their clients in the future by training their employees to become authentic and transparent with their controlled emotions, but using it as a tool for a better communication.

8.10.4 Value of Creativity

The value of a team and how to target a higher level of creativity is described in a publication by the HBR with the title "Creativity and the role of the leaders," by Amabile and Khaire (2008):

> Creativity has always been at the heart of business, but until now it hasn't been at the top of the management agenda. By definition the ability to create something novel and appropriate, creativity is essential to the entrepreneurship that gets new businesses started and that sustains the best companies after they have reached global scale... The shift to a more innovation-driven economy has been abrupt. Today, execution capabilities are widely shared and the life cycles of new offerings are short. As competition turns into a game of who can generate the best and greatest number of ideas, creativity scholars are being asked pointed questions about their research. What does it mean? How relevant is it? Does it offer guidance on the decisions that leaders in creativity-dependent businesses have to make? The first priority of leadership is to engage the right people, at the right times, to the right degree in creative work. That engagement starts when the leader recasts the role of employees. Rather than simply roll up their sleeves and execute top–down strategy, employees must contribute imagination. ...

In order to understand the value of creativity, according to this article, we need to closer look at the following facts: We do not manage creativity, but we manage for creativity. Creativity supports collaboration in its quest for radical innovations.

In order to achieve an excellent collaboration, a hierarchical structure should be avoided and we must ensure that every one can speak up. In order to achieve a higher level of creativity, one should avoid bringing people with identical backgrounds, same disciplines, and from the same areas to meetings. According to this article, sometimes the perspectives arising from another background support a break-through for another group's problem. This is why diversity enhances creativity.

This article discusses further interesting points:

- An organization should use the internet to facilitate the access to smart ideas of people who are working on the same issue. Use the personal interests of your employees so that they become more innovative. The organization must allow people to express their identities and if managers encourage their employees to integrate diverse identities, such as nourishing a culture where female engineers realize they do not have to dress like men would also support creativity in an environment.
- Motivated employees are vital for the organization and therefore allow people to pursue their passions. People who are revolutionary in their thinking are more likely to be better suited for radical innovations than a person who is happy to work on the 15th version of something.
- A manager must be crazy to believe that they can ignore this fact and mix-match a group without considering who would be better suited for their innovation ambitions. As a manager you can be an enthusiastic audience in order that a creative mind is motivated to become even more creative. A manager should dispel fears of failure. The goal should be a culture which allows failures, but to

learn as much as possible in the process. Failure should not be taken under the microscope.

- Management should provide for psychological safety and people should know that they will not be humiliated or punished for failure. Cultures must change their sensitivity to failure. The desire to avoid it will impede a company's vitality. By allowing failure, organizations will not suffer from missed opportunities.
- Failures in organizations fall into one of three categories: Unsuccessful tries, System breakdowns, Process deviation. All these categories must be analyzed and solved, but the first category must be considered as the most important one, which needs to avoid fear of failure in order that creativity is not inhibited. According to the article, people who feel well integrated will be a much better source of creativity. According to two experiments, Asian–Americans were asked to come up with a new form of Asian–American cuisine, while in another experiment female engineers were asked to invent the best phone for female users.

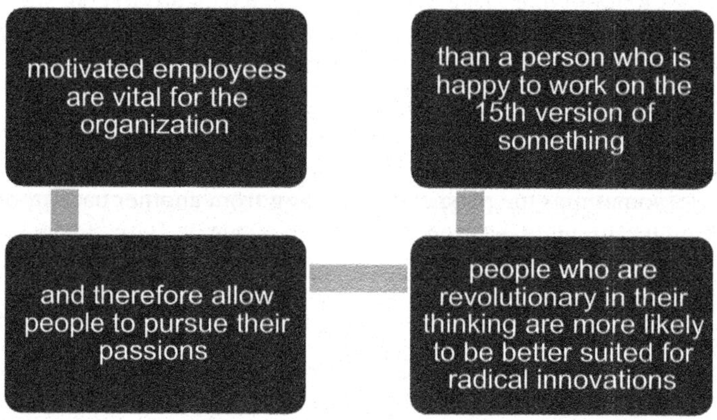

8.10.5 Possible Future Socializing

According to Lanier (2013) a siren server coordinates a network of powerful computers and they dominate the finance world, social media, and other companies and the information is distributed unequally as employees of social media, for instance, know more about the users than the users about them.

I think in term of exchanging information between friends, it would not matter too much if the information were distributed unevenly but in terms of company related information, there still will be some thoughts on how to use social media to exchange business-related information.

I think that the future banks will use a secure connection to social media to communicate with their clients. This connection allows using a special software but none of the information is ever recorded or stored on the devices of social media. Their windows only open a link but as soon as the company starts to communicate with its clients, the information will only be available on screen and only the company will be able to store it. This might be the way that the banks of future will use social networks to socialize with clients as many could be found there but there will be also a network with other banks.

There might also be that a special social media solution from an independent organization such as future banking club will be provided to the banks and clients to use for socializing and networking purpose.

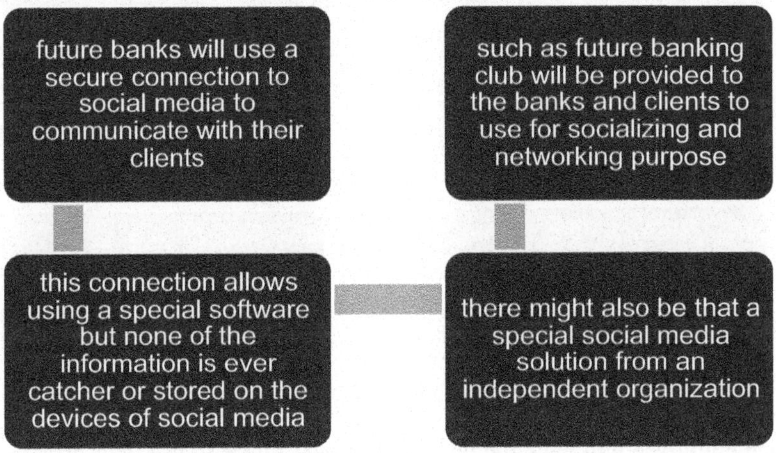

8.10.6 Communication

Video meetings and structured communication process will be the foundation of any business in the future, as the organizations can no longer afford the time consuming use of purely emails for communication to discuss or solve issues.

8.10.6.1 Communication and Risks

I think that communication is one of the key factors of causing hidden risks. Therefore there will be a revolution in the way information is transferred within the organization soon as today's way of communication needs an improvement urgently.

I think that in the future communication via email or any other form of text will be reduced to a minimum. New solutions similar to the concept of "Youtube" to serve internal information exchange will be created for internal purpose and be available on the intranet of the organizations. The information on the intranet can be searched by topic, owner of the content, or departments in organization. In the future conference calls will be replaced by video conferences.

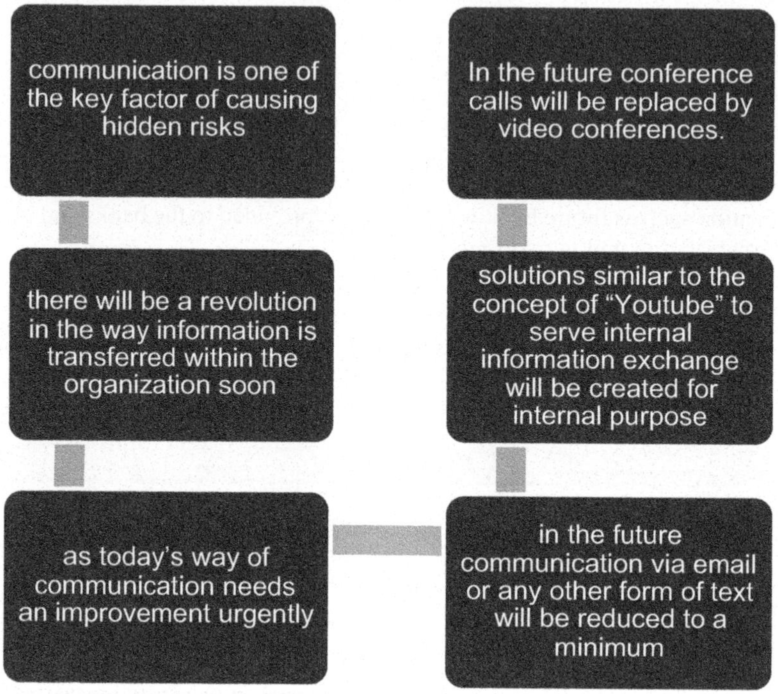

Each employee will have the possibility in the future to use their private phone for organization-related communication, as phones will provide a secure connection such as the app "Good" for iPhone today for exchange emails/texts as well as to exchange information based on audios.

8.10.6.2 Issues with Emails

We have all seen how annoying it is when we are in the middle of writing many emails regarding a simple subject that could be finished quickly via a face to face conversation or a call. We have all experienced when we had difficulties understanding a message in a project and sometimes, by exchanging many questions, we have accidently caused even more misunderstandings and maybe created conflicts.

I think that it is still the fact that projects that communicate mainly via email and only have phone conferences and very little face to face communication might fail or become very expensive or produce hidden risks, which will only be discovered after the project is finished.

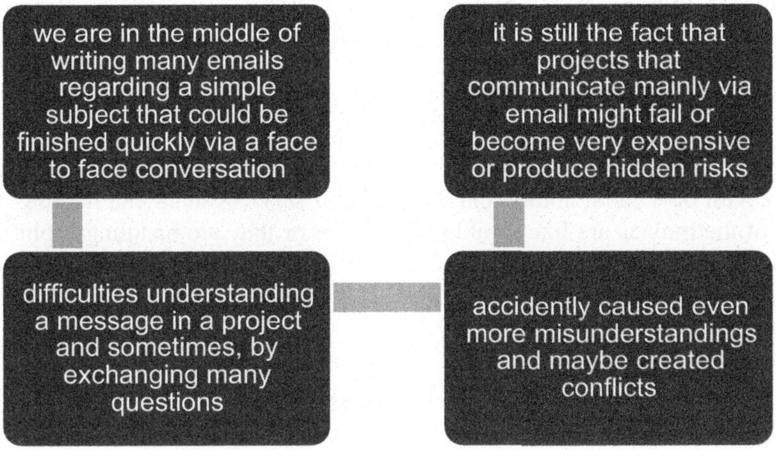

"The Pursuit of Unhappiness" is the book by Watzlawick (1993), which should be quoted here. Watzlawick's German version of the book was entertaining and also true for human's nature for interpretation. In most cases the project team is under a lot of pressure to deliver on time, and in many cases they are involved in many projects and sometimes the project members are a part of a matrix organization, which means that they already have two managers.

Using email and avoiding personal interactions make us pessimistic people over time. In Watzlawick's book, he says we will have many interpretations based on our current mood for something (e.g., the project) in order to understand the message fully. I think that in the near future emails will be seen as a tool which is "The Pursuit of Unhappiness" and will be only used to communicate 7 % of the information and 93 % of the communication will be done face to face or with the phone.

8.10.6.3 Online Communication

The website of some banks has the same old way of providing information to their clients like the past decade. Nothing seems to have changed and the information are mainly in text and black & white, and the appearance of the bank is very quiet. I have visited some and left quickly as the information were provided in a boring way. The transformation to the new age online communication has not been taken place.

In April 2014 the largest Icon on the first page of a traditional well known bank was "Design & Win" by clicking the icon the visitor was forwarded to the website of one of largest sport company. Next to finance related services the icon for sport shows and the link to the sport company was the most dominant icon on the first page. Although this bank has one of the strongest IT solutions in place comparing to any of large banks on the market and therefore could become attractive with their solutions that they offer to their clients, the website was not sending this message clearly to the visitors of the website. It would be confusing to see a sport shoe as a larger icon than icons and get forwarded to a sport company.

I am sure if a new client gets forwarded to another company's page, they will not return to the bank's website again. They will probably either design a sport shoe for fun and see if they win or buy a pair of sport shoe to remain fit or they search for other bank's website with simple way of understanding their services in maybe a more engaging or entertaining way.

In the web presentation of most of the large banks in the world, there are no videos with or without humor and explain their services in an entertaining movie. Most of the movies are like in old fashion way or they are handling sophisticated banking subjects and are very impressive as the vocabulary is mainly for experts and not for every person to understand. The question is who the audience of the video should be.

8.10.6.4 A Simple Way to Communicate

SIMPLE bank explains their benefits without using a word and Fidor bank explains all their wide rage services in about two and half minutes without using any complicated words. I think that these two banks have understood the desire of customer for simplicity/transparency and offer a first easy step to enter the banking knowledge and get a clear understanding of core services that these banks are offering.

8.10.6.5 Entertainment

I think that soon all information to the clients will be done with video massages and even with cartoons. The future banking will combine dry intellectual banking subject with simple explanation and maybe humor in order to ease customers' understanding and gain their attention. If we look at ourselves we will agree that we can combine humor in what we do only if we are relaxed and are convinced about ourselves.

I also know that allowing ourselves to be humor-full at work over a longer period of time also means that we must have a permanent trust in ourselves and transfer knowledge without over-complicating a subject that could be simplified. This is actually the reason why banks such as SIMPLE or Fidor Bank have gained so much admiration and trust. They have the confidence to provide a funny cartoon or a video without words about their services and let their clients to talk to each other. They are open to get their clients' feedback about weaknesses and new ideas and they present the kind of honesty and openness like in a friendship that we admire.

8.10.7 Future Bank as a Good Friend

I think that the future bank is also able to let its clients invite all other clients to their social events or set up a collaboration with each other at company level. The future bank is like a good friend, who is happy to introduce his network. They expect that their clients have the same appreciation for values like they would hold up in friendships and openness.

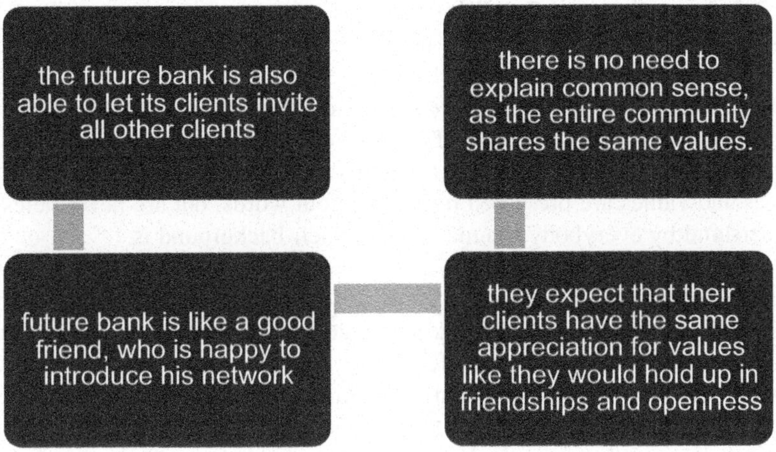

This will be the future bank—based on client relationships that are maintained by trust and common sense. There is no need to explain common sense, as the entire community shares the same values. There will be no need for heavy regulations, as the involvement of many authorities in the future as the understanding of right and wrong is easy for everybody and the price for a violation will be high for the individual and they do it right because of their own interest.

8.10.7.1 Human Nature

It is human nature to desire the correctness in everything we do or the desire of sharing all benefits with those who are excellent, trustworthy, and almost perfect. We seek for enriching encounters, for those encounters who make us feel a little more human and can nourish all those skills that strengthen us in our humanity. Why should be our expectation different to a bank than to a close friend? I think that the fact that we trust our banks with our money must confirm that we actually love to have an even closer relationship to our banks than to our closest friends. I have met many excellent private bankers, who have acted exactly like I have just explained. They are stressed and want to help if their clients are stressed with their business or anything else.

8.10.7.2 Understand Your Bank

We could trust our bank if we know that our bank values all those characteristics which make us human. A good check for us would be to visit the career page of a bank that you would like to select and research what they request as professional as well as personal skills from their new employees. By reading the carrier pages we could also have an understanding of how efficient the bank is or how modern are their systems, methods or how realistic their expectations are. However, it is not a good sign if job details are very long, almost like a document, or if they are expecting a super hero with a long track record of work experience and holds a MBA in a subject they expect and should not be older than 30.

8.10.7.3 Empathy and Confidence

I was once told that a bank with a higher self-confidence and a successful track record can afford to be different. If there are several banks with the same level of strong reputation, we will probably choose the bank which scores highest in terms of empathy. The empathy is coated if bank's stories are shared in a video message in an open and honest way with all their ups and downs. Additionally, the bank services and values are presented mostly without words, but are nevertheless easy to understand by everybody, no matter what their background is.

8.10.7.4 A Survival Tool

The simple possibilities to transfer knowledge to customers or employees became basically a tool to survive, but only few banks seem to recognize it. In today's time, customer behavior can quickly change to a more critical and less loyal attitude if they do not get the transparency they are maybe looking for in a new bank. Therefore, in case there is a lack of transparency, clients will be either unhappy and look for a different bank or they will wait to see if there are changes in the market and then make a decision. Fact is that many banks underestimate the power of transparency to either win new clients or keep old clients.

Financial institutions have hardly changed their ways of selecting consultants. They still have the same expectations compared to 10 years ago. There are also not many service providers, except for a few of them, such as IBM and Apple, who have the courage to engage their customers with emotions and art. The only change in selecting services, for instance, consultants, is that they request resources at a much lower price than in the past. These are consulting companies who have developed innovative approaches, such as taking two and paying for one, like a special sales offer in a super market. There are no innovative tools to measure the quality of the "take two, pay one" product or to measure the solution made the company to keep at least the old quality and save money. The measurement must be done in a longer period of time than just a couple of months. Is there any measurement of the risks from the dependency from an outsourced knowledge over a period of a minimum of 5 years? This period would make us recognize how much knowledge has left the organization and what the price is for these dependencies. I am not saying that outsourcing a solution should not be considered at all; I had to deal with developers from India in one of my projects, and they were excellent. I think that in the future outsourced solutions will only work for a certain period of time before making a permanent decision about outsourcing. In the future there will be many tools available to measure the exact benefits of outsourcing in term of costs, quality, and security.

8.10.7.5 Innovation

According to Bass (2012), president and CEO of Autodesk, "innovation is like a process that changes the world and is about making things better in significant and hopefully meaningful ways and taking risks and breaking the rules" he said at a TED talk. Innovation is fundamentally performed by individuals, as there are skills required such as imagination, creativity, and problem solving. Therefore the most important thing that a company can do is to hire the right employees. He believes that with innovation labs, innovation frameworks, and an army of innovation consultants the product is going to suck in the end.

How could the iPad create such a mass hysteria? Steve Jobs introduced the personal computer in the first place. Did he now open a new door for the end user by creating the iPad as the new personal computer of the future?

The media is talking about mobile banking and the new technology which will soon change the entire banking business. There is not so much talk around the security behind the usage of these devices and what would happen to the data from the old systems. I think that the future will bring along a new model of mobile banking, provided maybe by Apple or another company, which is hard coded in the way that only few changes are possible. It is programmed in a way that a security leak is not possible at all and has the stability of a host so that nothing can happen, as mobile banking is only based on a dummy window and can be replaced at any time. This device can have the size of an iPad, but can also be bigger or smaller.

8.10.8 BOFB as the Future Answer to Today's Insecurity

In the future, technology will be better structured and more intelligent than today as well as stronger through its excellent alignment with control procedures of the organization. It is unimaginable for us today, as we deal with unstructured IT landscapes, and maybe it is unimaginable, because we don't know if an organized and structured IT is possible at all, like in the same way as it was with the iPad. Suddenly, Apple's Steve Jobs introduced us to an experience that we could not even imagine before. Groom et al. (2014) argue the following in an FT article titled "London leads way in services recruitment": "We went through a major financial crisis, but confidence has come back into financial services perhaps even faster than in some other industries, said Chris Cummings, TheCityUK's chief executive." The fact is that IT is easing our business lives, but it also became a pain point. A future secure IT can certainly eliminate risks, as it can be used to control human weaknesses.

8.10.8.1 The Brain of the Future Bank

I think there are many enthusiastic and smart people like Steve Jobs, and one of them will provide the solution around monitoring daily processes that will eliminate unwanted risks in banks. Shareholders, clients, and executive managers of a bank make decisions on how the risk should be controlled and handled, based on a signed document by the responsible parties. An external or internal group of experts will develop a new AI system for banks, which will be called, as mentioned before, the "Brain of the future bank" in order to control the entire risk. After the implementation, the BOFB will become the highest authority of the bank and will monitor daily activities so that risks are eliminated before they even emerge.

Examples

Here are some examples of what the brain or BOFB is able to do without recognizing it:

- Clients have an agreed contract with their bank. The BOFB is taking over the control of the contract and monitors the portfolio managers' activities and ensures that the agreements are compliant with the contract. An activity is performed after the BOFB confirms it. The client has a contract with the bank, which confirms that he is a risk-friendly person, but also gives the risk a limit. As the client has his own opinion about the financial instrument, in the contract it is clearly explained what the limit of a loss should be, in which financial instrument it should be invested in and at what percentage and with further details. The BOFB will have all this information and knows how to monitor it automatically.
- Let's assume that the portfolio manager is doing everything right and that the BOFB will control its activity and ensures that only correct activities are accepted. The client calls his bank and will, with immediate effect, change his loss limit and allows his portfolio manager to invest more in one particular product that he thinks would be good. In the future, this process will be controlled by the brain. The client has the possibility to contact the brain directly, provides the needed information with his own unique identification code, and confirms the action. The brain is able to make the requested changes immediately or at the time requested by the client without the portfolio manager noticing. There will be a notification to a senior manager of a number of pre-defined areas, a documentation of the request, and what has been changed.
- The brain will also ensure efficient communication between the organization, employees, clients, service providers, and all needed IT infrastructures. In the future there will be no sign of weak communication, as the brain will send messages to executive manager, shareholders, clients, or service providers. The communication uses different sources, for instance, Facebook, to send clients general, one-way information, like when a monthly report is sent to your home address. It is one way, as the users are not able to answer this email. A communication between clients and their bank is only done in a pre-defined, secure environment, which will be provided to the clients through their banks.
- The BOFB is also able to communicate with the IT department in a way that misunderstandings are eliminated. In the IT departments, IT employees have a closer interaction with the BOFB, as the brain eases their daily work and eliminates risks around everything they do. In case a change is requested from a business and there is a change in system necessary, the BOFB creates a road map for a particular IT expert. The BOFB sends out a report to the IT expert and leaves a voice message with a short summary of how a person should understand the report. In fact, the BOFB is controlling IT and the IT

department and ensures that the information exchange between IT and business areas is done in a more effective way.

Furthermore, it is the BOFB that will monitor, for instance, tax regulations and will communicate with regulators and tax authorities around the world. The BOFB will be able to receive information from regulators and authorities around the world, prepare the information, and send it out to a pre-defined group of experts.

8.10.8.2 IT vs. Coca Cola

The BOFB can be based on different purposes, with the highest purpose of a financial institution being security. A future blue chip company who will provide a BOFB based on online security to banks will become one of the most desirable service providers, as they will have put an end to the chaos and insecurity in the internet. This future blue chip company will use basically the same strategy like Coca Cola and has developed in a way that an outsider is never able to understand and, as the programming part is done in a newly designed language, the knowledge is only partly available even within the organization. Even their hardware and operating system is developed in a way that outside the organization there would be no chance to access the knowledge behind it.

The operating system is strong and provides the organization with a lot of flexibility in controlling their system, and it's complex, but based on logic like Unix. In the organization there is a separate group that understands the operating system and a separate group for the applications installed. Based on their strategy, they have implemented a strong matrix-oriented organizational setup for their experts so that there are only people who are trained to understand the dependencies. This small group has no knowledge about the application or operating system, but can see the connections and dependencies. These people act as the company's team leaders, line managers, and project managers. A matrix organization in a company like this would make sense in the industry, as it will be able to protect the company's knowledge, provide higher quality solutions, and remain competitive.

8.10.9 Prediction of the Future

According to Watson (2008), in order to predict the future, we need to look beyond current limits or our current goals. He thinks that our future will become less transparent than it is today and we will become more tractable for governments in the future.

The virtual interaction will even affect our money and tax, as he thinks that we will pay with cell phones and pay taxes based on our need for energy etc. The virtual world will, for some people, reduce the interaction with the real world, as these people will do everything online, such as shopping and communicating. He sees this group of people as restless. He also thinks that technology will continue changing the way we define entertainment today.

The most effective teamwork will still be based on communication with text, voice, and body language. Only virtual communication will increase unnecessary risks, which is already the case today, and will be reduced in the future. Even if technology will become so perfect that virtual pictures and voice can be sent so that the person appears to be in room, this will not replace the value of real human interactions and the stimulation of collaboration by patting somebody on the back.

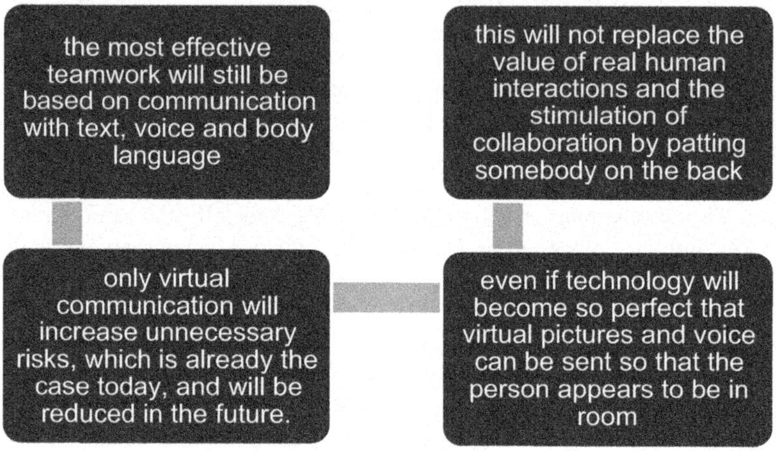

As an external consultant I have followed the evolvement of many IT solutions. One thing I know for sure is that IT will become the key to eliminate the risks in financial institutions of the future forever. This process has already begun and will probably be accomplished either by the current generation or a generation afterwards. Many tools are already available in the market, and only the usage needs adjustments. Maybe this generation will also set an end to IT viruses by either new operating systems, a new hardware solution, or simply by a new way of thinking that we have not discovered yet.

References

Alloway T (2014) Finance parts way with economic reality. Financial Times

Amabile TM, Khaire M (2008) Creativity and the role of the leader. Harv Bus Rev 86(10):100–109

Barber H (2008) Secrets of Swiss banking: an owner's manual to quietly building a fortune. Wiley, New Jersey

Bass C (2012) The new rules of innovation. TEDx, Berkeley

Beckwith H (2003) What clients love. Business Plus, New York

Bleeke N (2013) Conversations that sell: collaborate with buyers and make every conversation count. American Management Association, New York

Burstein DD (2013) Fast future: how the millennial generation is shaping our world. Beacon Press, Boston

Callaway J, Callaway JA (2012) Clients first: the two word miracle. Wiley, Hoboken

Christensen CM, Raynor ME (2003) The innovator's solution: creating and sustaining successful growth. Summarized by permission of Harvard Business School Press, Harvard Business School Publishing Corporation, Boston

Cienski J (2013) Growth will depend on invention and imagination. Financial Times

Cooke-Davies T (2011) Aspects of complexity: managing projects in a complex world. Project Management Institute, Newtown Square

Dawson R (2011) Secrets of power problem solving. Career Press, Pompton Plains

Dyer J, Gregersen H, Christensen CM (2011) The innovator's DNA: mastering the five skills of disruptive innovators. Harvard Business Review Press, Boston

Frei FX (2010) The four things a service business must get right. Harv Bus Rev 86(4):70–80

Groom B, Bounds A, Brown JM (2014) London leads way in services recruitment. Financial Times

Hansen MT (2009) Collaboration: how leaders avoid the traps, create unity, and reap big results. Harvard Business School Publishing, Boston

Kaku M (2011) Physics of the future: how science will shape human destiny and our daily lives by the year 2100. Allen Lane, a publishing division of Penguin Books Ltd., summarized by permission of the publisher

Krause MD (2013) Smart prospecting that works every time! McGraw-Hill, New York

Kuchler H (2014) How to preserve the web's past for the future. Financial Times

Lacity MC, Rottman JW (2008) Offshore outsourcing of IT work: client and supplier perspectives. Palgrave Macmillan, Basingstoke

Lanier J (2013) Who owns the future? Simon & Schuster, New York

Levine HA (2002) Practical project management: tips, tactics, and tools. Wiley, New York

Malik F (2006) Führen, Leisten, Leben: wirksames Management für eine neue Zeit. Campus Verlag GmbH, Frankfurt, M./New York

Marchewka JT (2009) Information technology project management: providing measurable organizational value. Wiley, Hoboken

Neale S, Spencer-Arnell L, Wilson L (2011) Emotional intelligence coaching: improving performance for leaders, coaches and the individual. Kogan Page, London

Nelson B (2012) 1501 ways to reward employees. Low-cost and no-cost ideas. Best practices. Latest trends. Proven strategies. Ways to motivate the millennial generation. Workman Publishing, New York

Palin A (2014) Payments via mobile to open to 30 m bank customers. Financial Times

Picard R (2011) Emotion technology. TEDx Talks

Scannell K, Massoudi A (2014) NY attorney-general subpoenas high-frequency traders. Financial Times

Schäfer D (2014a) Banks fear effects of stress on workforce. Financial Times

Schäfer D (2014b) Banks' skills gap forces up pay for talented minority. Financial Times

Scholtissek S (2011) Innovation excellence: creating market success in the energy and natural resources sectors. mi-Wirtschaftsbuch, München

Shaikh N (2012) Our financial future, digitized. TEDx London Business School

Snee RD, Hoerl RW (2002) Leading Six Sigma: a step-by-step guide based on experience with GE and other Six Sigma companies. Financial Times Prentice Hall, Upper Saddle River

Thomas D (2014) Mobile devices open new front in battle. Financial Times

Tobis I, Tobis M (2002) Managing multiple projects. McGraw-Hill, New York

Vitasek K, Ledyard M, Manrodt K (2010) Vested outsourcing: five rules that will transform outsourcing. Palgrave Macmillan, New York

Watson R (2008) Future files: a brief history of the next 50 years. Nicholas Brealey Publishing, London

Watzlawick P (1993) The situation is hopeless, but not serious (the pursuit of unhappiness) (Reprint edition). W. W. Norton & Company, New York

Enriching Encounters 9

There is a synergy between writing a book and introducing a new financial instrument or managing a project. I think that the result of any work becomes more enriching, but also more stimulating if more brains are involved. This book is a summary of my research conducted over the last 16 months and covers ideas from great innovators, from experts about innovation, and from thinkers about the future, such as Steve Jobs, Michio Kaku, etc.

In have projected some of these ideas and concepts into potential bank business models of the future and added in the previous chapters of this book. For this chapter I decided to include ideas from a close group of experts and I am happy to present some of these ideas here:

9.1 Sylvia Stocker: Creative Director

Innovation-Create Your Future: I believe financial institutions ought to consider the following key factors going forward:

- innovation and creativity
- awareness and handling of risk
- flexibility and rapid reactions to changes
- internal company culture
- reduction of complexity

While many financial institutions intend to be innovative, while they seek to offer brand new solutions to their clients, and aim at going a step further, yet practice shows that innovation and creativity is not their common approach. Many financial institutions are rather conservative and top-heavy, which frequently hinders them to be innovative and reach their full potentials.

The approach of being innovative is very much the same as being creative.

© Springer International Publishing Switzerland 2015

S. Thuiner, *Banks of the Future*, DOI 10.1007/978-3-319-07554-9_9

To me, innovation doesn't start with considering regulations, clients' needs, or market situations. These are all external factors. Instead innovation emerges from within, from the inside of you and me. It has nothing to do with a classical brainstorming session. Innovation is neither a mental exercise nor a cognitive one. It starts with a gut feeling. There are two preconditions to innovation

1. set an intention (not financial)
2. connect to your gut feeling and observe carefully

A common approach to innovation is to detach oneself from everyday life patterns and all knowledge that has been accumulated over the years. One is to become a curious child again for a moment. When we assume that we know nothing and become like a blank sheet of paper, then and only then do we open ourselves to creativity.

Here's an example from the creative world. A movie that is released touches thousands even millions of people worldwide. Now, why does this certain movie touch all these people? Why is it such a masterpiece? Why is it also one of the most profitable movies? Not because the movie was created in the brain with a financial goal in mind, but because the movie was created from a gut feeling with a clear intention of the outcome. It is precisely this gut feeling that was present during production and this feeling is transmitted to everyone that watches the movie. We all have made such an experience in the past.

An example of an innovative successful company is "Google." They urge their employees to be innovative from a to z, every day, every hour, to constantly be creative and present new ideas! For an employee, to be part of that, it is an honor, to love what you do, to believe in what you do can change the future, to believe that each one of us is capable to bring out something of significance to the world.

Google is in a different sector of business, nevertheless the initial intention of "I am curious," I believe that what I do enables my company to reach the greatest potential, that what I do could significantly change my company's values!

Please note that being creative doesn't mean to have a good idea, decide on it and then plan it through mentally, probably losing its exact value. It is very important to precisely define what exactly the idea is and then stick to it to avoid getting sidetracked by many other ideas and influences during the project. To clearly define the idea at the beginning of a project will avoid disappointment and lack of success.

Innovative employees are like a secret ingredient to a company's performance, now and in the future.

9.2 Jacques Ambühl: Meteorologist

Computers are disappearing from our sight, algorithms are becoming smarter, and the number of software developers, as well as their interconnection around the planet, is exploding. What are the consequences of this evolution for meteorologists?

Numerical weather forecasting models are global: they simulate and forecast the behavior of the atmosphere over the whole planet. Through our smartphones, they deliver to any location on earth reliable weather forecasts up to 8 days. Weather forecasting models remain, however, unseeable. Who knows the existence of the European Center for Medium range Weather Forecasting, or of the Consortium for small Scale Modeling, both institutions Switzerland is member of? Weather forecasting models are fed by thousands of airborne, as well as surface observing systems and as much as 45 satellites. To quote only one figure, the COSMO model operated at MeteoSwiss is a system of 78 millions of simultaneous, nonlinear differential equations, smoothly integrated eight time a day at the Swiss Center for Scientific Computing.

Algorithms are becoming smarter, even in meteorology, where a vast array of decision schemes has burgeoned around and mostly downstream of numerical models. Taking into account gross forecasts delivered by the models, these algorithms catch local climatological properties of the weather and enable the elaboration of products tailored to specific customers' needs, as for example for aviation, surface transportation, energy management, agriculture, tourism. Initially based on standard statistics (as well as Bayesian schemes, Kalman filters, or stochastic optimization techniques) these algorithms increasingly use methodologies emanating from bio-inspired AI: neural networks and, gradually, genetically evolved algorithms.

Furthermore, everybody knows the butterfly effect, by which the flapping of a wing in Alaska triggers a storm over Europe. This metaphor depicts the chaotic behavior of the atmosphere. Is any tentative to produce reliable forecasts accordingly doomed? No. Meteorologists developed during the last two decades ensemble prediction techniques that convey portfolios of probabilistic forecasts taking into account the uncertainty of the weather evolution. These portfolios can be treated in a similar manner as their financial counterparts and enable the measurement of risk, predictability, and economic impact of weather forecasts on customers' business.

This threefold evolution leads to an apex in algorithmic intelligence: techniques emanating from classical number-crunching, stochastic dynamical programming, Bayesian decision schemes, aspects of financial mathematics, bio-inspired AI, converge.

Where do humans stay in such an organization? In classical weather services, bench forecasters are working on the production chain of weather information. In the new paradigm, they are located above the chain and oversee it. Such a transition occurred in ancient navigation: on an antic galley, most of the propulsion was provided by enslaved rowers. Later, on sailing boats, sailors rigged sails and let wind propel their boats. Transposed in our context where, instead of force, intelligent work is taken over by machines, the shift induces an awkward dilemma: "either was my work intelligent, and then the machine must be at least as intelligent as I have been, or the machine is stupid, but then, how was my job . . .?"

The real situation is far of being as Manichaean as sketched here. Forecasters remain invaluable advisors for customers. Outstanding visualization software integrating all incoming information enables them to provide critical information, chiefly in case of extreme weather events. Their role, however, has been shifted and newly requires outstanding communication skills.

Such transformations depend upon carefully designed business process engineering. In this respect, it is known that costs of IT projects are shared in 10 % in hardware, 90 % in software, documentation, process redesign, and subsequent training. The share of risks is even more unequal with perhaps 1 % for the risk of a project failure on the hardware side and 99 % on the other side. One solution consists in dividing software development in two layers, at least for post-processing systems located downstream of numerical models. The first layer accommodates the development of the algorithms with the help of high-end prototyping tools. Applied mathematicians and statisticians are required at this level. The algorithms delivered and documented in this level are then prepared in a second layer for the operational suite in OOL languages of the Java category. Computing engineers and programmers are involved in this layer.

Finally, of course, not all the staff working on a project is lined up next door in an open space office. Developers and key people are usually spread around the world, linked by internet, thus emphasizing the interconnection issue raised in the introduction. Such endeavors, encompassing communication, organization, processes, staff, and hardware are framed through two overwhelming concepts: intelligence and aesthetics, both being two-faced. The obverse face of intelligence has already been discussed. Its reverse face, emotional intelligence, is an inalienable ingredient in any project involving human beings, structures, and IT. Only emotional intelligence provides the project leader with the energy bundle required to succeed. Aesthetics, whose obverse face frames the realm of arts, encounters on its reverse face a sensible echo in sciences: mathematicians can judge whether the proof of a theorem is aesthetically appealing, or ugly. Paul Dirac, the physicist who demonstrated the existence of anti-matter prior to its discovery, considered the aesthetic of a solution a prerequisite for its truth before its discovery. Similarly, any experienced programmer can judge whether a piece of code is aesthetically written, or if it looks awry. In the latter case, it will certainly not work properly, on any computer or application. In business too, seeking for aesthetically appealing solutions is a component of success.

Let us now reconsider the global weather forecasting systems. Are they likely to morph into kinds of supra-human intelligence at any time before 2040? Indeed a dared question that would provide an example of emergence, if positively answered. "How the body shapes the way we think," a cult AI book by R. Pfeiefer and J. Bongard, delivers a clue: intelligent systems are imbedded in the body they are driving. Look at a cat, or even at a Predator UAV to be convinced! Accordingly, even a global intelligent system should be embodied. Thus for us, meteorologists, is a weather forecasting system either dull, or there is a body. Where is it? In my understanding, the body is the whole society, which is increasingly weather dependent.

The question can be asked mutatis mutandis for financial systems that spin almost unconnected from the real economy: where is their body?

9.3 Anu Chhabra: Associate Partner, Swiss Banking Advisory

The world of hedge funds is ever evolving. With constant regulation, the changing investor appetite, and market conditions it has become a very challenging and competitive market. Furthermore, with recent trading scandals to hit not only banks but also hedge funds, it has become a market that is highly scrutinized.

Clients are looking to external consultants and the regulation framework for assurance that strategies they look to invest in are not going to be the next Madoff! That is where I think external auditing services can be very useful—where they have the finance background and the IT know—how. The combination of these two things can really help to make sure robust processes are in place in the first instance and it gives the investor the reassurance they are after.

9.4 Cyril Demaria: Private Equity Specialist and Lecturer

Finance is at the forefront of innovation. This movement is driven by the high level of competition between financial institutions. To differentiate themselves, these institutions launch regularly new products and services, which get replicated fast. They also invest heavily in technology and marketing, though the output gives them only a temporary advance on the competition. To truly innovate, banks would have to experience a Copernican revolution: change their culture. As it is impossible to change corporate culture by decree, financial institutions would have in effect to take the time, effort, and commitment to change the mentality of their executives. This would be a major innovation, a long lasting differentiator, and probably foster a necessary (but fading) requirement: employee loyalty and commitment to the long term. To achieve this goal, financial institutions themselves have to be loyal to their customers and employees, and commit to the long term. This in itself would be a major change.

9.5 Bernhard Moestl: CEO Brainworx Europe

In their golden years the monks of Shaolin monastery, Shaolin being a brand for more than 1,500 years, were known for their ability to connect imitation of successful concepts with their own, innovative ideas. Be it animals' fighting techniques that were adapted to human needs, be it the ideas of Taoism, Buddhism, or Zen: Demanding to be the best fighters in the by then known world, bringing up concepts unknown to the opponent were a must. Shaolin used to be a center of innovation, a place where all new ideas were welcome and processed to new, path breaking products. A master always had to be better than his students who could challenge him whenever they felt to do so. Thus spoken, innovation was crucial. And, following the words of Lao-Tse who was the first to realize that movement means life but stagnation is a symbol of death, they lived the idea.

The manufacturer's authorised representative in the EU is Springer Nature Customer Service Centre GmbH, Europaplatz 3, 69115 Heidelberg, Germany. If you have any concerns regarding our products, please contact ProductSafety@springernature.com

Printed and bound by CPI Group (UK) Ltd, Croydon, CR0 4YY
22/09/2026
02221065-0002